Activities

FOR A COMPREHENSIVE APPROACH TO

LITERACY

Nancy Lee Cecil

CALIFORNIA STATE UNIVERSITY, SACRAMENTO

Holcomb Hathaway, Publishers
Scottsdale, Arizona

Library of Congress Cataloging-in-Publication Data

Cecil, Nancy Lee.
   Activities for a comprehensive approach to literacy / Nancy Lee Cecil.
      p. cm.
   Includes bibliographical references.
   ISBN 1-890871-52-4
   1. Language arts (Elementary)—United States.   2. Education,
Elementary—Activity programs—United States.   3. Literacy—United
States.   I. Title.
   LB1576.C36 2004
   372.6—dc22

                                                    2004007026

Illustrations on pages 15, 31, 37, 39, 41, 43, 63, 69, 73, 75, 99, 105, 119, 121, 123, 175, 219, 239, 257, 261, and 283 by Diane Perruzzi. Other artwork by John Wincek.

Holcomb Hathaway, Publishers, Inc.
6207 North Cattle Track Road
Scottsdale, Arizona 85250
(480) 991-7881
www.hh-pub.com

10 9 8 7 6 5 4 3 2

ISBN 978-1-890871-52-4

Printed in the United States of America.

Brief Contents

For the complete Contents, see page iv.

Contents

3 *Activities for Phonics Instruction*   57

4 *Activities to Promote Oral Language and Fluency*   85

5   *Activities for Spelling*   111

6   *Activities to Increase Vocabulary*   139

7 Activities to Foster Reading Comprehension   169

8 Activities to Inspire Young Writers   199

9 Activities to Develop Literacy in the Content Areas   225

10 Activities to Promote Recreational Reading   249

11 *Activities for Working with Parents*   271

Appendices   293

Preface

The goal of *Activities for a Comprehensive Approach to Literacy* is to provide teacher-tested instructional strategies, coupled with effective reflection activities, to preservice and inservice teachers of literacy. This goal underscores the premise that the teacher is an educational leader and decision-maker in the classroom who influences how literacy instruction will be presented and who ultimately affects the students' enjoyment of reading.

In this book, which complements the more theoretical *Striking a Balance: Best Practices for Early Literacy* (Holcomb Hathaway, 2003) and *Literacy in the Intermediate Grades: Best Practices for a Comprehensive Program* (Holcomb Hathaway, 2003), I offer a broad spectrum of methodologies, techniques, and approaches for literacy instruction that have been found to be highly effective in today's diverse classrooms. I hope that prospective teachers will find this book valuable as a basis for identifying sound educational practices and as a guide for making systematic, logical, and humane instructional choices about literacy both in their teacher-training placements and, later, in their own classrooms. Although *Activities* is intended primarily for literacy courses for preservice and inservice teachers, it may be used as a reference book for a variety of other purposes as well. For example, students in tutoring classes who have not yet decided to become teachers will find in the activities and reflection questions valuable guidance for preparing effective literacy lessons for individual children. Seasoned teachers will find the book helpful as a "refresher," or as a source of interesting new activities to bring to their classrooms. The activities also are ideal for preservice courses using a reflective teaching approach. The teachers in training can try out activities on each other and then analyze the results of their teaching effectiveness through the reflection questions presented in this book.

The activities have been chosen specifically according to three discrete criteria:

1. They are designed expressly for, or are adaptable to, English language learners (ELLs) and therefore have the prerequisite sheltering necessary for this diverse population.

2. They are highly motivational activities that will complement the more structured nature of currently-in-use literacy materials.

3. They incorporate state-of-the-art understanding of the best practices for teaching young children to become literate human beings.

Each activity offers a suggested grade level, although this may be adjusted according to the achievement level of the group of students in question. Each activity also includes the materials needed for the activity, carefully delineated step-by-step instructions, the educational purposes for selecting the activity, and how the teacher can evaluate the effectiveness of each activity. Reflection questions at the end of each section may be used to determine the teacher's effectiveness, to ascertain changes that should be made in subsequent implementation of the activities, and to examine insights the teacher might have gained about the topic of instruction. The reflection activities also can be very useful in helping teacher education instructors meet the IRA/NCTE reflective standards for teacher candidates.

Throughout *Activities,* I have made reference to materials or discussions that can be found in the textbooks, *Striking a Balance* and *Literacy in the Intermediate Grades* (also available from Holcomb Hathaway, Publishers). These references are for your information only and need be pursued only if you wish to do so.

Acknowledgments

Reviewers of the manuscript provided critical feedback that I welcomed and incorporated into the final product. Classroom teachers field-tested the activities and offered many ideas about clarity, scope, and additions. I extend heartfelt thanks to them for their invaluable guidance: Betty Dean Newman, Athens State University; Laurie Williams, University of Pittsburgh; Catherine Kurkjian, Central Connecticut State University; Clara Carroll, Harding University; Diane Barone, University of Nevada, Reno; Sherron Killingsworth Roberts, University of Central Florida; Claudia Peralta-Nash, Boise State University; David M. Lund, Southern Utah University; Leah Kinniburgh, Lynn University; Cindy Dooley, Western Illinois University; Susan Dillard, Mississippi State University; Merry Boggs, Tarleton State University; and Evelyn Taylor, Southeastern College.

I also would like to thank Linda Toren, California State University, Stanislaus, who used a draft of the manuscript in her professional development seminar. We wish to thank the following teachers for providing feedback about the activities from the perspective of the classroom teacher: Marjorie Borgquist, Sousbyville, CA; Rita R. Millsaps, Mokelumne Hill Elementary; Heather L. Holland, Jenny Lind Elementary; Kathleen Davey,

Avery Middle School; Gretchen Johnson, Plymouth Elementary School; Mary Gylide, Sonora Elementary School; A. Zgraggen, Jameston Elementary School; Liz Miller, Curtis Creek School District; Sandy Fisher, Curtis Creek School District; and Gennalee Young, Cooperopolis Elementary School. Thanks go to Diane Perruzzi, who brought her expertise in working with children to the creation of a number of illustrations for this book.

The support of my publisher has been helpful beyond words. Colette Kelly, acquisitions editor, worked day and night to bring this book to fruition. She continues to share my vision of a literacy program that is balanced, creating readers who can read and who want to read.

Finally, I again extend my eternal gratitude to my husband, Gary, and daughter, Chrissy, who were infinitely patient as I took time away from coffee chats and other family activities to think about, write, and edit this book. Your feedback and interest in what I do is astounding—even when all of life appears to revolve around my writing.

Activities to Develop Early Literacy

Introduction

E mergent literacy is said to begin the moment a child enters this world. In fact, some reading experts say that literacy learning occurs at a certain level even while the child is still in the womb! Early in life, as children hear sounds, utter their first words, ask questions, listen to stories and conversations, and pretend to read and write, they are deeply involved in the process of becoming literate.

To help children become ready for more formalized instruction in the basics of reading and writing, teachers and parents can do much to ensure later success. By helping children to become fluent speakers and by encouraging them to become familiar with how print works—whether by calling attention to the sounds of words, their shapes, or the way words are put on a page of text—we are encouraging children in their ability to acquire a good foundation for future literacy.

The activities in this section are expressly designed to foster the process of literacy acquisition for the very young child in a preschool or kindergarten setting. The activities are appropriate for most preliterate children. Some are designed especially for the needs of children who are grappling with the English language and are busy acquiring a receptive and speaking vocabulary in English—English language learners (ELL). Other activities may be more appropriate for children who already have received a wide variety of experiences in conversation, listening to sounds, and book handling—such children may benefit from the greater challenge that these activities offer. The detailed activities are followed by some brief, practical classroom suggestions and selected references to children's literature for further reading about this special stage of development.

Draw a Story

SUGGESTED GRADE LEVEL *PreK–K*

PURPOSE Through drawing as a precursor to writing, children can respond to literature, develop story ideas, reflect on what they know about a topic, and demonstrate their understanding of sequence. In this activity, preliterate children can draw instead of write to compose their ideas.

MATERIALS
- Paper folded into quarters
- Pencils
- Inspirational object (optional, but helpful for ELLs)

PROCEDURE

1. With the children, brainstorm some interesting ideas they have about their lives, their families, their toys, their friends, or topics from books that have been read to them or television programs they have seen. Optionally, show the children an interesting object and allow them to describe it. On the chalkboard, write a word or several words for each of these ideas, sounding them out for the children.

2. Give each child a large piece of construction paper folded into quarters. Ask the children to choose one of the ideas that have been discussed, or any others that occur to them, and draw pictures to show how they feel about the topic they have chosen. Ask them to draw the pictures in the four boxes in order (demonstrate this idea by modeling your own four pictures; show children through thinking aloud why you are choosing this order).

3. Go around to each of the children, asking them to tell about their pictures. Above or below each picture, write a caption containing a key concept or an important word from what the child tells you, saying the word aloud slowly and segmenting the letters (sound-

ing out the word) in front of the child. Review the words with each child by saying them along with the child.

4. Have the children share their drawings with the rest of the group.

ASSESSMENT Take anecdotal notes on how each child was able to follow directions and draw four pictures corresponding to people and other important things in his or her life. Place these in the child's file. Allow each child to create oral sentences to go with pictures you show them from magazines.

Notes for next time . . .

_____

_____

_____

_____

_____

_____

_____

_____

_____

_____

_____

_____

_____

_____

_____

_____

_____

Treasure Hunt

○○○○○○○○○○○○○○○○○○○○○○○○○○○○○○○○○○○○○○

SUGGESTED GRADE LEVEL   *PreK–K*

PURPOSE   Children's success in decoding depends largely on a basic understanding of how written print works. This gamelike activity will help children become familiar with the parts of a book and how print is arranged in text, or "concepts about print."

MATERIALS
- A Big Book of an unfamiliar story
- The same story in small texts, enough for every other child in the group
- A pointer

PROCEDURE

1. Have a small group of children sit in a semicircle on the floor. Sit facing the children in a chair so all can clearly see the Big Book.

2. Before reading the story aloud, point out to the children the author's and illustrator's names and the dedication. Explain each of these features. Then, during the reading, call the children's attention to the following concepts of print:

   - The beginning of the book
   - A word
   - A letter
   - The first word on a page
   - The last word on a page
   - Punctuation
   - An illustration

3. After reading the story to the children, explain that you are going to ask them to go on a special "treasure hunt," searching for different things that can be found in a book.

4. Pair the children.

5. Beginning with the author, the illustrator, and so forth, ask each pair of children to find one book feature at a time. When each pair has located the feature requested, invite one child to come up and, using the pointer, indicate that same feature in the Big Book. Let the other child in each pair tell how he or she discovered the feature asked for.

6. Use the same procedure for *all* the concepts of print listed. Make this treasure hunt a part of your regular read-aloud routine until all the children are familiar with all of the book-related features.

ASSESSMENT   Using the corresponding small books, go around to each child and ask whether each can find the items discussed in this lesson. Use a checklist for each item, or use the Concepts about Print Assessment (Cecil, 2003). Place the checklist in each child's file. For children having difficulty finding specific orthographic items, offer direct instruction using the pointer and a different Big Book.

Notes for next time . . .

_____

_____

_____

_____

_____

_____

_____

_____

_____

_____

_____

_____

Same or Different?

(Adapted from Gentry & Gillet, 1993)

SUGGESTED GRADE LEVEL *PreK–K*

PURPOSE Children in the early stages of emergent literacy need to be able to discriminate sounds that are similar and dissimilar as a prerequisite to direct instruction in phonemic awareness and later reading and writing of the letters that accompany these sounds.

MATERIALS
- One white and one colored index card for each child
- A list of 20 word pairs, some beginning with the same and some beginning with different sounds
- Two pictures of a cat and two of a dog

Example of 20 word pairs:

pear, pony	ball, meat
cup, camp	zoo, tree
sun, sad	pink, farm
mouse, man	dark, king
bird, bat	game, house

PROCEDURE

1. Introduce the concepts of "same" and "different" by holding up pictures of a cat and a dog. Ask the children, "What are these animals called?" Follow up by asking, "Are these the same animals or different animals?" Encourage them to chant the answer.

2. Pass out the index cards, one colored and one plain for each child. Explain that they are to hold up the white card if the pictures are the same and the colored card if the pictures are different.

3. Hold up the two identical pictures of the cat. Ask the children, "Are these the same or different?" Check to see that the children are holding up the white card as they chant "same."

4. Hold up the identical pictures of the dog and ask the same question.

5. Repeat the procedure while holding up a picture of a cat and a dog, checking to see if the children hold up the colored index card and chant the word, "different."

6. Tell the children they are now going to play the same game, but this time they will have to decide if two words that you say begin with the same or different sounds.

7. Articulate two words that begin with the same sounds. Ask the children to hold up the appropriate card and chant the word that goes with it.

8. Articulate two words that begin with different sounds and ask the children to hold up the appropriate card. Repeat until the children understand what they are supposed to do.

9. Go through all the words on the list using this procedure.

VARIATIONS The children could use one reversible card with "same" written on one side and "different" on the other, or they could use "thumbs up" and "thumbs down" to indicate same or different.

ASSESSMENT Make a checklist for the skill of discriminating beginning sounds by listing 20 different word pairs. After the children understand how to play the game, ask individual children to respond to the words on the list as you check their competence in this skill. Place the checklist in each child's file. Revisit the game several times for those children having difficulty hearing beginning sounds.

Notes for next time . . .

_____

_____

_____

_____

_____

_____

_____

_____

Adapted from *Teaching Kids to Spell,* by J. R. Gentry and J. W. Gillet (Portsmouth, NH: Heinemann, 1993).

Words in the World

SUGGESTED GRADE LEVEL *PreK–1*

PURPOSE By having children talk about the words with which they are familiar, they begin to grasp the concept that print carries a message and represents concepts they know.

MATERIALS
- Chart paper
- Markers
- Stop sign made from red construction paper
- Labels for common objects in the room (desk, table, door, closet, computer, etc.)
- Masking tape

PROCEDURE

1. Hold up the stop sign for the children to see. Tell them this is a sign they see almost every day when they are in the car with their family. It contains a message for drivers telling them what they must do. Ask if anyone knows what the sign says.

2. Say the word "stop" with the children as you point to the letters in sequence.

3. Ask the children if they can think of any other signs they know about and can recognize. As they mention signs, such as Kmart, McDonald's, or Chevrolet, for example, write these words on the board, asking the children to contribute any letters they know. Later, place these words on a Word Wall.

4. Tell the children they now are going to put signs on the things they use every day in the classroom.

5. With each label, read the word to the children while pointing to each letter slowly. Ask for a volunteer to tape the label on the appropriate classroom item.

ASSESSMENT   Make a checklist containing all the signs and labels in the room. Have each child "read" the signs and labels as you check off the ones each child is able to read. Additionally, if a child is unable to say a word by sight, indicate if he or she is able to recognize any of the letters or sounds. Place the checklist in each child's file. For children having problems, follow up with practice recognizing signs and corresponding letters.

Notes for next time . . .

_____

_____

_____

_____

_____

_____

_____

_____

_____

_____

_____

_____

_____

_____

_____

_____

_____

_____

Oral Vocabulary Builder

5

SUGGESTED GRADE LEVEL   *PreK–3*

PURPOSE   A young child learns most words from hearing them spoken in conversation or through media, or having heard them being read in the context of a story. If children have a limited English vocabulary, they need much practice in oral language, both through listening and by attempting to generate thoughts in English. This activity provides practice for English language learners (ELL) and also offers a challenging opportunity for native English speakers to think about selecting appropriate words in a sentence.

MATERIALS
- Simple phrase cards or phrases written on the chalkboard
- Paper and crayons for each child

PROCEDURE

1. On the chalkboard each day, write a phrase containing a simple subject and predicate familiar to native English speakers but possibly new vocabulary to English language learners. Hand out cards containing the same phrase to each child. Examples:

   Baby cries.

   Boy ran.

   Dog sat.

   Bird sang.

   Door closed.

The baby girl cried when she saw the tiger growl.

2. Read the phrase aloud to the children as they point to each word and say it after you. Repeat this step several times until each child can say the phrase accurately.

3. Give the children crayons and two sheets of paper each, and have them draw a picture depicting the action in the phrase. Invite the children to share their drawings.

4. Explain to the children: The words I gave you don't tell us much about the baby and why she is crying. Can someone add a word or words to the phrase that will tell us what the baby looks like or why she is crying? (If the children have trouble getting started, offer ex-

amples, such as: The little baby is crying because she got stung by a bumblebee.) After allowing children a few minutes to think, go around the room soliciting new sentences from the children that add words, phrases, and clauses to the original phrase.

5. Ask the children to use their second sheet of paper to create a new drawing that incorporates some new descriptions of why the baby might be crying, what he or she looks like, and any other new information that emerged from the new sentences.

6. As the children are drawing, go around the room and ask each child to tell you what new sentence he or she is illustrating. Transcribe the revised sentence for the children underneath their pictures. Encourage the children to share their revised drawings. Discuss which drawing they like better and why.

ASSESSMENT Assess each child's ability to tell you the exact sentence he or she is drawing. Write down the exact sentence offered by each child, and place in the child's file. On subsequent occasions with this activity, note increases in the number of words (e.g., adjectives, adverbs, and clauses) the child uses to elaborate on the sentence.

Notes for next time . . .

_____

_____

_____

_____

_____

_____

_____

_____

_____

_____

_____

Nursery Rhymes

SUGGESTED GRADE LEVEL *K–1*

PURPOSE Young children enjoy the joyful rhymes, rhythm, and repetition of nursery rhymes. Rhymes can be simply read to the children, or they can be chanted chorally, used to inspire creative drama, or serve as the basis for composing unique language experience stories.

MATERIALS
- Nursery rhyme anthology book(s), such as Mother Goose, or a collection of rhymes in Spanish/English (see the Children's Literature List at the end of Section 1)
- Language experience chart and paper
- Triangles or wooden sticks (optional)

PROCEDURE

1. Read aloud a nursery rhyme, such as Jack and Jill, several times for the children. Invite them to chime in as they feel comfortable saying it with you.

2. Introduce the children to some choral speaking experiences. Because most nursery rhymes are easily memorized, the children do not have to be able to read. Practice different choral arrangements, such as the boys speaking every other line; or soloists speaking certain lines and the others becoming the chorus who speak the remaining lines. Have the children recite the rhyme in a whisper but say the rhyming words loudly, or recite the rhyme in a loud voice but whisper the rhyming words. Also, rudimentary instruments, such as triangles or wooden sticks, can be used to keep time to the rhythm or meter.

3. Use nursery rhymes to help the children identify the parts of a verse—beginning, middle, and ending—such as in Jack and Jill:

   > Jack and Jill went up the hill to get a pail of water. (beginning)
   >
   > Jack fell down and broke his crown. (middle)
   >
   > And Jill came tumbling after. (end)

   Ask the children to identify the first event in the rhyme, the second event, and the last event.

4. Divide the class into pairs and have them act out what happened in the beginning of the verse, the middle of the verse, and the end of the verse. Encourage the children to extend their parts by adding dialogue to accompany each event. Allow each pair an opportunity to act out its interpretation of the rhyme for the rest of the group.

5. After reading each nursery rhyme, write a story about it using the Language Experience Approach format. For example, after reading Jack and Jill, ask the children: What do you

Jack got a bump on his head when he fell down the hill. Jill helped him up. Their mom was angry because they got dirty. They did it again the next day but they didn't fall down.

think happened after Jack and Jill fell down the hill? Were they hurt? Did they ever climb the hill again? Did they ever get the water they were after? Transcribe the children's answers to these questions to create a piece of shared writing.

6. Provide copies of the shared writing for each child in the class. Place the story at the top of the paper and leave plenty of space at the bottom for the children to create illustrations to accompany their cooperatively composed story.

ASSESSMENT Using a tape recorder, ask individual children to retell the story in their own words using their illustrations as a guide. Select certain words at random and ask them to find the words in the story. Summarize this data to include in the child's file. Provide direct instruction in story structure for those children having problems.

The Alphabet in Five Senses

SUGGESTED GRADE LEVEL *K–1*

PURPOSE

Because the basic elements of all reading and writing are the letters of the alphabet, being familiar with these letters is crucial to becoming literate. Using all five senses instead of simply the child's auditory and visual senses makes learning accessible to all kinds of learners, especially those for whom English is a second language.

MATERIALS

- Overhead transparency of the alphabet in lowercase letters
- Sandpaper cards, one for each letter of the alphabet
- Scissors
- A quart of fine sand or salt
- Canned whipped cream
- Waxed paper

PROCEDURE

1. Teach the children the alphabet song (for some children, this may be a review). Then ask the children to sing the song slowly as you point out the letters on the overhead transparency. Sing the song slowly a third time, inviting individual children to come up and point out the letters on the transparency as they are sung.

2. Present a new letter each day, calling the children's attention to its characteristic shape and any ascending or descending features. Have the children look at the letter carefully and then draw the letter in the air with their imaginary "sky pencils."

3. From the sandpaper, cut out each of the letters and hand them out to the children as you introduce each letter. Have individual children touch the outline of the letter on the sandpaper, feeling the rough shape of the letter as they say aloud the name of the letter.

4. Place a thin layer of salt or fine sand in a shoebox lid or other container and have the children, one at a time, trace the letters in the sand or salt as they say the letters aloud and hear the teacher and classmates say them.

5. Finally, tape a piece of waxed paper to each child's desk. Squirt a small amount of whipped cream onto the waxed paper on the children's desks. (Make sure the children's hands are clean for this activity!) As you call out the letters, invite the children to trace the letters in the whipped cream. As you go around the room and check the letters, invite the children to smell and taste their letter. When they have done this, offer an alliterative phrase for them to announce. For example: Y (or whatever letter has been introduced) tastes yummy! or E is excellent! or T is tasty! This is a way for children to eventually associate sounds with letters.

6. Use the above multisensory method to introduce and reinforce all the letters of the alphabet in an enjoyable way.

ASSESSMENT Follow the lesson with an individual assessment of letter names and sounds. To do this, write the names of all the letters in large block letters, lowercase, leaving room for a check mark beside each letter. Run off enough copies for each student. Ask each child to tell you the name of the letter and its sound. Alternatively, use the Knowledge of Sounds and Letters Checklist (Cecil, 2003).

Notes for next time . . .

_____

_____

_____

_____

_____

_____

_____

_____

_____

_____

_____

Rebus Rhymes

**SUGGESTED
GRADE LEVEL** *K–1*

PURPOSE Being able to identify the rhyming element in a word (early phonemic awareness) is a first step toward becoming ready for phonics instruction. This
activity asks the children to identify rhymes in one-syllable words and to construct their own rhyme cards with matching pictures (rebus cards), as well as
act out the pictures. This makes the activity an ideal multisensory experience
for English language learners as well.

MATERIALS
- Rebus chart
- Cards with pictures of rhyming
  elements (from magazines)
- Blank 3 × 5 cards for children to make their own
  rebus cards

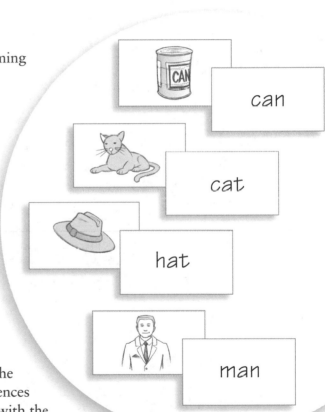

PROCEDURE

1. Discuss with the children that rhyming
   words are words with the same ending
   sounds. Give enough examples so the
   children are familiar with the concept
   (examples: cat/hat; man/can; get/wet).
   Display charts showing sentences with
   rebus pictures illustrating the words for
   rhyming (see illustration).

2. Introduce the rebus rhyming chart to the
   class. Explain that you will read the sentences
   and the class will find pictures that rhyme with the
   picture in each sentence. Have the children watch as
   you read the first sentence. For example, encourage them to
   look at the pictures on the individual cards and select the pictures that
   rhyme with cat. Ask them if they can think of other words that rhyme with cat.

3. Continue reading the rest of the rebus chart, selecting appropriate rhyming pictures and
   having the children identify other words that rhyme with the picture.

4. In a follow-up lesson, show the children how to make their own rebus game. Create another rebus chart story and encourage the children to draw pictures, on cards, of items that rhyme with the rebus pictures in your story. Optional: You could make another rebus chart as a group activity.

5. Finally, play a pantomime game with the rebus cards. Group the children into teams of three to act out rhyming words. One child from the team is chosen to be "it." That child might draw the card "mop," for example. The child might tell the group that the word rhymes with "top." The other children on the team whose turn it is then must guess the word and act it out. For example, the word "mop" might be acted out by having team members pretend to swab the floor.

The [man] has on a [hat]. The [cat] ate food from a [can]. You [can] get wet when it rains.

ASSESSMENT After modeling the concept of rhyming for the children, ask each child to provide two rhymes for some common three- and four-letter words. As a resource, use Rimes and Common Words Containing Them (Cecil, 2003). Record the child's answers on a note and place in the child's file.

For children having problems creating rimes, regroup them and do "Flannel board Rimes" or "Nursery Rimes" with them.

Notes for next time . . .

_____

_____

_____

_____

_____

_____

Flannelboard Rimes

9

SUGGESTED GRADE LEVEL   *K–1*

PURPOSE   To become ready for the recognition of common word patterns, children first need to be able to hear isolated sounds in words, such as "rimes," or the ending parts of words. This activity allows children to listen for common rimes and then manipulate colorful flannelboard characters to actively participate in creating a story containing many rhyming words.

MATERIALS
- A flannelboard consisting of a 3-foot × 4-foot piece of tagboard covered with flannel
- Three similar characters made of flannel—two boys and a girl
- Another character made of flannel—a man
- A can, a van, and a pan made of flannel

PROCEDURE

1. Start a discussion about word endings by introducing the triplets Nan, Jan, and Dan on the flannelboard.

2. Ask the children to tell you how the names of these three characters are alike. Tell the children that these three characters want to find other words that rhyme with their names.

3. Introduce the story "The Plan of Nan, Jan, and Dan" (below). Ask the children to listen carefully with their eyes closed and to raise their hand every time they hear a word that rhymes with Nan, Jan, and Dan.

Nan, Jan, and Dan

The Plan of Nan, Jan, and Dan

Nan, Jan, and Dan are triplets. One day they see a strange man. He is selling something in a can. It is something tan. None of the triplets has money, but they want to know what is in the can. Jan says, "I have a plan. Let's pick some berries in this pan. We will trade the berries for what the man has in the can." The others agree. They run after the man. Too late! The man has left in a van.

4. Ask the children to say the words they heard that rhyme with Nan, Jan, and Dan. Write the words on the chalkboard or add them to a Word Wall.

5. Invite the children, in groups of four, to act out the story as you reread it. Assign each child to become one of the four characters by manipulating the corresponding character on the flannelboard. Ask the other children to raise their hand every time they hear a word that rhymes with Nan, Jan, or Dan.

6. After all the children who wish to do so have had a chance to participate, ask individual children to retell the story while you manipulate figures on the flannelboard.

ASSESSMENT   Give each child the key word "Nan." Tell the children that the word "can" rhymes with "Nan." Then ask them to say as many other rhyming words from the story as they can remember.

Notes for next time . . .

_____

_____

_____

_____

_____

_____

_____

_____

_____

_____

_____

Accordion Book

SUGGESTED GRADE LEVEL *K–1*

PURPOSE   This art and language arts activity allows children to use the structure of an actual book as a vehicle by which to draw pictures and talk about their families, homes, and pets. The children are not only engaged in drawing but also are given the opportunity to talk about their books, listen to their classmates talk about theirs, and compose meaningful text that the teacher writes down. The contextualized oral language is especially helpful for English language learners.

MATERIALS
- Large sheets of construction paper, cut into four narrow rectangles (see illustration)
- Crayons or colored pencils

PROCEDURE

1. Ask the children: What is a family? Discuss the idea that a family can be any group of people who live together and are committed to and care about each other. Demonstrate the product of the activity by showing children the front of an accordion-pleated book with your picture on the front, entitled, "My Family and Me." Read the title of your book to the children as you point to the words.

2. Ask the children: What do you think might be inside this book? Discuss and validate their answers.

3. After they have made predictions, open the book. Each page has one illustration with a short sentence explaining the picture. Read your book to the children, showing them your illustrations of family members, pets, cherished items, your home, and so forth. Then tell the children they will have an opportunity to make their own books about themselves and their families.

4. Pass out the construction paper and show the children how to fold their sheets into accordion-pleated books.

5. Invite the children to illustrate their covers. As the children are drawing and coloring, go around the room asking the children individually what they want their title to be and transcribe it for them, sounding out each phonemic element as you do so. Have the child then read back the title.

6. On a later day, have the children illustrate one page for each family member, pet, cherished item, or other element of their life. After they have drawn each item, transcribe a sentence they compose about the person, pet, or item.

7. When the books are complete, give the children an opportunity to share their family books orally with the other children in the class. Encourage classmates to ask the author questions.

ASSESSMENT Take anecdotal notes on each child's ability to tell the main topic in each picture. Place these notes in each child's file. Provide direct instruction for those children who are not able to caption each picture.

Notes for next time . . .

_____

_____

_____

_____

_____

_____

_____

Cumulative Story

SUGGESTED GRADE LEVEL *K–3*

PURPOSE

Telling a cumulative story provides crucial practice in listening, sequencing events, and developing language. Auditory memory also is enhanced as the children have an authentic reason to listen carefully to one another so they can make an appropriate addition to the story. Moreover, the concept of story structure is highlighted as children attempt to build a story beginning, middle, and end.

MATERIALS

- A bag of various props (toys, household items, interesting objects)
- Tape recorder

PROCEDURE

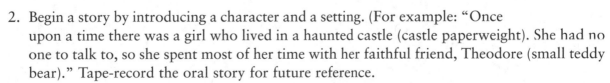

1. Show the children the objects from the bag, one at a time, naming them for English language learners. Keep these items in plain view for the children to use for inspiration. Say: We are going to tell a story about a little boy (or girl, dog, lion, etc.) using these things. I will tell the beginning of the story. Then I will call on a volunteer to continue telling the story. What happens will be anything you want, anything you can imagine. Your ideas might come from stories you have heard, experiences you have had, or even television programs or films you have seen. The objects we looked at also might give you some ideas.

2. Begin a story by introducing a character and a setting. (For example: "Once upon a time there was a girl who lived in a haunted castle (castle paperweight). She had no one to talk to, so she spent most of her time with her faithful friend, Theodore (small teddy bear)." Tape-record the oral story for future reference.

3. Invite a volunteer to add another sentence or two to the story. Allow all who want to contribute to do so. Before the last volunteer begins, tell him or her: Could you give us an ending for this story now?

4. After the cumulative story has been completed, the children will be eager to hear the entire story again on the tape. To enhance listening comprehension, the following extension activities are suggested:

- After listening to the recording of their cumulative story, ask the children to summarize the story in their own words.
- Read the children a list of the events in their story and ask them to put these in order of occurrence.
- Have the children answer questions about who did what in the story.
- Invite the children to act out the story.
- Have the children draw a picture of what they consider the most important event in the story.

ASSESSMENT   Record each child as they retell a story you have read to them. Create a checklist with the following features: ability to retell the story's beginning, middle, and end; the number of details mentioned; whether the retelling contained the main idea of the story; and the number of new vocabulary words used. Place the checklist in each child's file. Provide follow-up direct instruction on story structure for those children having problems.

SAMPLE CHECKLIST

Student Name: _____   Date: _____

	YES	NO
1. Able to retell the story's beginning, middle, and end.	☐	☐
2. Mentioned the story's significant details.	☐	☐
3. Contained the main idea of the story.	☐	☐
4. Used new vocabulary words.	☐	☐

Notes for next time . . .

_____

_____

_____

_____

Other Ideas & Activities

- **PICTURE CAPTIONS.** After each child draws a picture, have him or her tell you about it so you can print one or two sentences below it. Then read the sentences back to the child.

- **I'M GOING TO BETSY'S.** Play this game with the children. Have the first child begin by saying, I'm going to Betsy's and I will take a ball. Ask the next player to repeat that sentence, replacing the word "ball" with another word that begins with the same sound. Continue until no one can think of another word with that sound. Then work with another beginning sound (I'm going to Carol's and I will take a cow).

- **EXCURSIONS.** Take your students on brief excursions (walks around the school, park, playground, shopping trips, visits to the park, farm, firehouse, zoo, and so forth). Discuss these adventures with the students to increase their vocabulary and choice of words. When community members have been involved, write a collaborative thank-you note to that person using the Language Experience Approach format (see the "Nursery Rhymes" activity in Section 1).

- **TELEVISION DISCUSSIONS.** Tape-record television programs with educational value. Discuss them with your students. Ask questions that require children to think: Why do you think . . . ? What might have happened if . . . ? How did it make you feel when . . . ? Pursue the interest generated by programs with follow-up reading.

- **MODEL READING.** Read something (the newspaper, a novel, a magazine article, a how-to book, etc.) in the presence of your students every day, preferably during Free Reading time when they are engaged in browsing through books.

- **VISIT TO THE LIBRARY.** Visit the school library as often as possible. Help the children select books of interest to them as well as books you can read aloud to them. Acquire a classroom library where books can be checked out. Include books for all interest and ability levels and books of all cultures and genres.

- **BOOKS FROM OTHER SOURCES.** Obtain books through book fairs and book clubs. If you have Internet access, web sites such as www.amazon.com and www.barnesandnoble.com have massive collections of children's books and recommendations. Also, Chinaberry Book Service, a mail-order children's book service, will send a highly imaginative and descriptive catalog anywhere in the world (1-800-776-2242).

- **MAGIC WORD.** Play this enjoyable game in which everyone agrees on a magic word. During free time when children are conversing, ask your students to listen for the magic word. The first one to raise a hand when hearing the word gets a point. The person with the most points wins.

- **DAILY READING.** Read to the children every day. To get an idea of what to read, use the Reading Teacher's Children's Choice Award winners from *The Reading Teacher* or Newbery winners.

- **MOVABLE BOOKS.** For children who have trouble sitting still to listen to a story, try movable books. These books, such as Eric Carle's *The Very Hungry Caterpillar* and *The Very Quiet Cricket,* move, flip, or have texture, keeping active young children engaged.

- **WORDLESS BOOKS.** Sometimes select wordless books. These books, such as *The Bear and the Fly* by Paula Winter, show a story through the pictures, allowing children to increase their oral language by telling the story in their own words, in their own home language.

- **BOOKS ON TAPE.** Tape-record some of your students' favorite books so they can hear these whenever they wish. Although listening to a tape cannot replace a shared reading experience, this is a great solution for the teacher in a time crunch. As an alternative to taping stories yourself, many fine stories are available commercially featuring celebrities such as Cher, Meryl Streep, and Robin Williams as narrators.

Children's Literature List

Ada, Alma Flor, illustrated by Viví Escrivá. *Pio Peep! Traditional Spanish Nursery Rhymes.* (New York: Rayo/HarperCollins, 2003). Twenty-nine rhymes presented in both English and Spanish depict morning birds, elephants, and angels. Some are accompanied by finger plays and games to add to the usefulness of this resource. The book is richly illustrated with watercolor and colored-pencil illustrations by Spanish artist Viví Escrivá.

Baker, Alan. *I Thought I Heard: A Book of Noises.* (Brookfield, CT: Copper Beech, 1996). A sleeping child awakens to scary noises. By shining a flashlight around the room, she discovers that a clock, the cat, and a moth are making the noises. The repetition of, "I thought I heard . . ." and "it really was . . ." combined with the attention to environmental sounds, makes this an ideal book for preliterate children.

Berends, Polly Berrien. *"I Heard," Said the Bird.* (New York: Dial, 1995). Hearing that a new animal was coming, the other animals wondered what it was. They learned from a boy that the new one is a baby. Repeated lines provide an opportunity for choral or shared reading and also for predicting what the new animal is.

Jaramillo, Nelly Palacio (compiler), illustrated by Elivia. *Las Nanas de Abuelita/Grandmother's Nursery Rhymes.* (New York: Henry Holt, 1996). Lullabies, tongue twisters, and riddles are presented in both English and Spanish. The book includes whimsical, brightly colored illustrations in watercolor and ink.

Kirk, David. *Miss Spider's ABC.* (New York: Scholastic, 1998). Miss Spider's active alphabetical friends plan a surprise birthday party for her. This lovely book can be used to reinforce the letters of the alphabet in order in a most enjoyable way.

Schertle, Alice, illustrated by E. B. Lewis. *Down the Road.* (New York: Browndeer/Harcourt Brace, 1995). Hetty is going to the store by herself for the first time. When she breaks the eggs she has purchased, she climbs a tree to think. The language of sound words, vivid descriptive words and phrases, and lovely verbs makes this an excellent book for reading aloud to young children.

Weninger, Brigitte. *Ragged Bear.* (New York: North-South, 1996). A tattered teddy bear's rescue and repair by a loving child is portrayed in delightful watercolor illustrations. This tender childhood classic tale could be preceded by a "picture walk" to discuss book components and predict what might happen.

Other Resources for Developing Early Literacy

Beyond Storybooks: Young Children and the Shared Book Experience, by Judith Pollard Slaughter (Newark, DE: International Reading Association, 1993). A practical, hands-on book for working with emergent readers in preschool and kindergarten. Shared book experiences with Big Books versions of stories leads children to develop awareness of various concepts about print. An annotated bibliography of more than 100 children's books is included.

Facilitating Preschool Literacy, by Robin Campbell, editor (Newark, DE: International Reading Association, 1998). Considers the notion of young children constructing literacy; looks at literacy in the context of home and family; and presents ways to provide support for children as they begin the rudimentary tasks of beginning to read and write.

Linking Literacy and Play, by Kathleen A. Roskos, Carol Vukelich, James F. Christie, Billie J. Enz, and Susan B. Neuman (Newark, DE: International Reading Association, 1998). This video and facilitator's guide provides early childhood teachers, parents, and caregivers with ideas about how to use the natural environment and environmental print to foster emerging concepts about print, combining literacy with play.

Literacy in the Pre-School: The Roles of Teachers and Parents, by Bronwyn Reynolds (Herndon, VA: Stylus Publishing, 1997). An observation of the awareness children have about the relevance of signs, labels, notices, and directions. The author relates her experiences to theories of early learning and how concepts about print are acquired.

The Reading Environment: How Adults Help Children Enjoy Books, by Aidan Chambers (York, ME: Stenhouse Publishers, 1996). Concerned with practical aspects of creating an environment that supports young children as they begin to make sense of print. The author provides a multitude of stimulating ideas for introducing the pleasures of literacy to children.

A Sound Start, by Christine E. McCormick, Rebecca N. Throneberg, and Jean M. Smitley (New York, Guilford Publications, 2002). This book is an ideal resource for any teacher who wants to include explicit phonemic awareness instruction in an emergent literacy program. The lesson sets can be used independently or in combination with each other, and can be easily adapted to meet the needs of specific classes.

Starting Out Right: A Guide to Promoting Children's Reading Success, by M. Susan Burns, Peg Griffin, and Catherine E. Snow (Newark, DE: International Reading Association, 1999). Simplifies research findings to practical guidelines and suggestions and provides many ideas and examples about how to introduce children to print most effectively.

Striking a Balance: Best Practices for Early Literacy, by Nancy Lee Cecil (Scottsdale, AZ: Holcomb Hathaway, 2003). A companion text to this activities book, presents major research in and a theoretical overview of early literacy in an easily understandable, reader-friendly style. It guides readers in creating a comprehensive early literacy program that places direct skills instruction within the context of rich and varied reading and writing experiences.

Teaching Kids to Spell, by J. R. Gentry and J. W. Gillet (Portsmouth, NH: Heinemann, 1993). Many teachers question the usefulness of using spelling tests to teach spelling, since research on invented spelling suggests that spelling is best learned through reading and writing. The authors present a plethora of activities to teach children spelling in an authentic, research-supported way.

In Closing

○○○

1. After using the activities in this section, what insights have you gained about how children develop emergent literacy? What did you discover about yourself as a teacher of literacy by teaching these activities?

2. Which of the following activities do you think were particularly effective for reinforcing concepts about print? Why?
   - Understanding that text carries meaning
   - Ability to point to letters, words, and sentences
   - Understanding that text proceeds from left to right, top to bottom
   - Ability to identify punctuation
   - Understanding the parts of a story

3. Which activity do you think was the most effective in helping to develop the following skills? Why?
   - Vocabulary
   - Listening
   - Working cooperatively
   - Organizing ideas
   - Responding to literature
   - Experimenting with language

4. What did you discover about the need to determine what children already know about a concept before beginning an instructional activity? How did the assessment suggestions at the end of each activity provide you with insights into the strengths and limitations of your teaching of emergent literacy?

5. Select an activity that offered you the most insight into the literacy background of your learners. What did you discover? Cite examples of specific children with whom you worked.

6. Several of the activities asked you to transcribe words or sentences composed by a group of students. What concepts about print were reinforced as a result of these activities?

7. Several of the activities invited children to dramatize stories or role-play certain characters. How was early literacy developed through participation in these activities? Give some examples of specific children and what you think they learned as a result of this dramatic play.

8. Some activities asked children to draw pictures of events, objects, or people in their lives. What might be the advantages or disadvantages of such activities? What did you learn about a specific child's understanding of story structure based upon these drawings?

9. Which activities were difficult for ELL children? What did you observe about their difficulties? How could you revise these activities for them?

10. Identify a child you think has highly developed language ability. What are the characteristics of that child? Did his or her behavior during the activities differ from that of other children? Describe the differences, if any.

2

Activities to Develop Phonemic Awareness

Introduction

Phonemic awareness, the construction of a bridge between spoken and written language, is an important link to oral language understanding. A child who has a high level of phonemic awareness can segment and manipulate sounds in words, blend strings of isolated sounds together to form recognizable words, and tell where one word ends and another one begins. Phonemic awareness has been shown to be a crucial foundation for later instruction in phonics, or the relationship between sounds and letters. When integrated into a program rich with language and print, early instruction in phonemic awareness is often the instructional component that allows teachers to teach every child to read—even children who historically have fallen through the cracks.

Research suggests that phonemic awareness activities can maximize children's potential for a successful learning-to-read experience. Therefore, teachers of kindergarten and first-grade children should spend a few minutes each day engaging children in oral language activities that explicitly emphasize the sequence of sounds in the English language. The following activities have been chosen to do just that.

Counting Words

(Adapted from Cunningham & Allington, 1999)

SUGGESTED GRADE LEVEL *K–1*

PURPOSE Through this enjoyable activity, children learn to separate words in speech, which is an initial task in phonemic awareness. They also practice critical oral counting skills.

MATERIALS
- Ten items for each child, to be used as counters (beans, popcorn, blank tiles, raisins, etc.)
- Sentence strips, prewritten
- A square of colored paper, 8 inches × 8 inches for each child

PROCEDURE

1. Pass out 10 counters and a colored square to each child.

2. Begin by asking the children to help you count some common objects, such as several paperclips or pictures on the wall. Have the children put one of their counters on their colored square for each item counted.

3. Tell the children that you can count words in the same way. Explain that you will say a sentence once and then repeat it slowly, word by word. The children are to put a counter on the colored square for each word in the sentence. Begin with short sentences of no more than three words (example: The man laughed), and gradually lengthen the sentences (Example: Everyone liked the story we heard yesterday).

4. After each child has decided on the number of counters needed for the sentence, show each of them the sentence strip and have them count the words with you as you point to each word, moving from left to right. Make anecdotal notes of children who are having problems with this activity for later review.

5. As the children become proficient at this activity, encourage them to make up sentences for their classmates, saying them slowly, one word at a time, as they count them.

ASSESSMENT Review the anecdotal notes taken in step 4 and identify children who are having difficulty. Individually, read a five-, six-, and seven-word sentence. For each, ask the child to tell how many words are in the sentence. Record the information and place the record and anecdotal note in the child's file.

Notes for next time . . .

_____

_____

_____

_____

_____

_____

_____

_____

_____

_____

_____

_____

_____

_____

_____

_____

Adapted from *Classrooms That Work: They Can All Read and Write*, 2d edition, by Patricia M. Cunningham and Richard L. Allington (New York: Longman, 1999).

It's My Name!

(Adapted from Cunningham & Allington, 1999)

SUGGESTED GRADE LEVEL *K–1*

PURPOSE Through this activity, children can begin to understand the concept of *word*, that names are words, that words can be written, and that it takes lots of letters to write them. Finally, highlighting one child each day will boost self-esteem.

MATERIALS
- Box with cover
- Strips of paper each containing the name of a child in the class
- Blank strips
- Drawing paper
- Colorful cardboard crown (optional)

PROCEDURE

1. Reach into the box and draw out the name of a child in the class. Crown that child (optional).

2. Invite other children in the class to interview the child, asking, for example: Do you have a pet? What are your favorite activities? Foods? and so forth.

3. Call children's attention to the child's name, *Ramona,* as you point to the name strip, saying, "This word is *Ramona.* A name can be a word." Ask the children if the word is a short one or a long one. Tell the children it takes many letters to write the word *Ramona.* Ask the children to help you count the number of letters in this word.

4. Say the letters in *Ramona* one by one while pointing to each, and have the children chant them with you. Take a blank strip and have the children chant the spelling of the letters for you as you write them.

5. Give each child a large sheet of drawing paper and invite the children to draw a picture of the highlighted child—in this case, *Ramona*. Ask them to write the word *Ramona* underneath. Model on the board how to write each letter as they copy it. Optionally: With the class, brainstorm some words that begin like the first sound in the child's name. Place these words on a Word Wall.

6. On subsequent days, repeat this procedure with the name of another child in the class. Continue with the activity every day until all of the children's names have been highlighted.

ASSESSMENT Provide students with the opportunity to classify the names of the items in the box into two categories: long and short words. As they sort them, encourage them to say the names of the items aloud. Record the responses and place in each child's file.

Notes for next time . . .

_____

_____

_____

_____

_____

_____

_____

_____

_____

_____

_____

Adapted from *Classrooms That Work: They Can All Read and Write*, 2d edition, by Patricia M. Cunningham and Richard L. Allington (New York: Longman, 1999).

Sound Boxes

SUGGESTED GRADE LEVEL *K–1*

PURPOSE
By segmenting sounds and marking them on a sound box, children will develop one-to-one correspondence with a beginning, middle, and ending sound that make up a word.

MATERIALS
- Picture of familiar objects containing two or three sounds (examples: man, gum, bat, fish, boat, cane, dog)
- Tagboard rectangles, divided into three sections (see illustration)
- Three markers for each participant

PROCEDURE

1. Pass out three markers and a tagboard rectangle to each child.

2. Show the children the picture of the man and ask them to tell you what is in the picture. Tell them you are going to pretend the word is a rubberband and you are going to stretch it out. Have them say with you, "Mmmmm-mmaaaaaaannnnnnn."

3. Tell them that for each different sound they hear, you are going to put a marker on your tagboard sound box and they are to do the same. Demonstrate this by putting a marker in the first square for /m/, a marker in the second square for /a/, and a marker in the third square for /n/.

4. Ask the children to say the word slowly as they put a finger on each sound in the box as it is intoned.

5. Continue this procedure with the rest of the words the pictures represent. Adapt this activity to meet the needs of differing ability levels by using fewer sections for words with

only two sounds (e.g., me, go, at) or made more challenging by using four or more boxes for words containing four or more sounds (e.g., clown, frog, train, bottle).

ASSESSMENT Check competency for segmenting by asking the children individually to mark their sound box for 10 words, beginning with two-sound words and stopping when the task becomes too difficult for them. Record the number the child was able to segment correctly and place in the child's file.

Notes for next time . . .

_____

_____

_____

_____

_____

_____

_____

_____

_____

_____

_____

_____

_____

_____

_____

_____

_____

_____

_____

_____

_____

Toe Tappers

SUGGESTED GRADE LEVEL *K–1*

PURPOSE Tapping sounds is rhythmic fun for children. Furthermore, it is effective, requires little time, and entails no preparation or materials on your part. Tapping sounds helps learners become aware of the individual sounds in words. They are learning to segment words into their discrete, sequential sounds, an important phonemic-awareness task.

MATERIALS
- None
- Pencil for each learner (optional)

PROCEDURE

"m-e" "g-o"

1. Demonstrate for the children how to tap by saying a short word slowly, segmenting the two sounds and tapping your toe for each sound. Example: By: /b/ – /y/. In this example you would tap your toe only twice to indicate the two sounds.

2. Invite the learners to do the tapping. Begin with two-sound words (such as me, go, by, on, so, at), carefully segmenting the sounds so the children can hear each sound and tap once for each sound they hear.

3. Repeat the same words two or three times initially to make sure the children get the idea.

4. As the children gain proficiency, say the words slowly only once.

5. Introduce words with three sounds, and eventually four, stretching them out as above.

Toe Tappers *continued*

VARIATION   Instead of toe tapping, distribute a pencil to each child and allow the children to tap each sound on their desk.

ASSESSMENT   Assess each child individually by asking him or her to tap a toe to two-sound, then three-sound words, and finally to three- and four-sound words. Note where problems occur. Group children having problems identifying word parts and revisit the activity with the group, using different words.

Notes for next time . . .

_____

_____

_____

_____

_____

_____

_____

_____

_____

_____

_____

_____

_____

_____

_____

_____

_____

_____

Parts of the Body

**SUGGESTED
GRADE LEVEL**   *K–1*

PURPOSE   Through this activity, which uses an engaging story together with a physical activity, the children will begin to recognize the beginning parts (onsets) and ending parts (rimes) of words. English language learners will learn names for parts of the body.

MATERIALS
- *Tog the Dog,* by C. Hawkins and J. Hawkins
- Picture cards upon which are drawn parts of the body (hand, leg, thigh, foot, toe, waist, neck, head, nose.)

PROCEDURE

1. Explain to the children that you are going to play a game using words from parts of the body. Show the children the picture cards one at a time and have them chant the names of the body parts while pointing to them on their own body as they are depicted.

2. Tell the children you are going to put two sounds together to make one of the words we just said. Say: I will say the beginning sound of a word and then the rest of the word. The first part I hear at the beginning of the word *leg* is /l/. I hear /eg/ at the end of the word. /l/ and /eg/: (pause) leg. Say it with me. Leg. (Have the children repeat the steps of the procedure with the word *leg*.)

3. Using all the picture cards, have the children segment and then blend all the body-part words just as they did in Step 2. As the word is finally blended together, encourage the children to hold up, shake, or point to their body part.

4. Read *Tog the Dog* to the children. Encourage them to interact with the onsets and rimes in the story using the above steps by calling attention to new words as you turn each page.

ASSESSMENT   Individually, have children point to a part of their body and segment it as they did in the activity. Anecdotally, note strengths and needs and place the notes in the child's file. Provide direct instruction in segmenting for those children having difficulty with this skill.

Notes for next time . . .

_____

_____

_____

_____

_____

_____

_____

_____

_____

_____

_____

_____

_____

_____

_____

_____

_____

_____

_____

Speaking Martian

SUGGESTED GRADE LEVEL *K–1*

PURPOSE The children can practice the phonemic awareness task of blending sounds together to make words through this engaging activity. By listening to a series of longer and longer words stretched out in an exaggerated fashion, they will begin to understand that each word contains a sequence of sounds.

MATERIALS
- A list of words containing two sounds
- A list of words containing three sounds
- A puppet resembling a friendly Martian (optional)

PROCEDURE

1. Introduce the puppet to the children, explaining that it speaks a language that at first may seem strange but is a language that it hopes all the children will quickly learn to speak.

2. Tell the children that the puppet will say a word in the Martian language. The word will be just like a word they know, but they must "snap" the sounds together quickly to figure out what the word might be.

3. Have the puppet say the first word in an exaggerated, stretched-out manner ("Mmmmmmmaaaaaaannnnnnnn"), to which the children must blend the sounds into the word *man*, quickly.

4. Have the puppet slowly say all the rest of the words on the two lists in this manner while the children try to blend the sounds the puppet is saying in its "Martian language."

5. Invite children who think they have mastered the Martian language to come up and say a word in Martian for the other chil-

dren to guess. Ask each child to first tell the word to the puppet to have it determine if the word is indeed Martian.

ASSESSMENT   Take anecdotal notes on who is and who is not able to blend the words, being sure to give every child a turn. To assess the ability to segment, invite all the children to take a turn at saying a word in Martian (segmenting). Place notes in children's files. Provide additional instruction for children having problems in blending/segmenting.

Notes for next time . . .

_____

_____

_____

_____

_____

_____

_____

_____

_____

_____

_____

_____

_____

_____

_____

_____

_____

Sound Train

(Adapted from a lesson by Karen Gilligan)

SUGGESTED GRADE LEVEL *K–1*

PURPOSE Through this delightful phonemic-awareness activity, children will gain practice in isolating beginning sounds (onsets). Pictures are used as an aid to English language learners, and collaborative learning is encouraged.

MATERIALS
- Picture cards for beginning sounds
- Whistle

PROCEDURE

1. Seat the class in a circle.

2. Pass out picture cards, one for each child.

3. Ask the children individually to tell their neighbor what object is represented on their card, or to ask for help if they are unsure.

4. You, the teacher, are the "conductor." Blow the whistle and tell the children a letter sound that you know is represented by one of the pictures, saying, "The /m/ train is now boarding for /M/aine. The ticket to get on board is any picture that begins with the /m/ sound." Help the children determine if they have the required picture.

5. Have the children who have the "ticket" form a line and march around the outside of the circle as they make the /m/ sound and you blow the whistle intermittently.

6. As each child circles around to his or her original seat, have him or her say the word one more time, then "exit" the train.

7. Repeat the procedure with other letter sounds, going to places for which the first letter matches the target sound. When all the children understand the game, invite a child to be the "conductor."

ASSESSMENT As an individual assessment, call each child up to your desk. Lay out all the pictures for the child to see. Articulate a sound and ask the child to find a picture that begins with the sound. Do this for all the sounds represented by the pictures. Note in the child's file any sounds that are causing problems, for future direct instruction.

Notes for next time . . .

_____

_____

_____

_____

_____

_____

_____

_____

_____

_____

_____

_____

_____

_____

_____

_____

_____

_____

Shopping for Sounds

SUGGESTED GRADE LEVEL   *K–1*

PURPOSE   This enjoyable language-play activity can enhance the ability to hear and manipulate beginning sounds, or onsets, or, alternatively, to hear and manipulate ending sounds, or rimes. English language learners will be able to participate in the game because of its repetitive nature and the use of concrete objects.

MATERIALS
- Shopping bag with many items that have the same beginning sound (onset) or ending sound (rime)

PROCEDURE

1. Create a shopping bag full of six or so alliterative items, all beginning with the same first letter or letter combination. Example: bean, banana, basket, book, balloon, ball, biscuit, baby food.

2. Explain to the children that you are all going to go on a pretend shopping trip to the store and you will pretend to take home the items in the bag.

3. Start the game by holding up one of the objects and saying, "I went to the store and I bought a bean," exaggerating the initial /b/ in bean. Have children repeat this sentence.

4. Ask a volunteer to select an object from the shopping bag and create a new cumulative sentence, adding the new object to the previous one: "I went to the store and I bought a bean and a banana," while holding up the banana and pointing to the bean. Invite the rest of the class to repeat the sentence after the child.

5. Continue recruiting volunteers to select new objects, and add them to those that have been mentioned previously, pointing to each object as it is mentioned. If the children forget an object, have the child who is holding that object hold it up as a reminder.

6. When all the objects have been used, ask the children if they can think of any other objects that begin with the same sound.

7. After the children become proficient with beginning sounds they remember in this manner, do the same activity using objects that rhyme. Example: boat, coat, note, goat; or fan, man, can, pan. Or, try the game with ending sounds that are the same. Example: card, head, bed, sand.

ASSESSMENT Assess the children one at a time. Show them an object from this activity. Ask them to name as many items as they can think of that begin with the same sound. Record the number of correct responses and place in the child's file. Provide follow-up instruction on beginning sounds for those children unable to provide more than two additional items.

Notes for next time . . .

_____

_____

_____

_____

_____

_____

_____

_____

_____

_____

_____

_____

_____

_____

_____

_____

_____

Camel Chant

SUGGESTED GRADE LEVEL   *K–1*

PURPOSE   This advanced phonemic awareness activity requires children to chant or sing a whimsical rhyming poem and then manipulate the beginning sound or sounds of the rhyme to correspond to the beginning sound or sounds of a classmate's name. The repetition allows all children to catch on, at their own rate, to the idea of initial sound substitution.

MATERIALS
- Camel poem in large letters on chart paper
- Toy or stuffed camel (optional)

PROCEDURE

1. Tell the children they are going to learn a short poem about a camel. The first part of the poem will remain the same, but they are to change the second part by using the name of a classmate of their choice.

2. Teach the children the first part of the poem by saying it once for them while pointing to the words on the chart, then having them echo each line, and finally saying or singing the four lines together:

> Bibbety bobbety bee,
> The camel is looking at ME!
> Bibbety bobbety boo,
> The camel is looking at YOU!

Bibbety bobbety bee,

The camel is looking at ME!

Bibbety bobbety boo,

The camel is looking at YOU!

3. Review the concept of rhyme with the children. Ask them to tell which words in the poem rhyme.

4. Teach the children the remainder of the verse. Tell them: In the last part of the poem, the camel is looking at someone in the class and we must make the poem rhyme with that child's name. Let's use Sally as an example:

> Bibbety bobbety Bally,
> The camel is looking at Sally!

5. Now tell the children: Let's say the whole poem together and in the last part have the camel look at Tiffany. Chant the poem as follows:

> Bibbety bobbety bee,
> The camel is looking at ME!

> Bibbety bobbety boo,
> The camel is looking at YOU!

> Bibbety bobbety Biffany,
> The camel is looking at Tiffany!

6. Tell the children it is now Tiffany's turn. Class members will say the first part of the poem together, and then Tiffany must choose a classmate and rhyme the last word in the next to the last line with the name of the child she chooses. Help the children with this task until they are proficient with substituting beginning sounds.

ASSESSMENT Be sure each child in the group has a turn. Take anecdotal notes documenting who is able to make the appropriate initial consonant substitutions and who needs more practice. Provide direct instruction in phoneme substitution for those children experiencing difficulty in this area.

Notes for next time . . .

_____

_____

_____

_____

_____

_____

_____

_____

Beanbag Toss

SUGGESTED GRADE LEVEL   *K–1*

PURPOSE   This phoneme-manipulation activity develops social skills as well as large-motor skills while reinforcing targeted sounds.

MATERIALS   • Beanbag or small stuffed toy

PROCEDURE

1. To reinforce the idea of rhyme, say the following poem to the children and then ask them to repeat it after you, pointing out the two rhyming words:

   > I'll think of a word, I'll give you some time,
   >
   > I'll give you the word, please give me a rhyme.

2. Arrange the children, standing, in a circle. Say the above rhyme together.

3. Explain to the children that you will say the rhyme, say the word, then toss the beanbag to someone in the circle. When that child catches the beanbag, he or she must first say the word, then think of another word that rhymes with it. Offer examples (e.g., man/fan; get/wet) until everyone understands what they are to do.

Possible rhymes to use:

can, man, Nan, pan, Jan, tan, ran, fan, Dan

den, men, hen, when, Jen, ten, Len

bite, kite, light, night, sight, right, fight, bright

bug, jug, lug, tug, rug, hug, mug, snug, drug, dug

king, ring, wing, sing, thing, bring, swing, fling

hat, cat, bat, vat, chat, Nat, sat, fat, mat

sit, hit, mitt, bit, flit, wit, fit, pit

got, trot, not, rot, pot, shot, hot, plot, cot, dot, jot, lot

4. Say the rhyme and then a word that has many rhymes, such as *bug*. Toss the beanbag to a child and ask the child to say the word bug and a word that rhymes with it. Encourage children to also use "silly" rhymes for language play.

5. Instruct the child to choose another child to toss the beanbag to. That child must say the original word, the last child's word, and a new rhyme (nonsense words are acceptable).

6. When all the possible rhymes have been suggested, say the poem, select a new word, and again toss the beanbag to a child.

VARIATIONS After the game is familiar to all, encourage children to lead the game by selecting their own word to rhyme. In addition, use the game to reinforce beginning sounds by changing the rhyme:

> I have a word, I'll give it to you
>
> You give me a word that starts that way, too.

ASSESSMENT Make a chart of the rhyming words used in the game. Individually, have the children offer a rhyming word as you give the original word. Check off the words that each child is able to rhyme and those that give each child trouble. Regroup children who have difficulty hearing rhymes at all and provide direct instruction in this skill.

Notes for next time . . .

_____

_____

_____

_____

_____

_____

_____

_____

_____

_____

_____

_____

_____

_____

Apples and Bananas

SUGGESTED GRADE LEVEL *1–2*

PURPOSE This is one of the most challenging of phonemic-awareness activities. Through this catchy tune, composed by a well-known children's entertainer, the children will learn to substitute and manipulate the vowels of the two fruits for all the possible medial vowels.

MATERIALS:
- Tape or CD of Raffi's *Whale*
- Tape recorder or CD player

PROCEDURE

1. Play Raffi's "Apples and Bananas" (from *Whale*) for the children several times until they are able to sing it themselves.

2. Explain that they are going to now sing the song in a silly way by changing some of the sounds in the words. Ask the children what sound they hear in the word *eat*. Write on the board the letter that represents the sound. Exaggerate and stretch out the /ee/ until all can hear it. Tell the children you now are going to sing the song using that sound for all the words. Demonstrate by singing the following:

    I want to eat, eat, eat eeples and beeneenees.

    (repeat 3 times)

orple

bornornor

3. When the children are proficient with this vowel substitution, demonstrate how the song would be sung using a long /o/:

    I want to ote, ote, ote oples and bononos.

    (repeat 3 times)

4. Do the same song using all the short vowels as well as /oo/, /ar/, /er/, and /or/. Write the sound on the board.

5. Demonstrate how the words would sound using the focus sound, and then invite the children to sing along with the new version.

6. During subsequent sessions with this activity, encourage the children to name a sound. Then have the rest of the class sing the song with the substituted sound.

ASSESSMENT   Use Assessments for Phonological Awareness (Cecil, 2003) or ask the children individually to sing or chant the verse as you provide the target sound. Note sounds that are difficult for each child. Provide direct instruction in specific subskills of phonemic awareness for those children who need this help.

Notes for next time . . .

_____
_____
_____
_____
_____
_____
_____
_____
_____
_____
_____
_____
_____
_____
_____
_____

Other Ideas & Activities

- **JUMPING ROPE CHANTS.** Bring in a jump rope and encourage the children to jump to the chants they use on the playground. Have them listen for the rhyming words.

- **ROLL CALL.** When taking attendance and greeting children in the morning, select a letter they studied the day before and substitute that letter for the beginning sounds of all children (e.g., Mary Jones becomes Bary Bones).

- **NAME THE ANIMALS.** Brainstorm all the animal names the children know. Have them make up rhyming names, such as Trish the fish and Myrtle the turtle.

- **PICTURE SORTS.** Working in small groups, have the children sort magazine pictures on the basis of a selected beginning sound or ending sound.

- **RIDDLES.** Make up riddles giving the children phonemic information as clues. Example: I'm thinking of an animal that has the same ending sound as bat.

- **SOUND BINGO.** Make up bingo cards with pictures of common items. Call out the words. If children have items on their card beginning with the same sound, they place a marker on that picture.

- **TONGUE TWISTERS.** Have the children create tongue twisters by using the names of the children in the class in an alliterative phrase. Example: Mary made a merry monster mess on Monday.

- **SOUND ALERT!** When reading literature to the children, call attention to words that have interesting sounds (such as pumpernickel). Also, routinely point out words that contain sounds that have been recently introduced.

- **NURSERY RHYMES.** Teach the children common nursery rhymes, calling attention to the rhyming patterns. If you do not play a musical instrument, sing the rhymes along with a recording.

- **I SPY!** Adapt this popular children's game by asking the children to find an object beginning or ending with a certain letter. Example: I spy with my little eye something beginning with /r/ (radio).

- **LINE UP.** When releasing children for lunch or recess, have them line up by the beginning sounds of their first names. Example: Line up now if your first name begins with a /p/ sound.

- **PREDICTABLE BOOKS.** Read the children lots of predictable books in rhyme format, such as *Good Zap, Little Grog* (by Sarah Wilson, 1995). After the children recognize the pattern, have them predict the rhyme. Cecil (2003) provides a list of suitable predictable books.

- **RAP SONGS.** Using children's names and events in the classroom, create simple rap songs to which children chant along. The rhyme, rhythm, and repetition helps ELL children tune in to the cadence of the language.

- **NAME REVERSALS.** Have children practice manipulating beginning sounds by experimenting with the names of the children in the class. For example, "Bobby Jones" becomes "Jobby Bones" as they reverse the beginning sounds of the child's first and last names.

- **SOUND WALK.** Select a target sound the class has been studying. Take a short walk around the school looking for as many objects as the children can find that begin with that sound. Upon returning to the classroom, see how many objects with the sound the children can remember.

Children's Literature List

Edwards, Pamela Duncan, illustrated by Henry Cole. *Warthogs in the Kitchen: A Sloppy Counting Book*. (New York: Hyperion, 1998). Eight wild warthogs mix up 10 delicious cupcakes, along with lots of fun and a huge mess. Children will enjoy finishing the rhymes and counting the objects in each illustration.

Hoberman, Mary Ann, illustrated by Nadine Bernard Westcott. *Miss Mary Mack*. (Boston: Little, Brown, 1998). The classic rhyming chant about Miss Mary Mack and an adventure with an elephant. A hand-clapping game using the words of the rhyme on the inside cover is a great reinforcer for listening to the rhythm of our language as well as rhyme.

Robinson, Marc, illustrated by Steve Jenkins. *Cock-a-Doodle-Do! What Does It Sound Like to You?* (New York: Stewart, Tabori, & Chang, 1993). A lively, rhythmic text exploring the onomatopoeic sounds of animals, trains, and even dripping water in some of the world's languages. The book can provide a multicultural component as children listen for different interpretations of sounds for items they know.

Sturges, Philemon, illustrated by Joan Paley. *What's That Sound, Woolly Bear?* (Boston: Little, Brown, 1996). A simple story about a bear that tries to find a quiet place to sleep among many insects that make an assortment of noises, from "slish, slash," to "dash, dart." Full of playful language that can help children tune into beginning consonants and consonant blends.

Other Resources for Developing Phonemic Awareness

Assessing and Teaching Phonological Knowledge, by J. Munro (Herndon, VA: Stylus Publishing, 1998). Tests that enable teachers to decide whether a child's lack of phonological knowledge is contributing to reading difficulties and then to plan and implement a teaching-support system for children who need it.

Classrooms That Work: They Can All Read and Write, 2d edition, by Patricia M. Cunningham and Richard L. Allington (New York: Longman, 1999). A plethora of ideas for developing readers, writers, and thinkers using a variety of authentic narrative and expository texts. The authors share the viewpoint that phonics instruction is necessary, but it is not enough to create joyful readers who construct their own meaning from text.

Irresistable Sound-Matching Sheets and Lessons that Build Phonemic Awareness, by Janiel Wagstaff (New York: Scholastic, 2001). Children identify pictures from favorite books as you invite them to listen and match beginning sounds, ending sounds, vowel sounds, and more. Includes sheets for 24 books, lesson, and word lists.

Oo-pples and Boo-noo-noos: Songs and Activities for Phonemic Awareness, by Hallie Kay Yopp and Ruth Helen Yopp (New York: Harcourt Brace, 2001). Provided here are verbal games, such as tongue twisters, jump-rope rhymes, and think pinks, activities in which children manipulate objects that represent sounds and books and songs that draw children's attention to the sounds of language.

Phonemic Awareness in Young Children, by Marilyn Jager Adams, Barbara R. Foorman, Ingvar Lundberg, and Terri Beeler (Baltimore: Paul H. Brookes Publishing, 1998). A supplemental language and reading program to complement any prereading program with an entire year's worth of enjoyable and adaptable games and activities for rhyming, segmenting, and manipulating sounds.

Phonemic Awareness: Playing with Sounds to Strengthen Beginning Reading Skills, by Jo Fitzpatrick (Cypress, CA: Creative Teaching Press, 1997). A compendium of activities to help children become aware of the sequences of sounds in words—lesson plans, activity adaptations, and troubleshooting guidelines.

The Phonological Awareness Handbook for Kindergarten and Primary Teachers, by Lita Ericson and Moira Fraser Juliebo (Newark, DE: International Reading Association, 1998). Offers a practical and comprehensive means of teaching and monitoring children's development of phonological awareness in the classroom. The authors provide answers to frequently asked questions about phonological awareness, offer a possible teaching sequence, and suggest a variety of activities to enhance these important skills.

A Sound Way, by Elizabeth Love and Sue Reilly (Bothell, WA: Wright Group, 1998). Provides explicit ways to help children acquire clear concepts of sounds and letters and the critical association between the two.

Striking a Balance: Best Practices for Early Literacy, by Nancy Lee Cecil (Scottsdale, AZ: Holcomb Hathaway, 2003). *Striking a Balance,* a companion text to this activities book, presents major research in and a theoretical overview of early literacy in an easily understandable, reader-friendly style. It is written to help preservice and practicing teachers meet the challenge of today's diverse student population. It guides readers in creating a comprehensive early literacy program that places direct skills instruction within the context of rich and varied reading and writing experiences. The book includes numerous strategies as well as many practical tools for teaching and assessing early literacy.

In Closing

1. After using the activities in this section, what insights have you gained about how children develop phonemic awareness? What did you discover about yourself as a teacher of literacy by teaching these activities?

2. Which of the activities did you find particularly helpful in reinforcing the following skills related to phonemic awareness:

   - Awareness of words
   - Ability to rhyme
   - Ability to blend
   - Ability to segment
   - Ability to identify beginning sounds
   - Ability to substitute and manipulate beginning sounds
   - Ability to substitute middle and ending sounds

3. What did you discover about the need to determine what children already know about phonemic awareness before beginning a new instructional activity? How did the assessment suggestions at the end of each activity provide you with insights into the strengths and limitations of your teaching of phonemic awareness?

4. Select an activity that offered you the most insights into the phonemic awareness backgrounds of your learners. What did you discover? Cite examples of specific children with whom you worked.

5. Choose an activity that was difficult and one that was easy for your learners. Why do you think it was difficult/easy? What, if any, adaptations would you make the next time you teach the lesson?

6. Several of the activities asked you to sing or chant repetitive phrases with the children. What did these activities teach children about phonemic awareness? What did you discover about a specific child's phonemic awareness as a result of these activities?

7. Some activities asked the children to count words or syllables. Describe why you think these activities may be effective prerequisites to eventual instruction in phonics.

8. Several activities combined language play with a physical activity. How did the children respond to these types of activities? What are the advantages and disadvantages of these activities?

9. Which activities were especially difficult for your English language learners? What did you observe about their difficulties? How could you revise these activities for your English language learners?

10. Identify a child whom you think has a highly developed ability to hear and manipulate sounds. What are the characteristics of that child? Did his or her behavior during the activities differ from that of the other children? Describe the differences, if any. What instructional adaptations will you make for this child in future phonemic-awareness lessons?

Activities for Phonics Instruction

Introduction

Phonics is the study of the relationship between the letters in written words and the sounds in spoken words. Whenever you are helping readers decipher our alphabetic writing system, you are teaching phonics. This system of representing sounds with symbols is called the *alphabetic principle*. When applying the alphabetic principle to unknown words, the reader blends a series of sounds dictated by the sequence of the letters in the printed word. When the children are able to do this successfully, they are able to decode or unlock the code necessary to understand written language.

In general, proficient readers are better able than poor readers to use the alphabetic code. Research has shown this to be true in the early grades as well as in the later grades. Though reading entails more than being able to decode well, its contribution to reading with adequate comprehension is critical. Moreover, strong evidence suggests that children who develop efficient decoding strategies quickly find reading enjoyable and thus read more. Conversely, children who get off to a slow start in learning how to decode words rarely catch up to become strong readers who choose the activity.

The following activities have been selected to reinforce children's experience with the relationship between sounds and letters. The first part is composed of activities that will enhance the emerging phonics knowledge of all children in a class. The second part contains activities that also have vocabulary acquisition components and thus are expressly designed for the needs of the English language learner. The last part presents more challenging activities for children who possess rudimentary decoding skills.

Picture Dictionary

**SUGGESTED
GRADE LEVEL**   *K–1*

PURPOSE   By experimenting with pictures that begin with all the sounds of the alphabet, one at a time, the children will gain practice in matching sounds to symbols and create a picture dictionary. Moreover, children for whom English is a second language will enhance their vocabulary at the same time.

MATERIALS
- A supply of pictures, which can be secured from workbooks, magazines, catalogs, and the like
- Large pieces of white construction paper for each group
- Glue or paste
- Scissors

PROCEDURE

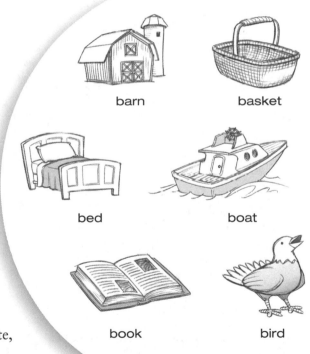

barn   basket

bed   boat

book   bird

1. Introduce a letter sound such as /b/ by having the children repeat the words ball, baby, and bag after you.

2. Ask the children if they can tell you what is the same about each of the three words.

3. Explain that each word begins with the same sound and that sound is /b/. Write the letter *b* on the board. Explain that this letter goes with the sound /b/.

4. Distribute construction paper, scissors, paste, and pictures to pairs of children.

5. Model how to write the letter *b* on the top of a piece of construction paper. Ask the groups to select one member each to write a letter *b* on the top of their paper.

6. Explain to the children that they now will look through their pictures for some animals, objects, and other items that begin with a *b*. When they think they have found one, they

are to discuss it with their pairs and, if both agree, they will paste it on their paper. Ask them to then write below the picture a *b* and other letters they hear in the word (demonstrate this sounding-out process for them). Tell them you will be coming around to answer any questions.

7. Follow the same procedure with subsequent letters as they are introduced.

ASSESSMENT Ask individual children from each pair to share their picture dictionaries with you. Have them tell you the letter and tell the names of the items on the page(s) that begin with the letter. Note any difficulties with specific sounds anecdotally and place them in the child's file. Revisit this activity, or another designed to practice matching sounds to symbols, with those children having problems.

Notes for next time . . .

_____

_____

_____

_____

_____

_____

_____

_____

_____

_____

_____

_____

_____

_____

_____

Eat Your Vowels

SUGGESTED GRADE LEVEL   *K–1*

PURPOSE   Short vowels are often the most difficult for children to hear and remember. This activity provides a concrete frame of reference for all the short vowels, making them easier to remember, especially for children for whom English is a second language.

MATERIALS
- Red Jell-O in small plastic cups, enough for every child
- Enough 1-inch Gummi insects for all children
- Apples, cut in half and cored, enough for all in the class
- Lollipops for all children
- Bubble gum for each child

PROCEDURE

1. Write an uppercase and lowercase letter *e* on the chalkboard. Explain that the letter can have different sounds. One is the /ĕ/ sound in elephant (exaggerate the beginning sound of elephant). Have the children repeat the word after you.

2. Tell the children that they are going to eat a food that will help them remember this sound of /ĕ/. Pass out a cup of red Jell-O to each child. Have the children chant r–ĕ–d j–ĕ–ll–o, elongating the short /ĕ/ sound, three times.

3. Ask the children to brainstorm some other words that have this /ĕ/ sound in them. Write appropriate words on the chalkboard and, eventually, on a Word Wall.

4. Invite the children to eat the red Jell-O. Then ask them, "What did you just eat?" encouraging them to chant, "Red Jell-O!" three times. Finally, ask, "And what is the *e* sound in red Jell-O?" They should answer, "/ĕ/!" three times.

5. Follow the same procedure for the remaining four vowel sounds, introducing, one at a time, "hălf an ăpple," "bŭbble gŭm," an "ĭnch of ĭnsect," and "lŏllipŏps."

ASSESSMENT   Using words on the class Word Wall as props, ask each child to say a word that contains each of the short vowels as you give them the target food prompt. For example, you might say "red Jell-O" and the child might respond, "gĕt" or "pĕppermint." Note children who cannot complete this task. Provide direct instruction using decodable texts targeting the short vowels that are problematic.

Notes for next time . . .

_____

_____

_____

_____

_____

_____

_____

_____

_____

_____

_____

_____

_____

_____

Alphabet Letters & Sounds

SUGGESTED GRADE LEVEL   *K–1*

PURPOSE   Knowledge of the alphabet is essential to early literacy. This activity makes the transition, in an enjoyable way, from knowledge of the letters, in sequence, to an understanding of the sounds those letters make.

MATERIALS
- Alphabet cards
- Tape recorder
- Tape of marching music
- Large hat

PROCEDURE

1. Seat the children in a circle on the floor.

2. Using capital letters to begin, and then mixing in lowercase letters, put the alphabet letters in the hat and ask each child to take a turn at drawing a letter out of the hat.

3. Have the children identify the letter and then think of something that begins with the sound the letter makes. If children have problems, offer several examples of something that begins with the sound until they are able to make the connection between the letter and its corresponding sound.

4. When all the children have had a turn, ask them to place their letter on the floor to mark their place.

5. Play a march tune and have the children march quietly around the circle until the music stops.

6. When the music stops, tell the children to sit down by the new letter they are closest to. Have the children, one by one, identify their letters and think of a word beginning with the new letter.

7. Repeat the above procedure several times.

VARIATION   The activity can be done using words; the children then think of rimes or other words with the same beginning letter(s).

ASSESSMENT   Use the Knowledge of Sounds and Letters Checklist (Cecil, 2003) or use letter cards from this activity to assess each child individually on knowledge of the letters, sounds, and ability to produce a word with the sound. Place checklist in each child's file. Provide direct instruction in letter/sound correspondence for those children experiencing difficulties.

Notes for next time . . .

_____

_____

_____

_____

_____

_____

_____

_____

_____

_____

_____

_____

_____

_____

_____

_____

_____

Silly Food Rhymes

SUGGESTED GRADE LEVEL   *K–1*

PURPOSE   This activity uses food rhymes such as "feetloaf" for "meatloaf," which children find hilarious. Besides participating in an enjoyable listening activity using a wonderful selection from children's literature, the children will gain practice in manipulating beginning sounds themselves to create silly nonsense words that rhyme with their favorite foods.

MATERIALS
- *The Hungry Thing*, by Jan Slepian (1976)
- Chalkboard or overhead projector and transparency

PROCEDURE

1. Read the children the book *The Hungry Thing*. To reinforce the concept of rhyme, stop when you get to the rhyming part of each phrase and allow the children to shout out the predictable rhyme. For example:

   "I know for sure," said a lady in red,

   "It's a cute little baby that stands on her [head]."

2. After reading the book and discussing it with the children, read it again, this time asking the children to name some of the foods rhymed in the book. Write the words on the board as the children say them.

meeza	=	pizza
blacos	=	tacos
rot hogs	=	hot dogs
bamburgers	=	hamburgers
mice scream	=	ice cream
falana	=	banana
ballad	=	salad
snake	=	cake

3. Explain to the children that they now are going to make up some rhymes for their favorite foods. Ask the children to raise their hand when they can think of a food that was not mentioned in the story.

4. Write on the board or overhead transparency, the foods that the children suggest, sounding them out in front of the children.

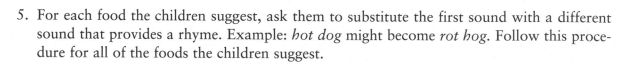

5. For each food the children suggest, ask them to substitute the first sound with a different sound that provides a rhyme. Example: *hot dog* might become *rot hog*. Follow this procedure for all of the foods the children suggest.

6. Reread the book using the new foods and rhymes the children suggest.

ASSESSMENT   Ask each child to write down on a piece of paper three new foods and corresponding rhymes that were not listed on the board. Note which children are not able to complete this task. Provide direct instruction in manipulating beginning sounds.

Notes for next time . . .

_____

_____

_____

_____

_____

_____

_____

_____

_____

_____

_____

_____

_____

_____

_____

_____

_____

Lonely Letter Poem

(Adapted from Cecil, 1994)

SUGGESTED GRADE LEVEL   *K–3*

PURPOSE   Through the use of alliteration in a poetic format, children can think of many words beginning with the same sound to tell about a topic, thereby experimenting with sound/letter relationships and expanding their vocabulary at the same time.

MATERIALS
- Overhead projector and transparency
- Dry-erase pen

PROCEDURE

1. Write the following poem on an overhead projector transparency and read it to the children, exaggerating the /t/ sounds in the words:

> Turtles
>
> Turtles are tame,
> Turtles are timid.
>   Ticklish, tiny,
>   Tender, tasty.
>   Terrible, tacky,
>   Teeny, tan.
> Turtles are timid,
> Turtles are tame.

Dogs

Dogs are dirty,
Dogs are dear.
   Dusty, dingy,
   Daring, dark.
   Delightful, dreamy,
   Ditzy, dry.

Dogs are dear,
Dogs are dirty.

2. Ask the children what they notice about the poem, guiding them to see that all the adjectives describing "turtle" begin with the same letter. Select a plural noun (such as *foods, pets, mothers, dogs, toys, cookies*). Write the word on the overhead projector transparency, segmenting the sounds for the children. Explain that they will be writing a poem about this topic.

3. Ask the children to tell you the first letter and sound in the word.

4. Invite the children to brainstorm some words that tell about, or describe, the topic. For foods, for example, the children might brainstorm the words *fine, fantastic, funny, fattening, fast, famous, fabulous, filling,* and *fussy.*

5. Using the brainstormed words, have the children help you write a new poem about their topic in the same format as in the turtle poem. Their poem might turn out to be, for example:

> Foods
>
> Foods are fattening,
> Foods are filling.
> > Fantastic, fine,
> > Fabulous, fast.
> > Famous, fussy,
> > Funny, familiar.
> Foods are filling,
> Foods are fattening.

6. Read the poem chorally several times with the children, inviting them to exaggerate the /f/ sounds.

7. Place the brainstormed words on a Word Wall.

8. Run off copies of the poem, leaving space at the bottom for each child to illustrate his or her class poem. Encourage the children to take their poems home to read to their families.

ASSESSMENT Have each child read his or her poem aloud to you, and offer assistance as necessary. Note, in particular, any inaccuracies with the targeted letter/sound.

Notes for next time . . .

_____

_____

_____

_____

_____

_____

Adapted from *For the Love of Language: Poetry Scaffolds for Every Learner,* by Nancy Lee Cecil (Winnipeg, Manitoba: Peguis Publishers, 1994).

Building Words

SUGGESTED GRADE LEVEL   *1*

PURPOSE   This hands-on activity helps children learn to look for the patterns in words, using individual letters—a useful decoding and spelling skill. Through active manipulation, they learn that changing just one letter or the location of a letter can change the whole word.

MATERIALS
- Letter tiles (commercial or made from file folders in 1-inch × 2-inch rectangles, enough sets for each child in the class)
- Letter holders (commercial or from Scrabble game)
- Plastic zippered bags for each set of letters
- Pocket chart and letter cards

PROCEDURE

1. In the pocket chart, display the letters *b, s, r, t, a,* and *i*. Ask the children to find these letters in their bag.

2. Say to the children, "Take two letters and make the word *at*. Put the word in your letter holder."

3. Ask for a volunteer to make the word in the pocket chart using the letter cards. Have the children look at the word in the pocket chart and check their words. Say the word together slowly and chant the spelling, pointing to each letter as the children say the sound.

4. Tell the children, "Now I want you to build a different word with two letters by changing the first letter to an *i*." Again, have a volunteer put the word in the pocket chart. Say the word *it* together and chant the spelling.

5. Say, "Now we are going to build a three-letter word by adding just one letter to the word *it*. Does anyone know what letter we can add to the word *it* to make *bit*?" The child with the correct answer goes to the pocket chart and makes the word with the letter cards as the

other children make theirs from their letter tiles, placing them in their letter holders. They say the new word together and chant the spelling.

6. Continue in this manner, adding and changing one letter at a time until the class has made the following words: *sit, sat, rat, bat.*

7. In subsequent sessions, use different letter combinations, generally including four consonants and two vowels to build new words. Add these words to a Word Wall for later reinforcement.

ASSESSMENT   Assess each child's ability to manipulate letters to form new words by asking them to respond to the following requests, using the letter tiles in their bags.

> "Find the word *it*."
> "Change the word to *bit*."
> "Change the word to *bat*."
> "Change the word to *sat*."

Place a record of each child's results in his or her file. Allow children having problems to practice this activity in small groups.

Notes for next time . . .

_____

_____

_____

_____

_____

_____

_____

_____

_____

_____

Word Wall Detective

SUGGESTED GRADE LEVEL *1–2*

PURPOSE   Word Walls are particularly effective for teaching the high-frequency words children will need in their everyday writing and spelling. This activity can be used to familiarize children with a new group of words that have been placed on the Word Wall.

MATERIALS
- Word Wall containing high-frequency words
- Individual chalkboards or paper for each child

PROCEDURE

1. Select six high-frequency words and place them on the Word Wall.

2. Introduce the words to the children, one at a time, using the following format:
   - Point to a word and say it distinctly.
   - Have the children repeat the word after you.
   - Spell the word for the children as you clap each letter.
   - Have the children clap for each letter as they chant the letter aloud.
   - Have the children write the word on their individual chalkboards or paper. Check.

morning	night
house	school
book	read

3. Tell the children they now are going to be "word detectives." Invite them to find one of the six words based upon the clues you give them and write on their chalkboards. Offer clues such as the following:
   - The word begins with /b/ and rhymes with *took*.
   - The word ends like *bead* and has four letters.

- The word begins like *skate* and rhymes with *cool*.
- The middle of the word sounds like *loud* or *sound*.

4. To check the answer, say the clue word and let the children say the word they wrote and chant its spelling.

ASSESSMENT Check answers on the individual chalkboards. Make anecdotal notes on difficulties with beginning sounds, ending sounds, vowel sounds, and finding rhyming words. Provide instruction on each of these subskills for those children experiencing difficulties.

Notes for next time . . .

_____

_____

_____

_____

_____

_____

_____

_____

_____

_____

_____

_____

_____

_____

_____

_____

_____

_____

Phonogram Fun

SUGGESTED GRADE LEVEL *1–2*

PURPOSE Children can demonstrate their understanding of phonograms, common ending patterns, by creating new words with the same ending through the enjoyable vehicle of a Dr. Seuss book, *The Sneetches*.

MATERIALS
- *The Sneetches,* by Dr. Seuss
- Cards with phonograms on them
- Tokens or markers

PROCEDURE

1. Review the concept of rhyme with the children by inviting them to participate in rhyming the following words: ball (call, fall, mall), can (tan, man, Dan, ran), etc.

2. Read the children the book *The Sneetches*. Read the book again, this time telling the children to listen for rhyming words as you read.

3. Pass out to each child three words containing phonograms, such as sock, clock, and rock. Tell the children the words on the cards are words they heard in the story.

"Sneetches!"

4. Ask the children to read their cards to their neighbor and then use each word in a sentence. (If a child has difficulty with a word, the partner may help them, or they may look at the page in the book and use the context of the pictures to decide what the word is.)

5. Read the story one more time, asking the children to put a token on their words when they hear them in the story.

6. Instruct the children that the first child to have all three words covered is to say, "Sneetches!"

8

7. Ask the child to find each word on the page of the book where the word appears, point to the word, and say the word in the text that rhymes with it.

8. Write the rhyming words on a Word Wall and have the children identify the ending part that the two words have in common. Ask them if they can think of any more words that have the same ending (phonogram or rime). Write them on the Word Wall.

9. Return to reading the book until another child calls out "Sneetches!" Continue the process until you reach the end of the book.

ASSESSMENT   Use anecdotal notes to record who was able to read the phonogram, who was able to create a sentence using the phonogram, and who contributed new rhyming words for the Word Wall. Place the notes in each child's file. Revisit this activity for children still having difficulty rhyming words.

Notes for next time . . .

_____

_____

_____

_____

_____

_____

_____

_____

_____

_____

_____

_____

_____

_____

_____

Word Wrigglers

9

SUGGESTED GRADE LEVEL *1–2*

PURPOSE As children create Word Wrigglers, they blend spoken language, think analytically about the alphabetic code, and strategically use knowledge of ending parts of words (rimes) to decode words.

MATERIALS
- 5-inch × 8-inch colored cards containing rimes
- Four large paper plates, decorated to look like wrigglers
- String
- Scissors
- Crayons
- Markers
- Masking tape

PROCEDURE

1. Write an onset (word beginning) on the board (*str,* for example). Also write this onset on one of the wriggler heads (paper plates). Write a word formed with this onset underneath (for example, *string*).

2. Explain that the word string is formed by adding the *str* blend to the rime *ing*.

3. Invite the children to think of other words that begin with the letter combination *str*—for example, *str aight, str ong, str uggle, str ay, str ipe*. Write the words under the word string, and on the 5' × 8' cards.

4. Do the same with other consonant blends and digraphs that serve as onsets (e.g., *bl, ch, tr*). Compare and contrast the *bl, ch, tr* sounds with the *str* sound, discussing the effect of each sound on pronunciation. Write these onsets on the other wriggler heads. Have the children also think of word endings for each of these onsets (e.g., blue, black, block; chain, chew, chalk; track, true, trust).

Word Wrigglers *continued*

5. Select four children and bring them to the front of the room. Tape a wriggler containing an onset—*tr, str, ch,* or *bl*—on each child. Tape a rime card on each of the remaining children.

6. Tell the children wearing rime cards that they now will become a "word wriggler" by finding the beginning letters that go with their ending letters. Ask them to look for the child with the wriggler head. For example, a child wearing the rime *ain* would look for the child with the *ch* onset on the wriggler to form the word *chain*.

7. After word wrigglers have been created, have the children chant the words formed by the wriggler (the onset) and the body part (rime) blended together.

8. When all the words have been chanted, invite the children who have body parts (rimes) to tape their cards behind the appropriate wrigglers (onsets), re-creating the word *wrigglers* on the chalkboard. If the sequence of body parts can combine to form more than one word, encourage the children to come up and move the body sections around.

ASSESSMENT Using flashcards of all the words created through the Word Wrigglers activity, ask individual children to decode them. To assess extra proficiency, ask the children to use the words in a sentence. Record the number of words each child was able to decode and place this information in the child's file. Provide direct instruction in blending for those children having difficulty with this skill.

Notes for next time . . .

_____

_____

_____

_____

_____

_____

_____

_____

_____

Syllable Patterns

SUGGESTED GRADE LEVEL   *1–2*

PURPOSE   Children who are familiar with the vowel patterns in one-syllable words (VC or CV or CVC) will be introduced to two-syllable words that also have discernible patterns.

MATERIALS
- Ten VC/CV twin consonant words on word cards (e.g., follow, happy, kitten, runner, butter, cotton, puppy, bonnet, dinner, saddle, manner)

PROCEDURE

1. Review one-syllable words (e.g., *hot*, *man*, *sat*) that have the CVC pattern. Ask the children to first identify the CVC sequence, and then ask them to tell you what happens to the vowel in these words. (The vowel is usually short.)

2. Show the twin consonant word cards to the children, one at a time. After you introduce each word, invite a child to write the word on the chalkboard, in a column.

3. Ask the children what they notice about all these words (they all have twin consonants).

4. Underline the first three letters in each of the words on the chalkboard. Ask the children to state what they notice about the vowel sounds in the beginning part of each of these words (they are short).

5. Guide the children to then state the generalization in their own words, paraphrasing the idea that in a closed syllable pattern (VC/CV), the first vowel is usually short. Ask the children: How will this pattern help you with spelling?

6. Try a few nonsense words with the children to see if they can apply the new rule—for example, how they would pronounce the following words: fobbit, sabber, rodding, lokker, jonnle, pobbie, bassop, nopple, cannet, wogger.

ASSESSMENT Create a checklist such as the one below containing new words that conform to the VC/CV pattern and ask the children individually if they are able to pronounce them. Ask them to tell you how they know. Use the following words:

Place the checklist in each child's file. Provide direct instruction for children not able to pronounce eight out of ten words correctly.

SAMPLE CHECKLIST

Name:	matter	gutter	sadder	paddle	hassle	bottom	gobble	winner	jiggle	fatter

Venn Diagram Sort

**SUGGESTED
GRADE LEVEL**   *1–3*

PURPOSE   Word sorts help children to focus on conceptual and phonological attributes of words and to identify recurring patterns. In this activity, pairs of children sort words according to two different features, for example, differing vowel sounds or common onsets or rimes.

MATERIALS
- Chart paper
- Markers

PROCEDURE

1. Compile two lists of three or four words each that have sound and letter similarities as well as sound and letter differences. For example, one list may consist of *drop, mop,* and *hop* and the other list might consist of *sleep, weep,* and *beep.* (Although the words in one list and the words in the other list all end with the letter *p,* the two lists have words with different beginnings/onsets and different vowels.)

2. Write the words from Step 1 on the board in no particular order. Say the words and have the children repeat them after you.

3. Draw two overlapping circles on the chart paper. Write a word from one list in one circle and a word from the other list in the other circle.

4. Write the feature that the words from both lists have in common (the letter *p*) on the overlapping portion of the diagram.

5. Ask the children to select a word from the board and tell on which circle it should go and why. Invite them to write the word on the appropriate circle (see illustration).

6. Repeat this procedure with several other pairs of lists until the children are proficient at identifying the similarities and differences between two sets of words.

7. For a further challenge, provide pairs of children with Venn diagrams drawn on chart paper. Encourage the children to do their own Venn diagram sorts.

ASSESSMENT Observe individual children as they place the words in the circles or overlapping portion of the diagram. Provide one-on-one assistance to children who have difficulty detecting patterns in words.

Notes for next time . . .

_____

_____

_____

_____

_____

_____

_____

_____

_____

_____

_____

_____

_____

_____

_____

_____

_____

_____

Other Ideas & Activities

- **BEACH BALL PHONICS.** With a laundry marker, print a consonant letter on each panel of a beach ball. Toss the ball to a child and have the child say a word beginning with the sound of the letter that his or her hand is touching or near.

- **PICTURE CARDS.** Use picture cards of animals, foods, or other familiar items to help children experiment with the sounds in language. Model some simple one-syllable words and have children practice saying, then writing, the words in two parts—onset and rime.

- **CARTOON WORDS.** With the children, brainstorm some of the sounds and nonsense words that cartoon characters say ("vroom!" "bam!" "aaaack!"). Have the children experiment with the sound/symbol relationship by helping you sound out these words as you print them on the board.

- **MARY WORE HER RED DRESS.** Chant the phrase with the children: "Mary wore her red dress, red dress, red dress. Mary wore her red dress all day long." Ask the children to change the chant by adding a new piece of clothing that has an alliterative name. Examples: Gary wore his blue blazer; Jenny wore her pink poncho; Jose wore his purple pants.

- **RHYME LISTS.** On a piece of chart paper, write a favorite poem of the children. Read the poem chorally with the children and discuss the rhyming words. Invite the children to write these words on the chalkboard. Encourage them to think of other words that rhyme with words in the poem and write them on the board.

- **CRAYON WORDS.** With a crayon, write several simple words on a large sheet of tagboard. In front of the children, trace the letters with your finger as you blend one sound with another (e.g., mmmmaaaannnn). Ask the children to write the same word with crayons in large letters on their own paper and practice blending the sounds while tracing each letter with their finger.*

- **FLOWER POWER.** Depending upon what you wish to emphasize, select a specific onset or rime and write it on the board. Give a sheet of colored construction paper to each child and have him or her cut out flower shapes. On these shapes ask them to write a word that has the same onset or rime. Tape the ends of these shapes into a circle. When several circles have been constructed with differing onsets or rimes, you have a brightly colored flower bulletin board.

- **BRICK HOUSES.** Make a brick house on the board by drawing a rectangle on the bottom of the board and writing within it a word that contains a phonological element you have introduced (for example, the *spr* blend). Tell the children they will help to build a house by adding bricks with words that begin with the same three letters. Make a rectangle beside or above yours and invite a volunteer to write a word beginning with *spr* on the brick. Repeat until you run out of words.

- **SOUND SEARCH.** Encourage the children to look through books they are reading to find words that have the same letters or sounds as the one you are studying—for example, /oo/. Make a list of these words and create a Word Wall from them.

* This activity has extra tactile/kinesthetic benefits.

- **CLOTHESLINE.** Hang a clothesline across a section of your classroom. Write a word on the chalkboard, such as the word moon. Give the children 3" × 5" cards. As the children think of words that contain the same sound symbol (soon, toot, poodle), have them write the word on their card, say it for the class, and pin the word on the clothesline with a clothespin.

Children's Literature List

Koch, Michelle. *Hoot Howl Hiss.* (New York: Greenwillow, 1991). Words and illustrations depicting sounds that animals make. Decoding skills are utilized as young readers decipher captions that go with the illustrations.

Raffi. *Down by the Bay.* (New York: Crown, 1987). A song celebrating silly rhymes: "Did you ever see a whale with a polka-dot tail, Down by the bay?" Lends itself to choral reading or singing. Reinforces rhyme and long /a/ and long /o/ patterns. Part of Raffi Songs to Read series.

Salisbury, Kent. *A Bear Ate My Pear.* (New York: McClanahan, 1998). A phonics pop-up book using beautiful illustrations and word families. Gives examples of short vowels, the silent /e/, two vowels together, and some consonants and blends. These phonics elements can be used for reinforcement after direct teaching.

Serfozo, Mary. *Joe Joe.* (New York: Simon & Schuster, 1993). Features Joe Joe, a small boy, who bangs a stick on a fence, bongs a garbage can, splashes, stops, claps, squishes, slips, and drips. Reinforces consonant clusters.

Snow, Pegeen. *Eat Your Peas, Louise.* (Chicago: Children's Press, 1993). A story about a parent pleading with a reluctant Louise to eat her peas. Nothing works—neither threats nor bribery—until he says, "Please." Reinforces long /e/ patterns.

Vaughn, Marcia. *Hands Hands Hands.* (Reading, PA: Mondo, 1995). Pictures children showing what they can do with their hands: tug, hug, tickle tiny toes, plant, pick, and so forth. Reinforces long /e/ and short vowel patterns.

Other Resources for Teaching Phonics

For the Love of Language: Poetry Scaffolds for Every Learner, by Nancy Lee Cecil (Winnipeg, Manitoba: Peguis Publishers, 1994). Ideas to help children explore many types of poetry. Each poetry activity includes a description, an easy-to-follow pattern, and a lead-in activity to help motivate children and help the teacher prepare for the session. Also includes samples of poetry written by children.

Phonics from A to Z: A Practical Guide, by Wiley Blevins (Jefferson City, MO: Scholastic Professional Books, 1998). An essential resource providing teachers with a balanced look at how to incorporate a phonics program into reading instruction.

Phonics Poetry: Teaching Word Families K–3, by Timothy Rasinski and Belinda S. Zimmerman (Upper Saddle River, NJ: Allyn & Bacon, 2001). This book shows elementary teachers how to make classwork more effective and fun through the use of phonogram poems to teach phonics. It includes many sample poems for the most common rimes in children's reading.

Phonics that Work! New Strategies for the Reading/Writing Classroom, by Janiel Wagstaff (Jefferson City, MO: Scholastic Professional Resources, 1998). A detailed, replicable description of how the author's integrated phonics program works in her second-grade classroom, including strategies, specific activities, and a minute-by-minute daily schedule.

Phonics, Too! How to Teach Skills in a Balanced Literacy Program, by Jan Wells and Linda Hart-Hewins (York, ME: Stenhouse Publishers, 1994). From consonant blends and lists of high-frequency words to sentence structure, all the background teachers need to make skills a part of a strong literacy program.

Ready, Set, READ: Building a Love of Letters and Literacy through Fun Phonics Activities, by Janet Chambers (Tucson, AZ: Zephyr Press, 2003). This book offers step-by-step instructions on how to introduce literacy skills to even very young children using a novel multisensory approach. The aim is for children to achieve a thorough comprehension of how print on the page and the words all around us relate to spoken sounds.

Striking a Balance: Best Practices for Early Literacy, by Nancy Lee Cecil (Scottsdale, AZ: Holcomb Hathaway, 2003). *Striking a Balance,* a companion text to this activities book, presents major research in and a theoretical overview of early literacy in an easily understandable, reader-friendly style.

Teaching Phonics Today: A Primer for Educators, by Dorothy S. Strickland (Newark, DE: IRA, 1998). Discusses ways in which reading instruction, particularly the teaching of phonics, has changed in recent years, and provides suggestions for helping children to use phonics as a key component of their overall reading development.

Whole-to-Part Phonics: How Children Learn to Read and Spell, by Henrietta Dombey, Margaret Moustafa, and the staff of the Centre for Language in Primary Education (Westport, CT: Heinemann, 1997). A set of detailed, practical suggestions for promoting the knowledge children need to learn letter-sound relationships while focusing on construction of meaning in both reading and writing.

Word Matters: Teaching Phonics in the Reading/Writing Classroom, by Gay Su Pinnell and Irene Fountas (Portsmouth, NH: Heinemann, 1998). A myriad of authentic and enjoyable activities to engage young children with the kind of personally satisfying word study that will lead to prolific readers and writers.

In Closing

1. After using the activities in this section, what insights have you gained about how children develop understandings about how sounds and letters correspond? What did you discover about yourself as a teacher of phonics by teaching these activities?

2. Which activity did you think was most effective in developing each of the following phonic understandings? Why?

- Phonemic awareness
- Identification of letters
- The relationship between beginning sounds and letters
- The relationship between ending sounds and letters
- The memorization of high-frequency words
- Blending of sounds into words

3. Choose an activity that was easy and one that was difficult for the children with whom you worked. What about the activity made it easy/difficult? What adaptations, if any, would you make the next time you teach this lesson? How do you think these adaptations would make the activity more accessible for your learners?

4. What did you discover about the need to determine what children already know about a specific phonic element before beginning an instructional activity to teach phonics? How did the assessment suggestions at the end of each activity provide you with insights into the strengths and limitations of your teaching of phonics?

5. Select an activity that offered you the most insight into the phonics background of your learners. What did you discover? Cite examples of specific children with whom you worked.

6. Several of the activities asked you to have the children look for patterns in words and group them according to the patterns they discovered. What do these activities teach children about a strategy to decode unknown words?

7. Some of the activities had, as a major component, much reinforcement of phonemic awareness. Why would it be important to continue this instruction when children are already able to identify letters and sound out words?

8. Several activities asked you to place high-frequency words on Word Walls. What do you see as the advantages and disadvantages of using Word Walls? Do you think the introduction of high-frequency vocabulary is compatible with phonics instruction? Why or why not?

9. Children from other language groups often have a difficult time hearing and articulating certain sounds in the English language. Analyze three of the activities that ask children to use specific sounds that may be difficult for some children. How can each of these activities be made more accessible to ELL children?

10. Identify a child who does especially well during phonics instruction activities. What are the characteristics of this child? What additional activities might you include to assure that this child is appropriately challenged in future phonics instruction activities?

Activities to Promote Oral Language and Fluency

Introduction

It is often assumed that children, especially if they are native English speakers, have developed their oral language abilities by the time they enter school. Unfortunately, we can overlook the importance of helping children further their ability to speak confidently in any situation. The basic curriculum cornerstones of reading and math usually take precedence over most other parts of the curriculum, and talk is not routinely interwoven effectively throughout the content areas. However, oral language must be continually nurtured in a balanced and comprehensive literacy program, for speech is the most widely used—and, therefore, arguably—the most critical of the modes of discourse. Moreover, proficiency in speaking enhances proficiency in all the other language arts.

The foundation for a sound oral language program is the variety of spontaneous and planned speaking situations that occur every day in most elementary classrooms. Opportunities for oral language include informal speaking, as in casual conversations and discussions, and more formal speaking, as in oral reports, interviews, panel discussions, and debates.

The activities in this chapter have been created to develop oral language as well as reading fluency in children. The first five instructional activities highlight the development of oral language; the latter five address fluency as the most prominent focus. Many activities include some form of drama, an effective and enjoyable activity that improves both oral language ability and fluency. Others involve choral reading or reading passages aloud and then discussing them, also activities that foster both oral language and reading fluency. All activities are ideal for the classroom that includes children at all stages of second-language-acquisition fluency.

Sock Puppet Scenarios

SUGGESTED GRADE LEVEL K–2

PURPOSE Children will develop oral language facility and appropriate vocabulary for a specific context in a motivational and stress-free situation.

MATERIALS
- Old, clean socks, one pair for each child in the group
- Buttons
- Colored markers
- Yarn
- Glue

PROCEDURE

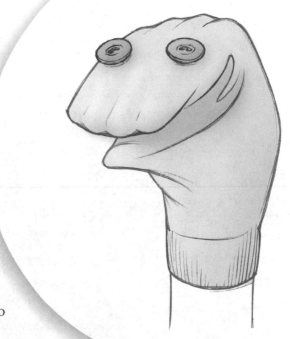

1. Distribute socks, yarn, buttons, and glue to the children. Explain that they will be making their own puppets to act out different scenarios for the other children in the group. Tell them their puppets will be made to look like people.

2. Put the children in groups of three or four. Spend one class period making the puppets as an art project. During this period, encourage the children to converse with the other members of the group about their puppet, what its name should be, and to imagine what its personality traits might be.

3. Write the following topics on the board and read them out loud to the children:

   a. A brother and sister want some candy before dinner and their mother says no.

   b. Three children are talking about some money they found on the playground.

   c. A man is telling two police officers that his car has been stolen.

   d. Four children are lost in a big city and don't know what to do.

e. Three children are taking a walk in the woods when they discover a baby dinosaur.

4. Have the children in each group discuss the five scenarios (or others the teacher creates) and decide which one they would like to act out in a three-minute skit.

5. Using a desk at the front of the room for the stage, invite groups to come up and act out their scenarios. Encourage the "audience" to applaud for the children when they have finished.

6. Continue in this manner until all groups have presented their scenarios. Optional: Have children create sets out of tagboard and bring in books with patterns to have children design more sophisticated puppets. Add props (e.g., toy car, plastic dinosaur, candy, etc.).

ASSESSMENT   Evaluate this activity by using a checklist to determine individual participation and how each child was able to explain the scenario through the puppet's words and actions; for English language learners, check for complete sentences and use of verbs. Use the sock puppets for subsequent oral language activities and note, anecdotally, any language growth in children who were originally not able to participate.

Notes for next time . . .

_____

_____

_____

_____

_____

_____

_____

_____

_____

_____

_____

Which Picture?

SUGGESTED GRADE LEVEL   2–6

PURPOSE   Children gain practice giving precise oral descriptions. Because pictures are being described, the activity is a vocabulary enhancer for English language learners as well.

MATERIALS   Ten large, mounted pictures or reproductions of paintings which can be placed on the chalk tray. Pictures should contain colorful characters, interesting backgrounds, or plentiful action. Sources include photographs of murals from the community, family pictures, photos from the community, pictures from *Gathering the Sun* by Alma Flor Ada, or old calendars. Optional: Pictures drawn by the children could be used. Pictures related to a curriculum unit based on literature, a holiday, an important event, or a multicultural concept could also be employed.

PROCEDURE

1. Place pictures on the chalk tray or on a bulletin board where every child in the group may view them clearly. Number the pictures.

2. Place the children in pairs.

3. Ask the children to look closely at each picture or painting and think about what that picture says to them, what it reminds them of in their own life, or what they particularly like about it. Encourage them to discuss these observations with their partners.

4. Tell the children you are going to show them how to use descriptive language to tell them about one of the pictures or paintings. Offer three sentences that tell about the picture without totally giving it away. Allow the pairs of children to guess which picture or painting you are describing.

5. The pair who guesses which picture or painting you have described becomes the "Orator," and selects a dif-

ferent picture or painting to describe, as you have just modeled. The two children discuss what three sentences should be used.

6. One child in the pair offers the oral description for their chosen picture and the other pairs of children, after quietly deliberating, guess. Note: Tell the children to be sure to look at the other children and not the picture when giving their description.

7. Proceed until each pair has had a chance to offer a description.

8. If a pair that has already described a picture guesses correctly, they may select a pair to create the description.

ASSESSMENT After the children have participated in the activity, have each child select a picture. Individually, ask each child to tell you three descriptive sentences about the picture he or she has chosen. Create a checklist for use of adjectives, complete sentences, and the ability to describe the most important aspects of the picture or painting. Place the checklist in the child's file. Revisit this and similar activities for the children needing help writing complete, descriptive sentences.

CHECKLIST FOR ORAL DESCRIPTIONS

Name _____ Date _____

	Yes	No
Uses adjectives	☐	☐
Writes in complete sentences	☐	☐
Describes important details	☐	☐

Notes for next time . . .

_____

_____

_____

_____

Help Me Find My Way

3

SUGGESTED GRADE LEVEL   *3–6*

PURPOSE   In oral communication, children must learn to quickly organize their thoughts in a logical, easily comprehensible way. This activity provides practice for all children—native speakers and English language learners—in organizing their thoughts within the context of dramatic play.

MATERIALS

- Cards containing suggested places such as the following:
  - on a street corner
  - in a new school
  - in a movie theater
  - in a grocery store
  - in a shopping mall
  - in the woods
  - in a city park
  - in a strange country
- Large sheets of poster board
- Colored markers
- Optional: If the children have access to computers and skills, PowerPoint can be used for the presentation

PROCEDURE

1. Lead a discussion about the situation of becoming lost. Encourage the children to contribute tales of times they have been lost and how they eventually found their way.

2. Divide the children into groups of four. Give each group one of the above place cards to indicate where they could become "lost." Invite the groups to create an alternative place of their choice if they wish.

3. Explain that each member of the group will first work individually, jotting down thoughts as to what he or she might do if he or she became lost in the proscribed place.

4. When each member of the group has come up with his or her ideas, tell the group to come together to formulate a plan that would tell a lost individual how to find his or her way in such a situation.

5. Ask each group to decide how they would like to present their ideas to the rest of the class. Advise them that *all* members of the group must take part in the presentation.

6. Ask for a volunteer to come up to the front of the room and act out the part of someone who has become lost at the first group's location. Invite the corresponding group to present their ideas on finding one's way in such a situation.

7. Subsequently, have different children act out the part of the lost individual in each situation as an introduction to each group's presentation.

ASSESSMENT Use a checklist to see if each child has participated in the initial whole-class discussion, problem solving, small group conversation, and the final presentation of the solution to the real-life possibility of becoming lost. Place the checklists in each child's file. Compare the checklists to those filled out in subsequent uses of the activity. Share growth with the students.

SAMPLE CHECKLIST

	Name:																		
Date:																			
Whole-Class Discussion																			
Problem Solving																			
Small Group Conversation																			
Final Presentation of the Solution																			

Family Interview and Report 4

SUGGESTED
GRADE LEVEL *4–6*

PURPOSE Children gain appreciation of their own heritage while learning how to interview, take notes, and formulate an oral report.

MATERIALS The book *Grandfather's Journey,* by Allen Say (Houghton Mifflin, 1993) or another trade book featuring an elder recounting his or her youth.

PROCEDURE

1. Read *Grandfather's Journey* to the children. Ask them to listen for ways this grandfather's life was different from, and similar to, their own.

2. After the reading, create a Venn diagram on a large sheet of chart paper with one circle labeled "Grandfather" and the other "Us" and an area of overlap. Discuss how the grandfather's life was similar and different from their lives and write their ideas on the board in the appropriate area.

3. With the children, brainstorm a list of questions they might ask their own grandparents, aunts, uncles, family friends, or other relatives about their lives when they were the age of the students in the class. For example:

   What did you do for fun?

   Where did you live?

   What were your clothes like?

   What music did you listen to?

   What was your school like?

   What did you care most about?

   If you came from another country, what did you miss about your old country, or appreciate about your new one?

4. Have the children select an older friend or relative whom they can interview, and choose four questions to ask this person. Ask them to take notes on the answers that are given.

5. Have the children volunteer to share orally the questions they asked and retell, in their own words, the answers given by the people they interviewed.

6. Invite the other members of the group to ask questions of each interviewer.

Grandfather

One-room school house

Born in Japan

Read or played games

Worked to earn money for family

Go to school

Large family

Liked to play

Had to work

Us

Big school

Born here, Mexico, or Vietnam

Played computer or video games

Do chores

7. Return to the chart paper. With the class, discuss the differences and similarities of the childhoods of the persons who were interviewed as compared with the children's lives. Write their answers in the appropriate columns.

ASSESSMENT As the children are sharing their reports, take anecdotal notes on their interview summaries. Much can be discovered about each child's ability to ask questions and summarize information concisely through this instructional activity. Place notes in each child's file. Provide direct instruction in summary writing for those children having problems in this area.

Notes for next time . . .

_____

_____

_____

_____

As Advertised

SUGGESTED GRADE LEVEL *4–6*

PURPOSE Children will develop oral communication skills, listening skills, and practice in thinking up a creative description and slogan to advertise a common household product.

MATERIALS Enough generic household products for each member of the group (e.g., pen, hairspray, perfume, cleaning product, dog biscuit, toy, battery, etc.).

PROCEDURE

1. Discuss how advertisers sell to people using techniques such as free giveaways, catchy jingles, and bandwagon appeal.

2. Ask the children to keep a log of television or radio advertisements they watch and summarize three of these, paying careful attention to how they influence people to buy their products.

3. In class, invite each child to tell about one advertisement they watched and the persuasive technique the advertiser used to sell the product. List these on the board.

4. Distribute the generic household products, one per child.

5. Give the children time to think up a slogan and/or a catchy device and a catchy name for their product that would get others to buy it. Ask them to include at least one persuasive technique that has been discussed in class.

6. Tell the children they will have one minute for a commercial to try to "sell" their product to the other members of the group with the devices they created.

7. After each child has performed his or her commercial, survey the class informally to see if they think they would buy the product. Why or why not?

8. Optional: Videotape the children as they advertise their products. Play it back for them to see.

ASSESSMENT Evaluate each child's advertisement by checking for (1) the inclusion of one persuasive advertising technique and (2) the ability to express him or herself in a clear, loud voice. If the performances were videotaped, allow the children to use the same criteria to evaluate themselves. Place the evaluations in the child's file. Compare each child's performance now to a subsequent lesson at the end of the school year. Discuss growth in these areas with each child.

SAMPLE STUDENT EVALUATION

Name _____ Date _____

	Yes	No	Technique:
1. I included one persuasive technique.	☐	☐	_____
2. I expressed myself in a loud, clear voice.	☐	☐	_____

Notes for next time . . .

_____

_____

_____

_____

_____

_____

Adapted from "Radio Reading," by Frank Greene, in *Reading Comprehension at Four Linguistic Levels,* edited by C. Pennock (Newark, DE: International Reading Association, 1979).

Reread Alouds

SUGGESTED GRADE LEVEL   *1–3*

PURPOSE   Current research suggests that children become more accurate and fluent when they read the same passage several times, and that their understanding of what they have read also increases. This activity will make repetition enjoyable for young children.

MATERIALS
- Tape recorder
- Blank tape
- Material of the child's choosing
- Simple bar graph to show progress
- Stopwatch or clock with second hand

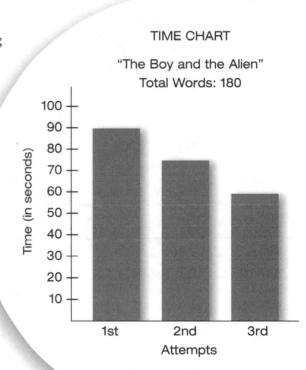

TIME CHART

"The Boy and the Alien"
Total Words: 180

PROCEDURE

1. Help the children each select a short passage that is a bit difficult for them (at their instructional level).

2. Have the children write down any words they cannot decode.

3. Have the children attempt to decode the problem words, then tell them the words. Record specific phonetic elements that are troublesome, and place in the child's file.

4. Ask the children individually to read the passage aloud as you tape-record it. Using a watch or clock with a second hand, record the time. Note any errors.

5. Tell the children that they are now going to beat their record by reading the same passage faster. Again, record the reading time for each child and note any errors. Repeat this process several times in a relaxed, gamelike fashion.

6. Help the children use a bar graph to compare the amount read and their accuracy between the first and last readings. Discuss the children's growth individually with them.

ASSESSMENT Photocopy the bar graph and place it in the child's file as an ongoing assessment of fluency and accuracy. Revisit the activity monthly to check that fluency is increasing.

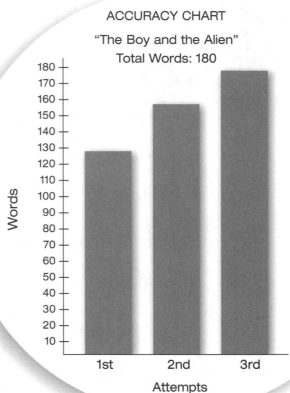

ACCURACY CHART
"The Boy and the Alien"
Total Words: 180

Notes for next time . . .

_____

_____

_____

_____

_____

_____

_____

_____

_____

_____

_____

_____

_____

_____

_____

Revised Radio Reading

(Adapted from Green, 1979)

SUGGESTED GRADE LEVEL   *3–5*

PURPOSE   This motivational approach to oral reading provides children with an authentic reason for repeated reading of a passage—to be a radio announcer—and also offers the other children assuming the role of "audience" a chance to listen critically in order to engage in subsequent discussion.

MATERIALS
- Literature from a basal reader or a children's trade book at the children's independent reading level. Suggested titles:

  Biggest, Strongest, Fastest, by Steve Jenkins (Scholastic, 1995) 4–6

  Welcoming Babies, by Margy Burns Knight (Tilbury House, 1994) K–3

  Peppe the Lamplighter, by Elisa Bartone (Lothrop, Lee & Shepard, 1993) K–3
- Optional: Karaoke machine or a microphone

PROCEDURE

1. Remind the children of a book they have all read by having them help you summarize the key points.

2. Divide the book into small numbered sections and give a section to each member of the group.

3. Ask the children to rehearse their sections by reading them out loud at home or at school.

4. Model asking an open-ended question for a section of the book. Example: What do you think you would do if you came face-to-face with a poisonous sun jellyfish? Invite the children to create one such open-ended question for the section they have been assigned.

5. Model reading a passage aloud, as a radio announcer might, while the other children listen with

their books closed. Then ask the student who has been assigned the first passage to read that passage as a radio announcer would.

6. Encourage the child to then ask his or her open-ended question about the section. (Allow sufficient time for a brief discussion, if the question engages the other children.)

7. When the first announcer is finished and the initial discussion has waned, have the other readers in the group read their sections in order as the other children listen. Follow each reading with the open-ended question and discussion.

ASSESSMENT   Create a checklist that includes the item's fluency, phrasing, and expression. Use a check, check plus, or check minus to indicate the degree to which each reading skill has been mastered. Place the checklist in each child's file. In subsequent uses of this instructional strategy, check for improvement in these skills.

SAMPLE CHECKLIST

Skill:	Name:																
Fluency																	
Phrasing																	
Expression																	

Notes for next time . . .

_____

_____

_____

_____

Adapted from "Radio Reading," by Frank Greene, in *Reading Comprehension at Four Linguistic Levels*, edited by C. Pennock (Newark, DE: International Reading Association, 1979).

Read Around

(Adapted from Tompkins, 1998)

SUGGESTED GRADE LEVEL *3–6*

PURPOSE Sharing favorite passages orally promotes fluency, critical thinking, and an ability to evaluate literature.

MATERIALS Reading material that all members of the group have recently read, including comic books, narrative, or informational text, or a magazine article. Post-it pads, or 3" × 5" cards.

PROCEDURE

1. Ask the children to skim over a selection they have recently read in order to find a sentence, phrase, or paragraph that particularly appealed to them. Explain that they can make their choice because it reminds them of something else they have read or know about, because it reminds them of something in their own life, or because they feel the passage was especially funny, sad, frightening, thoughtful, or well-written.

2. Have the children mark their selection with a sticky note or copy the passage onto a 3" × 5" card.

3. Give the children several minutes to rehearse their favorite passage by reading it quietly to themselves.

4. Ask for a volunteer to read his or her favorite passage while the other children listen. Invite the reader to explain why he or she chose the passage or what about it appeals to him or her.

5. Continue calling on volunteers until every child who wishes to has had the opportunity to share.

ASSESSMENT Take anecdotal notes on each child's ability to read fluently with accuracy, appropriate rate, and expression. Also, note each child's choice of passage as an indication of future reading interests. Place notes in each child's file.

Notes for next time . . .

_____

_____

_____

_____

_____

_____

_____

_____

_____

_____

_____

_____

_____

_____

_____

_____

_____

_____

_____

_____

Adapted from *50 Literacy Strategies Step by Step,* by Gail Tompkins (Upper Saddle River, NJ: Merrill, 1998).

Readers Theatre

(Adapted from Opitz & Rasinski, 1998)

SUGGESTED GRADE LEVEL 3–6

PURPOSE Children practice fluent, expressive, meaningful language while using their reading voices to perform a story or script for an audience. No sets, props, or costumes are required, thus minimizing distraction from the language activity.

MATERIALS
- A transparency of ready-to-use scripts such as those in *Readers Theatre for Beginning Readers,* by Suzanne Barchers
- Several reading level-appropriate selections from a piece of children's literature that contain plenty of dialogue, such as *Charlotte's Web,* by E. B. White. Copies for each child in the group.
- An overhead projector

PROCEDURES

1. Share a ready-made script with the children using the overhead projector. Show them how the narrator explains the action while the actors do the speaking. Explain the use of the colon after a character's name to denote who will be speaking.

2. Divide the children into groups of three to five. Pass out the copies of a three- or four-page selection of children's literature with plenty of dialogue for each child.

3. Within the groups, have the children discuss how the selection might be changed into a script by having the characters speak while the narrator explains the action.

4. Select a recorder for each group to rewrite the script in readers theater format with the input from other group members.

5. Give the group members adequate time to read the scripts both silently and orally, as a group, to develop the fluency and expression necessary to share it with the others.

6. As the small groups feel they are ready, allow them to share their revised scripts with the rest of the class. Alternatively, sharing can be done in the order the selection occurs in the book.

7. When each group has performed their script, conduct a group discussion of which facets of each performance were effective and why.

ASSESSMENT Construct a checklist to note each child's ability to read his or her part of the selection with fluency, expression, and in a clear, appropriately loud voice. Provide more practice of this and similar activities for children having problems in the area of fluency.

Partial readers theatre script

The Boy Who Cried Wolf (in children's manuscript)
Developed by second-graders and their teacher

Narrator: Once upon a time there was a little shepherd boy who lived in a village with his mother and father. Every morning he went to the hillside to herd his sheep. One day he got bored and decided to play a little joke.

Shepherd boy: I am tired of looking after these silly sheep. I think I will play a joke. I will get the village people to come and join me. They will keep me company.

Narrator: So the boy stood up and yelled as loudly as he could:

Shepherd boy: Wolf! Wolf!

Narrator: Soon all the village people came running up the hillside to see what was wrong.

Village person #1: So where is the wolf, young man? I don't see any wolf.

Village person #2: Yes! We were very busy and you disturbed us. There is no wolf here!

Village person #2: I don't see any wolf either. Let's go back down the hill. This was a waste of our time.

Narrator: So the village people went back down the hill. The next day the shepherd boy went to the hillside again. He got bored again. He wondered if his joke would work again.

SAMPLE FLUENCY CHECKLIST

	Name:																								
Date																										
Fluency																										
Expression																										
Clear, loud, appropriate voice																										

Adapted from *Goodbye Round Robin: 25 Effective Oral Reading Strategies,* by Michael F. Opitz and Timothy V. Rasinski (Portsmouth, NH: Heinemann, 1998).

Choral Reading of Poetry

**SUGGESTED
GRADE LEVEL**   *4–6*

PURPOSE   Children discover that poetry is meant to be read aloud and doing so encourages growth in fluency through the repeated readings that this activity affords. Also, children gain practice in speaking with clear, rhythmic voices.

MATERIALS
- Poetry suitable for the independent reading level of the group members. Suggested poems can be found in the following excellent anthologies:

  Where the Sidewalk Ends, by Shel Silverstein (Harper & Row, 1974)

  Preposterous: Poems of Youth, selected by Paul B. Janezco (Orchard, 1991)
- An overhead transparency of a selected poem

PROCEDURES

1. Select a poem from the suggested anthologies, or another of your choosing. Read the poem aloud to the children using appropriate expression and phrasing.

2. Discuss the poem's meaning, or theme, with the children, using open-ended questions such as:

   > What does this poem remind you of in your own life?

   > How does the poem make you feel?

   > What words and phrases in the poem appeal to you?

3. Have the children read the poem aloud with you.

4. Divide the class into different groups for a further reading of the poem. For example, a poem with dialogue may be divided as such: children with deeper voices may read big, gruff characters, such as giants, monsters, or large animals;

children with lighter, softer voices may speak the parts of fairies, butterflies, small animals, and so forth.

5. Practice the poem with the different voices several times, until the children seem fluent with the reading.

6. Optional: Invite the children to think of actions or gestures that would enhance the words and phrases, such as waving arms for the wind or fluttering fingers for butterflies. Such actions also make the words accessible for English language learners.

7. When several poems have been prepared in this manner, have the class perform their poems for parents, another class, or for a school function.

ASSESSMENT When several readings of the poem have occurred, ask the children to read the poem to you individually. Check for fluency, expression, and phrasing, using the sample checklist from the previous activity. Allow children having problems with fluency to practice reading their poem into a tape recorder, or invite them to practice reading their poem in order to read it to younger children.

Notes for next time . . .

_____

_____

_____

_____

_____

_____

_____

_____

_____

_____

_____

Other Ideas & Activities

- **KINDS OF SENTENCES.** Write different kinds of sentences on index cards, some containing strong feelings ("That makes me so sad!"), some commands ("I said shut the door!"), some questions ("Why on earth did she do that?"), and others declarative sentences ("I am having a birthday party soon."). In small groups, have the children practice saying the sentences at different rates, with differing pitches, and with different voice qualities to suggest alternative meanings.

- **QUESTIONS.** As an alternative to extemporaneous speaking, ask the children to brainstorm some common questions people ask when they are just getting to know one another, for example, "What is your favorite TV program and why?" or "Who is the person you most admire? Why?" Write the children's questions on slips of paper and put them in a jar. Have each child pick a question and provide a sixty-second response.

- **LET ME ENTERTAIN YOU.** Invite the children to practice reading picture story books with fluency and expression in order to be a guest reader in a classroom with younger children. Likewise, invite fluent readers from other classrooms in to present models of fluency.

- **INTRODUCTIONS.** Set up scenarios for the children where they are practicing making introductions. For example, tell the children they are introducing their friend to their mother, or a new boy in school to the class. Remind them to offer some information about each person so the two people can begin a conversation.

- **JOKE TIME.** Set aside time on a weekly basis for the children to share jokes they have heard or found on the Internet. Encourage all the children to contribute and remind other children what constitutes a polite audience.

- **PLAY IT AGAIN.** Have a tape recorder available at a learning center in the classroom. Direct the children to practice reading favorite book passages into the tape recorder. Have them listen to themselves, make notes on what they think needs improvement, and reread the selection trying to better their performance.

- **ASSUME A ROLE.** Have the children silently read a passage with plenty of dialogue. Ask them to think carefully about how each character might say what is written. Call on individual children to read lines of dialogue as he or she thinks individual characters might.

- **PROPS.** Divide the children into small groups. Give each group several common household materials, such as a mop, a toy, a dish, and so forth. Ask each group to devise a short skit, using the items as props, to perform in front of the rest of the class.

- **TELL A TALE.** Arrange the children in a circle. Begin telling a story, introducing the setting and main characters. Ask the child on your right to continue telling the story, for one minute, adding as much or little as he or she likes. When that child is finished, have the child on his or her right begin where the first child left off. Before the last child begins, tell him or her to provide an appropriate story ending. The story can be tape-recorded and transcribed.

- **GUESS WHAT I FOUND OUT?** Once a week, choose a topic that could be from current events, science, or social studies. The topic could be one the children are studying, or one that comes from the children's interest or discussion. For example, the topic might be lightning bugs: What makes them glow? Or thunder: Why does it make such noise? Have the children use the Internet, trade books, magazines, or adult resources to find one new fact to add to a discussion the next day.

- **NEWS REPORT.** Have the children responsible each night for keeping up with one topic in current events. They may get their information from the newspaper, magazines, an adult, the radio, or TV, but they should be prepared to participate in a discussion about the topic. Have the children share what they know.

- **TWO TRUTHS AND A LIE.** Have the children share three statements about themselves, but fabricate one of the three. For example: I have a cat named Julia (truth). I went on vacation to Hawaii when I was four (lie). I don't know how to whistle (truth). Invite other children to guess which of the statements are not true.

- **ORAL AEROBICS.** Write a simple subject and predicate on the board such as, "The boy laughed." Ask each child to elaborate on the sentence by adding adjectives, clauses, and phrases to create more interesting sentences such as, "The frail, freckle-faced boy laughed wickedly when he was told that the neighborhood bully fell in the mud."

- **DESCRIPTO.** Give each child material from which to make a collage that represents who they are. When the children have finished, display them without the children's names. Other children make three guesses for each collage. Then the child to whom it belongs makes a short oral presentation about what the collage represents.

- **TALL TALE CONTEST.** Help the children forget their self-consciousness when speaking in front of a group by seeing who can tell the tallest tale. Even the shyest child may enjoy participating when the presentation is make-believe and they have no fear of making a mistake.

Children's Literature List

Ada, Alma Flor, illustrated by Simon Silva. *Gathering the Sun: An Alphabet in Spanish and English.* (New York: Rayo/HarperCollins, 2001). This book is a beautifully illustrated alphabet book, which also includes poetry. Centered around the experience of Hispanic agricultural workers, the book contains color-saturated gouache illustrations, celebrating the lives of farmworkers. It is perfect for reading aloud to a group of bilingual students.

Ada, Alma Flor, illustrated by Lori Lohstoeter. *Friend Frog.* (San Diego: Gulliver Books, 2000). Poor Field Mouse is so impressed by Frog, who can jump, croak, and swim, that he doubts whether the two of them can ever become friends.

Bartone, Elisa. *Peppe the Lamplighter.* (New York: Lothrop, Lee & Shepard, 1993). Little Peppe wants to accept a job as a lamplighter in Little Italy, a New York City neighborhood, to help support his family. At first Peppe's father is upset, but he gradually becomes proud of his son.

Blos, Joan. *A Gathering of Days.* (New York: MacMillan, 1979). Written in journal format that makes it interesting for reading orally, this book tells the story of two years in the life of a nineteenth-century young girl.

Janezco, Paul B. *Preposterous: Poems of Youth*. (New York: Orchard Books, 1991). Janezco has selected a variety of poems to amuse youngsters of all ages.

Jenkins, Steve. *Biggest, Strongest, Fastest*. (New York: Scholastic, 1995). This informational text identifies the animal record holders in the world, such as the world's fastest, largest, and most poisonous animals.

Knight, Margy Burns. *Welcoming Babies*. (Gardiner, ME: Tilbury House, 1994). This informational book for all ages introduces readers to the ways families of all cultures welcome newborns into the world.

Say, Allen. *Grandfather's Journey*. (Boston: Houghton Mifflin, 1993). A Japanese–American man tells the story of his move to America and of his feelings of love and longing for both his native country and his newly adopted one.

Silverstein, Shel. *Where the Sidewalk Ends*. (New York: Harper & Row, 1974). One of the most popular books of children's poetry of all times. A must for every elementary classroom library.

White, E. B. *Charlotte's Web*. (New York: Harper & Row, 1952). The children's beloved and timeless classic about the friendship between a child and a pig.

Other Resources for Teaching Oral Language and Fluency

Readers Theatre for Beginning Readers, by Suzanne Barchers (Englewood, CO: Teacher Ideals Press, 1993). Barchers' book describes how to prepare scripts for readers theater, and provides prop, delivery, and audience suggestions. It also includes 17 ready-to-use scripts adapted from literature from a variety of world cultures.

Creating Competent Communicators: Activities for Teaching Speaking, Listening, and Media Literacy in K–6 Classrooms, by Pamela Cooper and Sherwyn Morreale (eds.) (Scottsdale, AZ: Holcomb Hathaway, 2003). The teaching activities in this resource have been tested in communication classrooms and found to be successful in helping students develop competencies in the fundamentals of communication, speaking, listening, and media literacy. They involve students in sending and receiving messages in a variety of contexts for a variety of purposes and provide for student interaction and involvement—important components of oral communication skill development. In addition, these activities make it easy for a teacher to integrate oral communication instruction across the curriculum.

In Closing

1. After using the activities in this section, what insights have you gained about how children develop oral language and fluency? What did you discover about yourself as a teacher of literacy by teaching these activities?

2. Which of the activities in this section did you find were particularly effective in teaching the following oral language and fluency skills?

- Making presentations
- Reading with expression
- Feeling comfortable in front of a group
- Participating in discussions
- Interviewing
- Listening to others

3. Choose an activity that was particularly easy and one that was difficult for the children with whom you worked. Why do think it was easy/difficult? What, if any, adaptations would you make the next time you teach the lesson? Why?

4. What did you discover about the need to determine what children already know about a subject before beginning an instructional activity? How did the assessment suggestions at the end of each activity provide you with insights into the strengths and limitations of your teaching of oral language and fluency?

5. Select an activity that offered you the most insight into the general knowledge background of the children with whom you worked. What did you discover about the importance of children having background knowledge about a topic before discussing it? Cite specific examples of this discovery in the children with whom you worked.

6. Several of the activities asked the children to elaborate on simple language or use language to describe a picture or a feeling. What speaking and writing skills are enhanced through the use of such activities? What did you learn about your learners' oral language facility as a result of these activities?

7. Certain activities asked the children to reread a passage or book in preparation for reading aloud or chorally. What might be the advantages or disadvantages of these activities? What did you learn about a specific child's oral language fluency as a result of these activities?

8. Some activities asked the children to act out certain scenarios in order to persuade the listener or to entertain. How do you think oral language can be improved through the use of these activities? Why? Give examples of specific children and how you feel their language fluency or confidence increased as a result of this activity.

9. Which activities seemed especially difficult for your English language learners? What did you observe about their difficulties? How could you revise these activities to make them more accessible for your English language learners?

10. Identify an English language learner who you think has quickly acquired a high degree of oral language and/or reading fluency. What are the characteristics of this child? Did his or her behavior during the activities differ from that of the other children? Describe the differences, if any.

Activities for Spelling

Introduction

Because spelling is one of the most visible manifestations of literacy, it holds an exalted place in our society. Therefore, teachers must understand the nature and function of spelling, or "sound mapping," and communicate to parents about how spelling proficiency actually evolves.

After many years of studying spelling, researchers have decided that spelling involves much more than simply memorizing the sequence of letters in a list of words. Just as the errors young children make in speaking or drawing get corrected after much practice, spelling will evolve after some direct instruction in how English orthography works. Spelling seems to develop in a fairly consistent and predictable way in all children, similar to the stages children pass through as they learn to speak. Knowing a bit about how this important literacy convention progresses will ease the anxiety that parents and others often have that the errors in early written work will become permanent.

J. Richard Gentry has analyzed the way in which children learn to spell and has identified five discrete stages that children go through:

1. The *precommunicative stage,* in which children are using strings of letters and various other symbols but have little or no idea which symbol stands for which sound.

2. The *semiphonetic stage,* wherein they realize a rudimentary relationship between sounds and letters but often use one letter to represent an entire word.

3. The *phonetic stage,* in which spellers tend to segment sounds according to what they hear.

4. The *transitional stage,* which finds children using rules and orthographic patterns they have been taught, and also becoming much more aware of the visual aspects of words.

5. The *correct, or conventional, stage,* when children have mastered many of the more sophisticated rules of orthography and also have acquired a large body of grade-appropriate words that they can spell correctly in their written work.

The following activities have been chosen because they allow children to focus on the rules of English orthography and, in younger grades, experiment with print in an enjoyable way. They are designed not to replace but, instead, to supplement a program of direct instruction in spelling.

Puzzlers

1

SUGGESTED GRADE LEVEL *K–1*

PURPOSE Spelling riddles, such as the ones suggested here, combine foundational elements of phonemic awareness, such as the manipulation of sounds and sound segmentation, with deliberate mapping of the sounds using letters, or spelling. Because the riddles are oral, children must use their visual memory to think about the sounds and the letters.

MATERIALS
- 5" × 8" word cards, one for each of the words used
- Create puzzlers in Spanish, or other languages spoken by children in the class (optional).

PROCEDURE

1. Tell the children you are going to play a riddle game with them. You will ask them a question about some words and the sounds within them, and they are to guess the answer.

2. Model the game, by saying: In this game, I might say three words—*bunny, bat,* and *bean.* Then I would ask you, "Which letter is in all three words?" You would say "b." Or I might say, "I am in *top* but not in *hop.* What letter am I? I'm the letter *t.*"

3. Begin with easier-to-hear questions containing only beginning sounds. Use the following riddles or add to them with your own:

> I am in tin, tomato, and tiny. What am I?
> I am in bag, bone, and bottle. What am I?
> I am in sun, soft, and sad. What am I?
> I am in land, loaf, and luck. What am I?
> Salgo en taza, té y tren. ¿Quién soy?

I am in truck, train, and trust. What am I?

I am in tin, tomato, and tiny. What am I?

I am in try but I am not in sky. What am I?

I am in call but I am not in ball. What am I?

Salgo en mar, moto y madre. ¿Quién soy?

Harder: I am in truck, train, and trust. What am I?

I am in call but I am not in ball. What am I?

I am in sing but I am not in wing. What am I?

Salgo en río pero no en tío. ¿Quién soy?

I am in time but I am not in lime. What am I?

I am in boy but I am not in toy. What am I?

Harder: I am in try but I am not in sky. What am I?

4. After each riddle has been discussed and answered orally, reinforce sound/symbol relationships by showing the word cards and pointing to the letters that are the same or were being manipulated.

5. For a greater challenge for children who are more capable spellers, invite them to create their own puzzlers to share with the rest of the class.

ASSESSMENT The riddles created for this activity can be used to assess either phonemic awareness or sound mapping ability by using the cards in two different ways.

1. Ask individual children who are not yet able to work with letters to tell only the sound represented by the words in the riddles (e.g., tin, tomato, and tiny all begin with the /t/ sound).

2. For children who are already working successfully with phonics, use the cards with individual students to ascertain which letters they are able to recognize, segment, and manipulate, and which letters require more work.

Notes for next time . . .

_____

_____

_____

_____

_____

Consonant Picture Match

SUGGESTED GRADE LEVEL   *K–1*

PURPOSE   At the initial stages of spelling development, children must begin to notice the visual differences in structure, as well as the sound differences, between letters that are dissimilar. This activity affords children enjoyable practice in discriminating between two letter sounds at a time.

MATERIALS
- Consonant picture cards
- Consonant letter cards

PROCEDURE

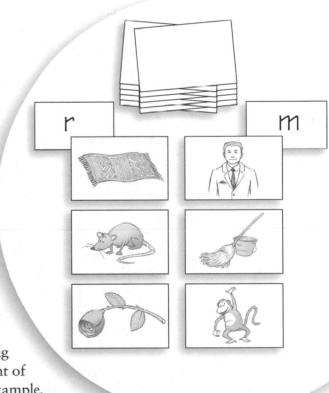

1. Begin with two letter sounds that are most dissimilar (e.g., r and m).

2. Choose two pictures, one each for the beginning sound corresponding to the two letters.

3. On a table or desk, place the pictures (e.g., rug and man) under the corresponding letter. Shuffle the remaining cards and say to the children: Now we are going to listen for the sounds at the beginning of these pictures. We will decide if the word begins like "rug" or like "man."

4. Model how you decide how the beginning sound is categorized by doing several in front of the children until they have the idea. For example, if the picture is of a mouse, say: Mouse: mmmmmouse begins like mmmman, so I'll put it under the letter "m."

5. Invite the children to take turns deciding whether a picture belongs under the "r" or the "m" by sounding out the picture's beginning sound, as you did.

6. After all the pictures have been sorted in this manner, have the children help you name all the pictures in each category from the top down, exaggerating the beginning sound of each.

ASSESSMENT Have individual children complete the sort while naming the picture and matching the letter with which it corresponds. Using a checklist, determine which children are able to complete this task and which children need further instruction in discriminating the targeted initial consonants. Place checklists in children's files.

Notes for next time . . .

_____

_____

_____

_____

_____

_____

_____

_____

_____

_____

_____

_____

_____

_____

_____

_____

_____

_____

_____

_____

Rhyming Race

SUGGESTED GRADE LEVEL *1–2*

PURPOSE
This activity gives young children practice in recognizing the patterns of rimes, or phonograms, in the English language, introduces the concept of homophones, and offers a welcome variation from the routine weekly spelling test.

MATERIALS
- Pencils
- Paper
- List of spelling words that have common rimes (e.g., call, sand, date, fold, fill, ran, pin, teach, grew, like)

PROCEDURE

1. Review the concept of rhyming with the children. Guide them to see that words that have the same ending sounds have rimes that are often spelled the same way. Offer examples such as the words *man* and *tan*. Invite the children to add new beginning letters to these words as you write them on the chalkboard or on a Word Wall.

bit	boat
fit	coat
split	float
wit	goat
sit	moat

2. Say the first spelling word (e.g., grew). Ask the children to write it on their papers.

3. Ask for a volunteer to write the spelling word on the chalkboard so all the children may see if their word was spelled correctly.

4. Invite the children to write down as many rhyming words as they can for the word on the chalkboard (for the word *blew*: flew, drew, few, stew, knew, crew, chew, threw).

5. Discuss words that sound the same but are spelled differently than the original word (for example: blew, blue; through, threw; see, sea). Introduce the concept of homophones (also called homonyms) for these word pairs.

6. Write the sets of rhyming words on a Word Wall, where they can be used for original poetry. Create a separate column for words that sound the same as the original word but are spelled differently (homophones).

ASSESSMENT Invite the children to create original rhymes using the rhyming words on the Word Wall. Note how each child is able to use rhyming patterns and decide when a word is a homophone. Place information for each child in his or her file. Follow up, for those children having difficulty creating rhyming words, with activities form the Phonemic Awareness section.

Notes for next time . . .

_____

_____

_____

_____

_____

_____

_____

_____

_____

_____

_____

_____

_____

_____

_____

Smoked Bacon

**SUGGESTED
GRADE LEVEL** 2–3

PURPOSE This activity forces children to attend to the exact sequence of letters that comprise words, to hold them in their visual memory, and then to actively form those words using their body as a "place holder."

MATERIALS • Two sets of large cardboard letters, each set containing each of the letters in the words "smoked bacon"

PROCEDURE

1. Divide the class into two teams.

2. Have the teams stand up and face each other.

3. Distribute one letter card to each team member. Ask the children to hold their letter up prominently so the other team can clearly see it.

4. Call out an anagram, or a word that can be spelled with the letters from these two words (there are at least 100).

5. Ask the members of each team to rearrange themselves to form the letters in the word in order. The first team to get in the correct position gets one point. One child from the winning team is selected to write the new word on the chalkboard. The team with the most points wins the game.

ASSESSMENT   For the final weekly spelling test, use the anagrams from the words "smoked bacon." As a bonus, use two different words, such as baby sister, and ask the children to see how many new words they can create from these.

Notes for next time . . .

_____

_____

_____

_____

_____

_____

_____

_____

_____

_____

_____

_____

_____

_____

_____

_____

_____

_____

Guess and Spell

SUGGESTED GRADE LEVEL *2–6*

PURPOSE The visual memory necessary for proficient spelling is highlighted in this activity, which asks children to spell the names of common objects in the classroom. The leader, a good speller whose prowess is highlighted, puts letters on the chalkboard as other students suggest them, allowing individual students to practice sound mapping in an enjoyable and nonthreatening gamelike activity.

MATERIALS • Chalkboard

PROCEDURE

1. Select a proficient speller to be "it." This child selects a common object in the room and whispers its name to the teacher.

2. The other children in the class raise their hands, and the leader calls on them to guess the first letter of the chosen object. As they guess the correct letters, the leader puts them on the chalkboard.

3. When the first letter is guessed, the children start trying to guess the second letter, then the third letter, and so forth, until the entire word is spelled.

4. When any student thinks he or she can spell the total word after only a few letters have been guessed, that student may challenge the leader by spelling the complete word. If the word is spelled correctly, that student becomes "it." Note: This activity can be adapted for intermediate grades by varying the spelling patterns and level of difficulty for the words.

Guess and Spell *continued*

ASSESSMENT   Make a list of the words the leaders chose and use these as a spelling list for the week. In small groups, the children can sort these words according to beginning or ending sounds, affixes, or other attributes. Make notes on children's strengths and needs observed through these activities. Place these notes in each child's file.

Notes for next time . . .

_____

_____

_____

_____

_____

_____

_____

_____

_____

_____

_____

_____

_____

_____

_____

_____

_____

_____

_____

Roots and Branches

SUGGESTED GRADE LEVEL *2–6*

PURPOSE
Children develop an understanding of the roots of words by seeing how the spelling of a word can change with the addition of suffixes. This activity can be adapted to any of the later spelling stages.

MATERIALS
- Sets of four word cards for each of several regular root words and their common derivatives—for example:

  march, marcher, marching, marched

  fear, feared, fearful, fearing

  dance, dancer, dancing, danced

  call, called, calling, caller

  play, player, playing, played

  ask, asked, asking, asker

  bake, baker, baking, baked

PROCEDURE

1. Make enough copies of each set of words to have four "books" (a "book" is all four cards with the same root) for each child. Divide the children into pairs.

2. Shuffle the cards and give six to each child.

3. Tell the children to sort their cards according to "roots," and give an example of how this would be done.

4. If a child holds four cards with the same root, that child has a "book" and lays down the cards on his or her desk.

5. At a given signal by the teacher, the children take turns asking their partner if they have a card with a certain root. Each

child may continue asking for a card as long as the other child holds other words with the desired root.

6. Reverse the roles. The partner asks for root cards in a similar manner.

7. At the next signal, the children select a different partner and repeat the procedure, laying down "books" as they are acquired.

8. A child wins the game when all of his or her cards are in "books."

Note: Care should be taken not to introduce elements for which the children are not developmentally ready—for example, doubling the final consonant of a root or completely changing the spelling, such as *teach* and *taught*.

ASSESSMENT Before the game, introduce the words to be assessed, and then use them for the weekly spelling lesson. When introducing more difficult stem changes, play the game again, incorporating the new spelling patterns.

Notes for next time . . .

_____

_____

_____

_____

_____

_____

_____

_____

_____

_____

_____

_____

Flower Chains

**SUGGESTED
GRADE LEVEL**   2–6

PURPOSE   This activity promotes interest in words, strengthens visual memory, and shows children how many words they are able to generate and spell. The integration with art makes this activity especially appealing.

MATERIALS
- Pencil
- Writing paper
- Colored construction paper
- Paste
- Laminating materials (optional)
- Vis-á-vis markers

PROCEDURE

1. Cut out a series of flower shapes from colored construction paper. The flowers can be laminated and a vis-á-vis used to write on them so they can be wiped off and used many times. Put these aside.

2. Explain that you are going to see how many words you can make into a flower chain by saying a word, spelling it, and then thinking of a new word that begins with the last letter of the first word. For example, you might say: "My word is man, m-a-n. My next word is nut, n-u-t. My next word is tan, t-a-n," and so forth.

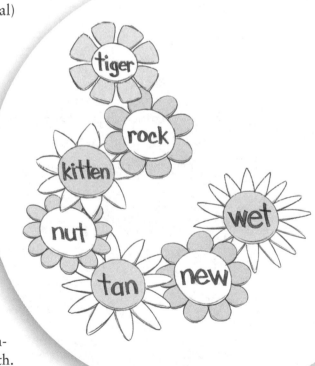

3. As you spell out the words, write them on the chalkboard, underlining the last letter of the first word, the first letter of the second word, and so forth. Keep adding words until all the children are able to tell you the letter the next word must start with.

4. Transfer the word list from the chalkboard to the flowers, one word per flower.

5. Paste the flowers together so corresponding beginning letters and ending letters follow one another.

6. Finally, connect the flowers when one word ending is the same as the first letter of the original word (see illustration).

7. Ask the children to write down a favorite word, perhaps from their weekly spelling list. Invite them to then write down as many words as they can think of using the first letter/last letter sequence. Encourage them to sound out unfamiliar words. Use these for future weekly spelling lists.

8. Pass out colored construction paper and have the children make flowers to correspond to their words. Help them to make flower chains by connecting the flowers where the first and last letters match.

ASSESSMENT As the children are creating their lists, walk around the room taking anecdotal notes on each child's ability to sound out words, as well as the words memorized. Note which high-frequency words are generally giving the class problems. Include these in the weekly spelling list, or create a special Word Wall for them. Place a list of high-frequency words that each child has not yet mastered in his or her file.

Notes for next time . . .

_____

_____

_____

_____

_____

_____

_____

_____

_____

Memory Game

SUGGESTED GRADE LEVEL   2–6

PURPOSE   Besides improving visual memory and motivation for spelling new and familiar words, this activity stimulates the acquisition of new meaning vocabulary for English language learners.

MATERIALS
- Picture cards for 10 to 15 objects
- Objects (marble, pencil, scissors, paperclip, ruler, yo-yo, stamp, tack, book, etc.)
- Pencils and paper

PROCEDURE

1. Put the children in groups of three, according to language proficiency.

2. Tell the children that you are going to show them some pictures, and later some objects, and that they are to study these carefully and try to remember each one.

3. Show the pictures to the children, one at a time. Clearly state the name of each object for the benefit of English language learners.

4. Conceal the pictures. Ask the children to write down the names of every one they can remember.

5. When the children have remembered all they can, allow them to consult with their other two group members to see if they recall these pictures and to check on the correct spelling. Have the groups form a new, corrected list with as many words as each group can remember.

6. Bring out the objects. Have members from each group take turns writing the name of an object on the chalkboard.

7. Create a Word Wall with these words.

ASSESSMENT   Collect the lists of initial spelling attempts from individual children before they receive input from their group. Analyze the spelling patterns of the children individually according to their stage of spelling development. Consider homogeneous regrouping according to the children's individual stage of spelling development.

Notes for next time . . .

_____

_____

_____

_____

_____

_____

_____

_____

_____

_____

_____

_____

_____

_____

_____

_____

_____

_____

_____

Favorite Words

SUGGESTED GRADE LEVEL   3–6

PURPOSE   Children learn to spell words more easily if they have special meaning for the children. In this activity, which can supplement the weekly spelling list or be used to supplant it for individual children who are struggling, children select their own words to learn to spell.

MATERIALS
- Word cards
- Magic markers
- Metal notebook rings
- Dictionary (optional)

PROCEDURE

1. Individually, take children aside and ask them to think of a word they would like to learn how to spell.

2. Write their word on a word card with a marker. Optional: Invite the child to draw a picture of the word next to it.

3. Ask the child to tell you a short sentence that contains the word. (They may use a dictionary.)

4. If the sentence is correct, ask the child to write the sentence on the back of the word card, underlining his or her word.

5. Have the child read the word and the sentence on the back of the word card.

6. Ask the child to look at the word while saying each letter aloud, and then spell the word to you without looking at it.

7. Punch a hole in the word card and put it on a metal ring.

8. Add more words as each child is ready.

ASSESSMENT Periodically, have each child read the words and sentences. Then ask the child to spell the words either orally or on paper. Keep a record of the words the child has "mastered," determined by whether the child is able to spell the word and use it in a sentence at a later date. Place this information in the child's file.

Notes for next time . . .

_____
_____
_____
_____
_____
_____
_____
_____
_____
_____
_____
_____
_____
_____
_____
_____
_____
_____
_____
_____

Find the Missing Letter

10

SUGGESTED GRADE LEVEL   *3–6*

PURPOSE   This activity can help children to pay closer visual attention to the specific sequence of letters in words, especially in words with elements that are commonly misspelled. The activity helps to develop a spelling consciousness ("The word looks right") as well as an awareness of English orthographic patterns.

MATERIALS
- Chalkboard
- List of grade-appropriate words with confusing letter sequences
- Colored chalk

PROCEDURE

1. Place two identical lists of words, each with a missing letter or letters, in separate columns on the chalkboard. Create teams and as many words as there are children on the team. An example of a word list with problematic letter sequences is:

piece	special
chief	beat
eagle	woman
wear	bear
believe	friend
receive	human

p_ece   speci_l
chi_f   be_t
e_gle   w_man
we_r   b_ar
bel__ve   fr_end
rec__ve   h_man

2. At a given signal, a child from each team goes to the board and writes the missing letter(s) in a word (each child may call upon teammates for help if stuck).

3. When each team has correctly completed all the words, the last member of the team uses different colored chalk to circle the words that are alike in their sounds or letter sequences, with help from teammates.

4. A member of each team explains to the other team how the categories were selected. Note: This activity can be easily adapted to the appropriate grade level by varying the spelling patterns and level of difficulty of the words.

ASSESSMENT Have the children write down the words they have worked with correctly, and place in each child's file. Take note of individual confusion with specific patterns. Create individual word study lists for children who demonstrate problems with specific patterns.

Notes for next time . . .

_____

_____

_____

_____

_____

_____

_____

_____

_____

_____

_____

_____

_____

_____

_____

_____

_____

_____

_____

_____

_____

_____

Word Detectives

**SUGGESTED
GRADE LEVEL**   4–6

PURPOSE   Many spellings relate to semantic function in the language rather than to phonetic representation. Some spellings represent meaning and therefore lead the speller and the reader directly to the word's meaning. Some spelling instruction, such as in this activity, should emphasize regularities in meaning between related words.

MATERIALS
- Lined paper
- Construction paper
- Staples

PROCEDURES

1. Discuss with the children the fact that many words give clues to spelling. If we understand the meanings of two similar words, we can improve our spelling ability.

2. Ask the children to pronounce and identify the relationship between "microscope" and "microscopic." Tell them that even though they are pronounced differently, there is a close relationship in meaning.

3. Ask the children to use the two words in sentences and have them compare the meanings so that they can identify the similarities in spelling. Discuss the parts of speech of each new word. Has it changed?

4. For guided practice, have them work with the following words in the same way:

nature	natural	gymnasium	gymnastics
photograph	photographer	biography	biographical
piano	pianist	library	librarian

5. Invite the children to become word detectives and have them search for their own examples of word families that share similar spellings and meanings.

6. Pass out lined paper and construction paper and encourage the children to create booklets of other spelling words that show a relationship between meaning and spelling.

7. Have the children use their words in sentences and share their word detective books with the rest of the class. Optional: Invite the children to share their booklets with younger children in other classes.

Word Detectives *continued*

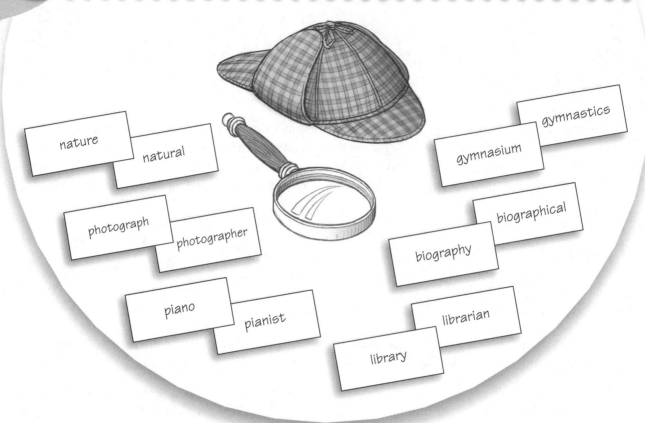

nature

natural

gymnastics

gymnasium

photograph

photographer

biographical

biography

piano

pianist

librarian

library

ASSESSMENT   Check word detective booklets for number of entries and different forms of the same words. Individually, ask the children to pronounce their words for you and tell you what each one means. See if they are able to identify the parts of speech. Place the number of correctly identified words in the child's file. In a subsequent implementation of the activity, note an increase in the number of words correctly identified. Use this increase as evidence of growth in spelling and morphological awareness.

Notes for next time . . .

_____

_____

_____

_____

_____

Other Ideas & Activities

- **CHALKBOARD SPELLING.** Have children with fine-motor coordination problems write spelling words on the chalkboard with paint brushes and water.

- **MNEMONIC DEVICES.** Use mnemonic devices to help children remember difficult words by making specific associations with the word. Examples: *All right* is like *all wrong*. I want a *piece* of *pie*. A fri*end* is with you until the *end*.

- **ALLITERATIVE SENTENCES.** In small groups, have the children produce sentences all beginning with the same first letter. Examples: Does David dig for dusty dinosaurs? Freda fries frog fritters on Fridays.

- **TREASURE BOX.** Write the weekly spelling words on slips of paper, fold them, and put them into a "treasure box." Invite each child in turn to draw out a slip to be handed to you unopened. Pronounce the word and have the child attempt to spell it. Hand misspelled words to the child to study. Two children can provide extra practice for each other as they play this game quietly in a corner.

- **NOVELTY SPELLING.** Instead of calling words from a spelling list, say, for example, "Spell a word that rhymes with *joint*," "Spell a word that contains a *ph* that sounds like *f*," or "Spell a word that means _____ ."

- **BALLOONS.** Draw balloons on the chalkboard. Write the first letter of spelling words, one in each of the balloons. Each child who can say and spell the word that starts with a beginning letter "buys" a balloon. Let the child select the balloon he or she wants. If the child spells the word correctly, write the word and the child's name on the balloon.

- **PEAR TREES.** Divide the class into three committees to develop trees that "grow" pears with pairs of antonyms (big, little), homonyms (pair, pear), or synonyms (evil, bad). Put the pairs of words onto light green or yellow pears and add dark green leaves and brown branches for effect.

- **SPELLING JINGLES.** Establish spelling of new words by having the children compose jingles using the new word in a rhyme, thereby learning the new word and similar words as well. Example: When it is night, we need a light.

- **CROSSWORD PUZZLES.** Make a crossword puzzle for the week's spelling words. For clues, use either the meaning or the word in context. (There are websites, e.g. PuzzleMaker.com, where the teacher or children can do this easily.)

- **BEANBAG TOSS.** Have a child stand in front of the room and toss a beanbag underhand to a seated child. As the beanbag is thrown, the child calls out a word that the catcher must spell. If the catcher spells the word correctly, it is that child's turn. A child may ask for help from a classmate.

- **SHAVING CREAM SPELLING.** As a tactile activity, squirt some shaving cream on children's desks and ask them to write words using their fingers. When they are finished, they can wipe off the desks with paper towels, thereby cleaning the desks at the same time!

- **CONTRACTION HUNT.** Have children look through newspapers and magazines for word pairs that can be changed into contractions, or contractions that can be changed into two separate words. Have children highlight these words and then place them on a Word Wall.

Children's Literature List

Brown, Craig. *City Sounds*. (New York: Greenwillow, 1992). Depicts the sounds that Farmer Brown hears when he comes into the city to pick up some baby chicks. Reinforces long /e/ patterns as well as the use of phonics skills to decode city sounds.

Gardner, Beau. *"Have You Ever Seen . . ."? An ABC Book*. (New York: BGA, 1986). Asks questions that incorporate the sound correspondence being presented: "Have you ever seen a banana with buttons?" Reinforces beginning sounds and their spellings.

Raffi. *Spider on the Floor*. (New York: Crown, 1993). A song telling about a spider that is on the floor and then crawls up the singer's leg, stomach, neck, face, and head. The book lends itself not only to choral reading and singing but also to recognizing the short /e/ pattern.

Roe, Eileen. *All I Am*. (New York: Bradbury Press, 1990). A little boy telling about his unique qualities and interests: "I am a friend. I am an artist. I am a dancer." Provides a writing model and also reinforces the "er" suffix.

Wilson, Sarah, illustrated by Susan Meddaugh. *Good Zap, Little Grog*. (Boston: Candlewick, 1995). The strange nonsense words and rhythmic patterns beg for repetition. Children will beg teachers to read the book again and again. The book can be used to create interest in words and encourage children to sound out or spell the nonsense words. After reading, children can be invited to tell other stories using made-up words.

Other Resources for Teaching Spelling

The Spelling Connection: Integrating Reading, Writing, and Spelling Instruction, by Ronald L. Cramer (New York: Guilford Publications, 1998). Emphasizes practical classroom issues in exploring effective instructional strategies and their conceptual underpinnings; describes criteria for selecting spelling words; presents case studies showing the stages of spelling development; and addresses frequently asked questions about spelling.

Spelling Inquiry: How One Elementary School Caught the Mnemonic Plague, by Kelly Chandler and the Mapleton Teacher–Research Group (York, ME: Stenhouse Publishers, 1999). A K–5 perspective on spelling development. Discusses how to foster inquiry-based learning about spelling and provides a detailed look at the workings of a schoolwide teacher–research group. Accessible and lively narrative blends the voices of a dozen of its members.

Spelling Instruction That Makes Sense, by Jo Phenix (Bothell, WA: Wright Group, 1998). A refreshing book that explores when and how to introduce spelling in the classroom. Presents ways to capitalize on the "teachable moment" with individual students, small groups, and the whole class.

Spelling K–8: Planning and Teaching, by Diane Snowball and Faye Bolton (York, ME: Stenhouse Publishers, 1999). Assists teachers in implementing specific types of spelling investigations, such as sounds and spelling patterns, by clearly outlining the general process involved in productive spelling explorations. Relates the teaching of spelling to reading and writing experiences in a variety of curriculum areas.

Spelling Strategies That Work: Practical Ways to Motivate Students to Become Successful Spellers, by Min Hong and Patsy Stafford (Jefferson City, MO: Scholastic Professional Resources, 1998). Secrets of success in teaching spelling with an integrated language arts program written by seasoned classroom teachers. Documentation of how four primary students developed in spelling over a two-year period illustrates the value of tailoring a program to individual needs.

The Spelling Teacher's Book of Lists, by Jo Phenix (Bothell, WA: Wright Group, 1998). A collection of interesting words, spelling patterns, and facts designed for teachers who want to help children make sense of spelling. Lists focus on consonants, vowels, confusing spellings, linguistic roots, and useful rules.

The Violent E and Other Tricky Sounds: Learning to Spell from Kindergarten through Grade 6, by Margaret Hughes and Dennis Searle (York, ME: Stenhouse Publishers, 1997). Uses detailed descriptions of growth in spelling by following children from kindergarten through grade 6. Reveals what children say and do as they come to understand spelling and its systematic nature.

Voices on Word Matters: Learning about Phonics and Spelling in the Literacy Classroom, edited by Irene C. Fountas and Gay Su Pinnell (Westport, CT: Heinemann, 1999). An exploration, by experts in the field, of letter and word learning in a variety of reading, writing, and language contexts—with articles ranging from detailed observations of individual readers and writers to full-scale analyses of classroom processes and student work.

In Closing

1. After using the activities in this section, what insights have you gained into how children learn to spell? What did you discover about yourself as a teacher of spelling by teaching these activities?

2. Which of the following activities did you think were particularly effective for children at each of the following developmental spelling stages? Why?

   - The precommunicative stage
   - The prephonetic, or preliterate, stage
   - The phonetic, or letter name, stage

- The transitional, or within-word, stage
- The conventional, or syllable juncture, stage

3. What did you observe about the nature of children's "invented" or temporary spelling as a result of using the activities in this section?

4. What did you discover about the need to determine what children already know about the sound–symbol relationship before beginning a spelling lesson? How did the assessment suggestions at the end of each activity provide you with insights into the strengths and limitations of your teaching of spelling?

5. Select an activity that offered you the best insight into the developmental spelling stages of your learners. What did you discover? Cite examples of specific children with whom you worked.

6. Several of the activities offered a gamelike format. What do you see as the advantages and disadvantages of this format for spelling lessons?

7. One activity (*Favorite Words*) invited children to choose some of the words they would like to learn to spell. Do you think there were any motivational benefits to having the children do this? Describe your observations.

8. Some activities asked children to identify patterns or specific word parts such as roots. How do you think this strategy compares with having children memorize spelling rules and generalizations? Why?

9. Which activities were particularly difficult for English language learners? What did you observe about their difficulties? How could you revise these activities to be more accessible to your English language learners?

10. Identify a child you think has a highly developed ability to spell unfamiliar words. What are the characteristics of that child? How did his or her behavior during the activities differ from that of the other children? How will you adapt future spelling activities to assure that these children are appropriately challenged?

Activities to Increase Vocabulary

6

Introduction

Learning the meanings of new words is without question crucial to a comprehensive literacy program for all learners. The more numerous the reading, writing, speaking, and listening activities, the more children will come into contact with a variety of intriguing new words. These experiences help the vocabularies of children grow; and, through the excitement of reading and writing, these children also blossom into proficient readers and writers.

Children add approximately 3,000 new words to their meaning vocabulary each year. This growth can be fostered through effective meaning vocabulary development activities such as helping children appreciate words, encouraging wide reading and application of new words, presenting strategies for figuring out new words, and the direct teaching of vocabulary and vocabulary-related skills. The ultimate goal of all vocabulary instruction should be to inspire children to become independent word collectors who actually enjoy encountering unfamiliar words. These children become those who comprehend best, and thus read the most, entering a self-perpetuating cycle of success.

The following activities are designed to foster a love for words, an appreciation for discerning just the right word when writing, and a better understanding of how words are formed in the English language. Many of the activities include pantomime or drawing to provide comprehensible input and thus enhance the participation of English language learners.

Words in Color

SUGGESTED GRADE LEVEL   *1–3*

PURPOSE   The definitions of words are remembered more easily when multisensory activities are used to focus children's attention on them. By sketching the meaning of a word, children are compelled to consider the context of that word; moreover, English language learners benefit from definitions, both by attempting to create the drawings themselves and by observing the drawings of their classmates. Articulating how the drawings fit the words provides an authentic purpose for critical thinking and oral language.

MATERIALS
- Colored markers
- White drawing paper
- Vocabulary words culled from text the children will soon read

PROCEDURE

1. To initiate this activity, demonstrate the end product by showing the children a drawing you have made that illustrates a word's meaning. Example: For the word "sad," draw a person frowning, perhaps near a dented car, or a rainy day, or a child with an ice-cream cone with the ice cream on the ground.

2. Introduce each of the new vocabulary words, explaining the meaning of each. Ask several volunteers for different ways each word might be represented through a drawing.

3. Divide the children into pairs. Distribute paper and pens and ask each group to discuss the meaning of each word and then agree upon an illustration for each word. The two children may choose to take turns drawing, or one may opt to simply offer suggestions.

4. As the children are discussing the words and the drawing, ask the groups to clarify the meanings of words about which they are unclear.

5. Have each pair select one of the words and explain to the rest of the class how their drawing illustrates the meaning of the word.

6. Taking each pair's favorite drawing, make a class book from the drawings, and title it "Words in Color."

ASSESSMENT   Children's drawings, as well as their explanations of them, allow an important qualitative assessment of how well they understand the meanings of the new words. As a follow-up assessment, later ask individual children to define the words without the drawings, orally for preliterate children and in written form for older ones. Tape-record their answers. Transcribe and place results in each child's file. Compare their ability with a follow-up assessment to determine vocabulary growth.

Notes for next time . . .

_____

_____

_____

_____

_____

_____

_____

_____

_____

_____

_____

_____

_____

_____

_____

_____

Describe the Character

**SUGGESTED
GRADE LEVEL** *1–6*

PURPOSE In this cooperative group activity, the children use oral language to discuss the outside features (appearance) and the inside features (feelings, personality, character) of major characters from stories they have just read.

MATERIALS
- 3" × 5" cards with the name of a literary character on each
- Book from which each character came
- Chart paper for each group
- Colored markers

PROCEDURE

1. Hold up the character cards, one at a time, for the entire class. Revisit their parts in stories that recently have been read.

2. Select one character from a grade-appropriate book, such as Amelia Bedelia, to use as a demonstration.

3. Make two columns on the chalkboard, one labeled "outside" and the other labeled "inside."

4. Ask the children to brainstorm the best words they can think of to first describe Amelia's outside, or her appearance. Write their suggestions under the "outside" column (e.g., thin, old-fashioned, dark-haired, grown-up). Do the same for their suggestions for Amelia's inside, or feelings and personality (e.g., confused, hard-working, funny, kind).

5. Place the children in small cooperative groups of three children each. Give one character card to each group.

Inside

confused
hard-working
funny
kind

Outside

thin
old-fashioned
dark-haired
grown-up

6. Invite the children to revisit their character in the story from which he or she came. Have them pay careful attention to the character's physical appearance and then, using colored markers, draw a picture of their character on the top of the chart paper.

7. Ask the groups to brainstorm as many words as they can think of for their literary character for both categories, inside features and outside features.

8. Have a member from each group share his or her chart with other members of the class, explaining their drawing, their word choices, and how they were selected.

ASSESSMENT   On an individual basis, ask each child to select one character from a book he or she is reading or has recently read. Using the inside/outside format, ask the child to list as many descriptors as possible for the character. Place the list in the child's file. Provide a mini-lesson on descriptive words (adjectives) for children who offer mostly "tired" words, or who are unable to list five words for both the inside and outside of their chosen character.

Notes for next time . . .

Strange Expressions

SUGGESTED GRADE LEVEL *2–4*

PURPOSE Figures of speech, homophones, and other unusual expressions in the English language are often confusing for English language learners, as well as native English speakers. This activity focuses on some commonly used figures of speech through a whimsical text and invites children to collect others for group discussion.

MATERIALS
- *A Chocolate Moose for Dinner,* by Fred Gwynne (New York: Simon & Schuster, 1976) or *The King Who Rained,* by Fred Gwynne (New York: Simon & Schuster, 1974)
- Word Wall
- White drawing paper
- Marking pens

PROCEDURE

1. Read any of Fred Gwynne's books to the children. Each of these concerns a little girl trying to visualize the strange expressions her parents use, such as a "car pool," or a "king raining" or a "gorilla war."

2. Discuss the actual meaning of these expressions and their literal connotations.

3. Revisit the book, directing the children's attention to the illustrations, in which the little girl's literal interpretation of the terms leads to some hilarious visualizations.

4. With the children, brainstorm some other confusing expressions, idioms, or figures of speech that Gwynne's book did *not* cover, such as "She has a frog in her throat," or "I am tickled pink!" List these on chart paper, to which new expressions will be added over the next several weeks as they are encountered.

5. Encourage each child to select one of the expressions the class has collected and have each child illustrate the literal interpretation of the term and write the expression underneath.

6. Have each child share his or her illustration with the rest of the class, explaining what the expression actually means, yet what it sounds like it means to them.

7. Collate the pictures and bind them together into a class book entitled "Strange Expressions" or another title of the children's choice.

I have a frog in my throat!

ASSESSMENT Understanding of these expressions can be determined by using the class book. Ask each child to read the expression and explain what each statement means and how each can be misinterpreted. Calculate the percentage of expressions each child was able to explain and place this information in each child's file. Repeat this exercise with an alternate Gwynne book for those children scoring less than 80 percent.

Notes for next time . . .

_____

_____

_____

_____

_____

Definitions

SUGGESTED GRADE LEVEL *2–4*

PURPOSE This writing activity allows the children to use the poetic form of blank verse to define an entity by free-associating their personal feelings and reactions to it, and also considering what the entity is *not*.

MATERIALS
- Pencils
- Lined writing paper
- Sample poem written on an overhead transparency or chalkboard

PROCEDURE

1. Select a common state of being about which to brainstorm with the children. Examples: happiness, anger, jealousy, loneliness, confusion. (Younger children may be more comfortable using concrete entities such as lions, toys, friends, brothers, stars, or shoes.)

2. Stimulate thinking about the chosen word by asking questions such as, "What is it? What is it like? What is it not like? What are some examples of it?"

3. Have the children follow along as you read the sample poem or another of your choice, to inspire children and demonstrate the format.

4. Have the children select a topic, such as *puppies*. Write a group poem together on the chalkboard, with each line beginning with, "Puppies are . . ." and alternating lines beginning with "But puppies are not . . . ."

5. When the children have run out of ideas on the topic, read the poem together chorally, using a left-to-right motion to help children follow along.

Vacations

Vacations are fun and relaxing
But vacations are not being really bored.

Vacations are sleeping late
But vacations are not going to bed early.

Vacations are going to the lake or camping
But vacations are not staying home and doing nothing.

Vacations are fishing and hiking
But vacations are not cleaning up and doing chores.

Vacations are fun
But coming home to my pets is good, too!

6. Brainstorm some other ideas for topics that can be defined in this manner. Write them on the chalkboard and ask the children to select one.

7. Distribute the writing paper and ask each child to write a definition poem using the format of one line telling what the entity is and the next line telling what it is not. For younger children or children struggling with writing, provide sentence stems for each line ("Puppies are ___. But puppies are not ___"), allowing them to write as much or as little as they can.

8. Have the children illustrate their definition poems and read them aloud in small share groups.

ASSESSMENT   Examine the individual poems to determine if each child is able to use the contrasting format to define his or her chosen feeling or concrete entity. Place the poems in the children's files. Compare quality of contrasting words to those used in a repeat of this activity later in the school year to determine writing and vocabulary growth.

Notes for next time . . .

_____

_____

_____

_____

_____

_____

_____

_____

_____

_____

_____

_____

Teakettle

5

SUGGESTED GRADE LEVEL 2–6

PURPOSE This activity shows children that many words are polysemantic—that they have multiple meanings—and therefore can be used in different ways.

MATERIALS
- Polysemantic words, each on a separate slip of paper (for example: ball, fast, change, rock, bank, miss, hand, sink, key)
- Box in which to put slips of paper

PROCEDURE

1. Use the word "ball" to explain to the children that some words can have different meanings depending upon how they are used. Ask them to consider the following sentences as you write them on the board:

   We had a *ball* at the party.

   The princess danced all night at the *ball*.

   The boy hit the *ball* with his bat.

2. Discuss how the word has different meanings in each sentence.

3. Explain that you are going to select a slip of paper from the box. On it will be a word that has several meanings. Make up a different sentence for each meaning, similar to the way you did with the word "ball." Instead of saying the word, however, say the word "teakettle." Offer the example:

   The princess danced all night at the teakettle. Can you think of the word?

   We had a teakettle at the party. Can you think of the word?

   The boy hit the teakettle with his bat.

   Now do you know the word?

4. Select another word from the box. Give the children a sentence using one meaning of the word, then another, then another, always substituting the word "teakettle" for the word on the slip of paper.

5. Ask the children to raise their hand and guess as soon as they think they know the hidden word.

6. When the children seem to understand the concept of the game, invite them to select a word and make up sentences giving the different word meanings.

The boy moved *fast*.
The man held *fast* to his beliefs.
The family did not eat during the *fast*.

I got *change* from the five-dollar bill.
I had to *change* my clothes.
We had pudding for a *change*.

I didn't want to *rock* the boat.
I sat on the *rock* to think.
The boy enjoys *rock* music.

The teacher has the answer *key*.
I need a *key* to open the door.
Hard work is the *key* to success.

The boy sat on the river *bank*.
Don't *bank* on being home early.
I keep my money in a *bank*.

I *miss* my old friend.
I had to *miss* school when I was sick.
Miss Jones is a good teacher.

We washed our hands at the *sink*.
I watched the girl *sink* the basket.
I saw the boat *sink* in the water.

The audience gave the performer a *hand*.
I wear a ring on my right *hand*.
I will *hand* over my books.

VARIATION   Have the children draw an illustration for each meaning of each word.

ASSESSMENT   Ask the children to write as many sentences as they can using different meanings for the following words: ball, fast, change, rock, bank, miss, sink, key. Provide direct instruction in polysemantic words for children who are not able to create at least two different sentences for each word.

Notes for next time . . .

_____

_____

_____

Beef It Up

SUGGESTED GRADE LEVEL   3–6

PURPOSE   With this activity, children can see how adding descriptive language and replacing "tired" words and phrases with more interesting vocabulary makes writing come to life. The activity is one of the few that also provides opportunities for group writing for young children, as well as an important experience in the evaluation of writing.

MATERIALS
- Simply written, short paragraph on an overhead transparency
- Overhead projector, blank transparency, and overhead writing instrument

PROCEDURE

1. Make a transparency of a simply written paragraph and put it on the overhead projector for the children to see.

2. Read the paragraph aloud to the children as they follow along (for younger children, provide a hard copy and allow them to "track" as you read).

3. Ask the children if they think the first sentence could be improved by adding words, feelings, details, or by changing some "tired" words (such as "good," "happy," or "nice") without actually changing what the author was trying to say. Solicit some ideas from the children. Write the "improved" version of the sentence on a blank transparency.

4. Divide the class into groups of three. Assign one or two sentences from the paragraph to each group. Ask each group to "improve" their sentences by adding words, feelings, details, or by changing "tired" words.

5. When all the groups have finished editing, ask a child from each group to read his or her revised sentence. Write the revisions on the blank overhead transparency under the first sentence. Continue in this manner until the entire rewritten paragraph has been read.

6. Place the rewritten paragraph(s) alongside the original paragraph. Read the revised one first, then reread the original paragraph.

7. Ask the children to tell, in their own words, the difference between the two paragraphs. (The revised paragraph should appear more lively, descriptive, and interesting to the reader.)

8. Revisit this activity several times to ready the children to take part in a Writer's Workshop as helpful peer editors and self-evaluators.

Beef It Up continued

Original paragraph:

Danny was a boy. He lived with his family in a small town. He always wanted to be in the circus. He thought it would be fun. One day he met a clown. The clown told him that living in a circus was hard work. You also have to travel from place to place. Danny changed his mind. Now he wants to be a firefighter.

Revised paragraph(s):

Danny was a friendly eight-year-old boy with sandy brown hair and freckles. He lived with his mother and father and seven brothers and sisters on a small, tree-lined street in a little Midwestern town. He dreamed of joining a circus in a far away city. "Becoming a circus performer seems like an exciting way to live," Danny blurted to his little sister.

One sunny afternoon Danny met a clown who was performing in a circus nearby. The clown, whose name was Bubbles, told Danny that becoming a circus performer took lots of difficult work. "A circus performer also has to travel from one location to another, all around the country," Bubbles whispered to Danny.

Danny thought about that for a while and finally decided not to join the circus after all. "I guess I will become a firefighter just like my dad!" he exclaimed.

ASSESSMENT After implementing this activity several times, use the sample original paragraph in the illustration to see how well the children are able to revise the writing individually. Ask them to rewrite the paragraph, as they did in the activity, adding fresh words and phrases, dialogue, feelings, and other colorful details. Place these paragraphs in the children's files. Provide direct instruction in the use of descriptive language for those children experiencing difficulty.

Notes for next time . . .

_____

_____

_____

Matrix

7

SUGGESTED GRADE LEVEL   *2–6*

PURPOSE   Certain meaning vocabulary is easily forgotten because it pertains to a specific subject area and is not used in everyday conversation. To teach children domain-specific vocabulary, the following graphic is helpful and can lead to rich comparison-and-contrast discussion about the topic.

MATERIALS
- Chalkboard or overhead projector

PROCEDURE

1. A matrix, also called a Semantic Feature Analysis, can be used to discuss attributes of items in a specific class and to discriminate between them. Example: You are preparing to take the children to the zoo and you want to discuss some animals they will see.

2. Brainstorm with the children all the animals they might expect to see in the zoo. (For children who may lack background knowledge, provide picture books as aids.)

	monkey	snake	ostrich	elephant	camel	panda	lion	shark	duck	polar bear
legs	✓		✓	✓	✓	✓	✓		✓	✓
fur	✓				✓	✓	✓			✓
mane							✓			
hump					✓					
gills								✓		
lungs	✓	✓	✓	✓	✓	✓	✓		✓	✓
tail				✓	✓	?	✓			✓
hooves					✓					
webbed feet										✓
bill			✓						✓	
trunk										

3. On the chalkboard or using an overhead projector transparency, write horizontally across the top of the board the names of animals the children have brainstormed, sounding out the spelling with the children.

4. In a vertical column to the left of the line of animals, create a list of attributes, or features, that animals could have. Define domain-specific vocabulary that might be unfamiliar to children, such as gills, mane, scales, hooves, webbed feet, bill, trunk, plumage, and hump.

5. Examine the cells one by one and, after you explain the attribute, ask the children to decide whether the animal in question possesses that feature. Write "yes" in the cell if the animal does and "no" if it does not. If the attribute is a quantifiable feature such as "legs,"

write the number in the cell. Rich discussion can ensue when children try to determine, for example, if a snake has a tail or if an elephant has fur.

6. Have each child select an animal and write one or more expository sentences describing it, using information contained in the matrix.

Note: For English language learners or preliterate children, you may want to provide pictures of the animals and their attributes while retaining the same level of discussion and vocabulary development. Older children may actually construct their own graphic organizers.

ASSESSMENT As the children are busy writing their sentences, use the time to do individual vocabulary assessments. Taking notes, ask the children to tell you everything they know about each of the animals as you mention their names one by one. Assess how the children use the new vocabulary words. Place a sample of words they used in the children's files.

Notes for next time . . .

_____

_____

_____

_____

_____

_____

_____

_____

_____

_____

_____

_____

_____

Peer Teaching

(Adapted from Blachowicz & Fisher, 1996)

SUGGESTED GRADE LEVEL 2–6

PURPOSE
Some researchers believe children can learn vocabulary best from other children because they are at the same cognitive level of operations. This activity allows children to teach words to each other, thereby benefiting from figuring out how to explain the word to another child.

MATERIALS
- Three index cards per child
- Writing instruments

PROCEDURE

1. Divide the children into groups of three. Give three index cards to each child in each group.

2. As the children are doing recreational reading, ask them to select one word they come across for which they do not know the meaning.

3. When the reading session is over, ask the children to prepare to discuss their word in a small group by writing the word and the sentence in which it appears on all three of the cards.

   > **EXHAUSTED**
   >
   > "Jeremy was exhausted after completing the 10-mile hike in the Sierras."
   >
   > very tired

4. Invite the children to try to determine the meaning of the word by (a) using the context of the sentence, (b) asking a resource person to explain it, or (c) using the dictionary, for those who are able to do so.

5. Have the first child in each group pass out his or her cards to the other members of the group. Have that child begin by reading his or her word in the context of the sentence as the others follow along.

6. Ask the other two students to discuss the possible meaning of the word from the context. They decide the final meaning in collaboration with the child who brought the word to the group.

7. Ask the other children to write the meaning of the new word on their index cards underneath the sentence in which the word appears.

8. Have the children retain these word cards in a personal word box to which they add on subsequent executions of this activity.

ASSESSMENT   Have the groups teach their words to the other children in the class. Utilize the words the children have compiled into lists for weekly spelling words. In addition to spelling these words, ask the children to write a simple definition for each. Place their spelling tests, with definitions, in their files, as samples of spelling ability.

Notes for next time . . .

_____

_____

_____

_____

_____

_____

_____

_____

_____

_____

_____

_____

_____

Adapted from *Teaching Vocabulary in All Classrooms,* by Camille Blachowicz and Peter Fisher (Upper Saddle River, NJ: Merrill, 1996).

Verb Gradient

SUGGESTED GRADE LEVEL 2–6

PURPOSE   Through this holistic activity, children can visualize and actively discuss the fine shades of meaning possible in a continuum ranging from one verb to its opposite. This is an especially appropriate activity for use with English language learners.

MATERIALS
- Overhead projector or chalkboard
- Blank Word Wall

wail

sob

cry

weep

smile

giggle

laugh

bellow

roar

PROCEDURE

1. On an overhead projector transparency or chalkboard, write the word "laugh" at the top and the word "cry" at the bottom, leaving plenty of room in between for adding new words.

2. Ask the children, "If you are not laughing but you're not crying, can someone tell me what else you might be doing?" Solicit answers that fall somewhere between these two behaviors, such as "smiling" or "whimpering."

3. Continue to solicit other responses, placing them closer to "laugh" or closer to "cry," depending upon their meaning.

4. Ask the children to think of words that might be more intense than "laugh" (for example, "roar") and more intense than "cry" (for example, "sob") and place these words in the appropriate spaces.

5. When the children have run out of ideas, suggest that they act out the words, beginning with the bottom word ("sob") and continuing up to the top word ("roar").

6. Write two other pairs of antonyms on the overhead projector: walk/run and whisper/shout.

7. Divide the children into groups of three and ask them to fill in the space for one of the sets of antonyms with words they think of.

8. When the children have finished, invite each group to read its list from bottom to top slowly while other members of the class act them out.

9. For each of the three verb gradients, create a Word Wall, upon which the children may add new verbs in appropriate spaces as they think of them.

ASSESSMENT Take anecdotal notes on the groups' discussions as they decide upon words and determine where to place them on the continuum. Some of the richest discussions take place during this activity. In addition, you can select other antonyms (for example, good/bad; hot/cold; slow/fast) and ask the children to create gradients independently, for individual evaluations of their understanding of the concept. Place each gradient in each child's file. For children not able to think of ten or more words on the gradient (select a lower number for lower grades, a higher number for higher grades), provide a mini-lesson on synonyms and antonyms.

Notes for next time . . .

_____

_____

_____

_____

_____

_____

_____

_____

_____

_____

_____

_____

_____

_____

Cloze Capers

SUGGESTED GRADE LEVEL 3–6

PURPOSE Increase children's ability to comprehend sentences as well as their facility with fine shades of meaning by using this critical-thinking activity. The activity is especially useful to help English language learners focus on the syntax of English.

MATERIALS
- Overhead projector and transparencies
- Brief passages (50–100 words), at children's independent reading level

PROCEDURE

1. Take out either verbs or adjectives from a brief passage, leaving blanks where the words have been deleted. Retain the original passage.

2. Write the following sentence on the overhead transparency: The boys ____ down the street after winning the ball game. Ask the children what action words, or verbs, would best tell how the boys were moving as they went down the street. (Guide the children to see that "cartwheeled" or "leaped" would be more appropriate word choices than "walked" or "strolled.")

3. Read the passage to the children as they follow along, saying "blank" for each of the words that have been deleted.

4. For each blank, invite the children to brainstorm a word that might fit in the blank, soliciting words that best describe the action in the passage, as they did in the example. Decide upon a "best" word for each blank through consensus.

5. When the children have filled in each blank in this manner, read the "new" passage to the children as they follow along. Place the original passage alongside the new passage. Ask the children which passage they prefer and why.

When the children and their father _reached_ the middle of the forest, the father _built_ a good fire. Then the stepmother _demanded,_ " _Wait_ by the fire while we _collect_ fire wood. We will _return_ to collect you later." Hansel _comforted_ Gretel, who became frightened by the dark. Later, they _recalled_ the pebbles that Hansel had _discarded._ They _followed_ the pebbles all the way home.

6. Divide the class into groups of three. Give them a similar brief passage and, through group discussion, ask them to fill in the missing blanks with appropriate verbs.

7. Have each group read its revised passages and compare the word choices.

VARIATION   Try this same activity using deleted adjectives.

ASSESSMENT   After completing the group activity, distribute a third passage with verbs (or adjectives) deleted for the children to complete individually. Assess on the basis of percentage of appropriate words they used. Provide daily cloze capers for those children who have difficulty choosing appropriate words, or for those who score below 80 percent.

Notes for next time . . .

Super Word Discoveries

11

SUGGESTED GRADE LEVEL 2–6

PURPOSE   For children to stretch the storehouse of words in their reading vocabulary, they can be urged to look for new words, decoding them by using the analogy strategy of comparing them to shorter, known words.

MATERIALS
- A "ballot" for each child, on which to write his or her discovered word
- A ballot box in which to collect ballots during the day
- A Word Wall, chart, or bulletin board space on which to retain all the discovered words

PROCEDURE

1. Continue this activity throughout the school year. To introduce the activity, tell the children they are to be looking continually for interesting, unknown words, or "Super Words," to share with the class. Although they should try to figure out the meaning of the new word by comparing it to words they already know, they may find the meaning by asking someone. Discovered words may come from anywhere—books, newspapers, environmental print, and so on.

2. When the children discover a word, they are to write the word on a ballot that is kept in a specific place in the room, put their name under it, and place it in the ballot box.

3. At a certain time at the end of each school day, read all the Super Words aloud to the class.

4. Have the class vote on the word they think is the most interesting, and then ask the child who discovered that word to explain what the word means, how he or she figured it out, and why he or she selected it.

5. Add the Super Word of the day, ceremoniously, to the Word Wall, chart, or bulletin board created for this purpose.

ASSESSMENT Encourage each child to participate in selecting the words, and note how each child attempts to decode unknown words. At various intervals, revisit the Super Word chart and have the children say the words and discuss their meanings. As an individual assessment, ask the children to write down the words from the Super Word chart, define them, and use them in a sentence. For children who are unable to do this for 80 percent of the words, pair them with students who are successful at this activity. Have them work together to discover and define future Super Words.

Notes for next time . . .

_____

_____

_____

_____

_____

_____

_____

_____

_____

_____

_____

_____

_____

_____

_____

Camouflage

SUGGESTED GRADE LEVEL   3–6

PURPOSE   Children will stretch their speaking vocabulary by using many words they have seldom used orally while explaining an autobiographical incident.

MATERIALS
- Lists of words in the meaning vocabulary of learners but slightly above their normal speaking vocabularies.
- Slips of paper containing one word each

PROCEDURES

1. Explain the meaning of the word "camouflage" and tell the children that in order to play this game, they must camouflage, or hide a specified word.

2. Give each child a slip of paper, each of which contains a word that is just above the normal speaking vocabulary; that is, words that they rarely use in everyday conversation, but words they may have encountered in a text.

3. Ask the children not to show their word to another child, but they may consult a dictionary to obtain a broader sense of the word's meaning.

4. Select a child to begin. That child will solicit autobiographical questions from the other class members, such as the following:

   What was your favorite summer vacation?

   What is your favorite animal?

   What did you do last weekend?

   What have you done that makes you proud?

> What was your favorite summer vacation?

> What is your favorite animal?

5. After considering the question for a moment, the first child must loosely answer the question, being sure to slip in the word that is contained on the slip of paper. (An obvious strategy is to utilize all the "big" words the child can think of to throw the other children off.)

6. When the child is finished answering the question, other members of the class raise their hands and try to guess which word was camouflaged. The first child "wins" if the number of children who guess the camouflaged word is fewer than the total number of incorrect guesses.

ASSESSMENT   Over time, children will become more facile at using more varied and interesting words when speaking. The first time the activity is introduced, make a note of the new words each child is able to use correctly in context. On subsequent revisiting of the activity, note any increase in the number of new words each child uses in context. Place both numbers in each child's file.

Notes for next time . . .

_____

_____

_____

_____

_____

_____

_____

_____

_____

_____

_____

_____

Other Ideas & Activities

- **TORTURE THE TEACHER.** Have the children take turns daily, finding a new word they think you will not know. Have them write their word on the top right-hand corner of the chalkboard while you decide whether you know it or not. (Tell them the definition, simply, if you know it.) Keep a running tally of the words you know and the words you miss, showing the children that even teachers can learn new words!

- **DESCRIBE THE OBJECT.** Place a common object (e.g., scissors) in a bag and give it to a volunteer, who peeks in the bag. Have that child use words to describe the object without naming it. From the child's description, other children may try to draw the object or simply guess what it is.

- **FAVORITE WORDS.** Share your favorite word(s) with the children and encourage them to collect their own favorites. Keep a tally of these words on a prominently displayed Word Wall.

- **WORD BANKS.** On colored 3" × 5" cards, have the children write new words they encounter in reading or in discussions. Provide time in class to discuss these words.

- **HINKY PINKY.** Provide clues for words that are rhyming synonyms, such as "a small insect" (wee bee) or "an unhappy father" (sad dad). When the children are facile at figuring them out, have them create their own.

- **PICTURE DICTIONARIES.** Have the children create and alphabetize their own colorful picture dictionaries for new words they have learned. This is especially helpful for English language learners.

- **WORDS FROM OTHER LANGUAGES.** As words are encountered through reading and discussion, collect them from other languages and cultures (e.g., bazaar, ballet, fiesta, patio). Have the children make a bulletin board illustrating these words and their country of origin.

- **BEANBAG PREFIXES.** Select a common prefix (e.g., *in, re, sub, un, com*) and ask the children to think of a word that begins with this word part as you throw a beanbag to them. Allow them to get help from a classmate. When ideas have been exhausted, change the prefix. Write new words on a Word Wall.

- **WHAT'S THIS WORD?** Daily, ask the children to bring in words they have heard or seen for which they would like to know the meaning. Utilize these words in your weekly spelling list.

- **PASSWORD.** Select one student to be "it" and have that child face the class, away from the board. Select a vocabulary word that has been recently introduced and write it on the board. Have other children try to help the chosen child guess the word by providing synonyms for the word. Write these synonyms on the board and discuss them after someone has guessed the word.

- **WORD OF THE DAY.** Choose a "stretch" word that is just above the children's meaning vocabulary. Explain its meaning and offer a small prize to every child who uses that word correctly during the day, either orally or in written form. Example: procrastination.

- **WORD PICTURE HUNT.** Challenge the children to find pictures from old magazines that illustrate their new vocabulary—for example, a picture of a desert might illustrate the word "desolate"; a picture of a cat watching goldfish might illustrate the word "captivating." Make "pictionary" scrapbooks from these pictures.

- **LISTENING WALKS.** Take children on a listening walk around the school. Tell them to be very quiet as they listen to the rhythms of the cafeteria, office, playground, and so forth. When they return to the classroom, have them use a variety of juicy words to describe the sounds they heard.

- **CATEGORIES.** Invite one child to choose a category, such as trees or cars. Other children take turns contributing a word that fits the category. When children have finished offering as many words as they can think of, the words are written down and categorized.

Children's Literature List

Antoine, Heloise, illustrated by Ingrid Godon. *Curious Kids Go on Vacation: Another Big Book of Words* (Atlanta: Peachtree, 1997). A delightful book written in the format of a themed pictionary, exploring a family vacation. More than 40 small objects are labeled, each relating to something one does or needs on a vacation.

Gwynne, Fred. *Chocolate Moose for Dinner.* (New York: Simon & Schuster, 1976). A hilarious book featuring a compendium of familiar expressions that are often confusing to young children, such as "We need to set up a car pool," and "Lions prey on other animals." Colorful illustrations show what children hear from the expressions. The book can lead to discussion about the expressions, and the children can create another book with other expressions that confuse them.

Kessler, Leonard. *Old Turtle's Riddle and Joke Book.* (New York: Greenwillow, 1986). Favorite riddles, which include classics such as: What fish chase mice? Cat fish. What happens when ducks fly? They quack up. Reinforces awareness of multiple meanings of words.

Most, Bernard. *Pets in Trumpets and Other Word-Play Riddles.* (New York: Harcourt, 1991). Riddles with the answer to each as the key word in the riddle and bold-faced in the text: Why did the musician find a dog in his trumpet? Because he always finds a **pet** in his trumpet. Reinforces seeking pronounceable word chunks in words.

Young, Selina. *My Favorite Word Book: Words and Pictures for the Very Young.* (New York: Random House, 1999). An irresistible introduction to words and reading by Zoe and Toby. More than 500 nouns are depicted in detailed drawings that feature an adorable cast of recurring characters. Can be used to build vocabulary, especially for English language learners, in an enjoyable way.

Other Resources for Teaching Vocabulary

Bringing Words to Life: Robust Vocabulary Instruction, by Isabel L. Beck, Margaret G. McKeown, and Linda Kuean (New York: Guilford Publications, 2002). This text provides a research-based framework and practical strategies for vocabulary development with children through the earliest grades all the way through high school. Many concrete examples, sample class-room dialogues, and exercises for teachers bring the material to life.

Classrooms That Work: They Can All Read and Write, by Patricia M. Cunningham (New York: Addison-Wesley, 1998). Loaded with classroom strategies and activities to teach children to read and write through extensive exploration of the English language in an enjoyable way.

Easy Mini-Lessons for Building Vocabulary: Practical Strategies That Boost Word Knowledge and Reading Comprehension, by Laura Robb (Jefferson City, VA: Scholastic Professional Books, 1998). Mini-lessons and activities covering vocabulary discussion charts, linking new words to children's lives, learning about roots, prefixes, and suffixes, conquering contextual clues, building word banks, and other strategies.

Let the Shadows Speak: Developing Children's Language Through Shadow Puppetry, by Franzeska Ewart (Herndon, VA: Stylus Publishing, 1998). Intended for teachers who are looking for exciting and effective ways to help children express themselves and enhance their vocabulary, be they bilingual children, children with language difficulties, or gifted children bored with traditional approaches.

Literature-Based Reading Activities, by Hallie Kay and Ruth Helen Yopp (Boston: Allyn & Bacon, 1996). Uses children's literature as a vehicle through which to reinforce vocabulary development as well as personal response to what is read.

Stretching Students' Vocabulary: Best Practices for Building the Rich Vocabulary Students Need to Achieve in Reading, Writing, and the Content Areas, by Karen Bromley (New York: Scholastic, 2002). In this text, you'll find more than 70 strategies drawn from the language arts, science, math, and social studies to help students excel in content-area reading and writing. Lively examples, illustrations, and photographs show the strategies in action.

Teaching Vocabulary in All Classrooms, by Camille Blachowicz and Peter Fisher (Upper Saddle River, NJ: Merrill, 1996). Explores independent means of learning vocabulary and the value of word play, as well as teacher-directed techniques that have the broader goal of enhancing the acquisition of new knowledge.

What's in a Word? Vocabulary Development in Multilingual Classrooms, by Norah McWilliams (Herndon, VA: Stylus Publishing, 1998). Develops children's word power. This book offers practical approaches and strategies based on the linguistic, cognitive, and social principles affecting children's use of words and their meanings in English as an acquired language.

Word Matters: Teaching Phonics and Spelling in the Reading/Writing Classroom, by Gay Su Pinnell, Irene Fountas, and Mary Ellen Giacobbe (New York: Heinemann, 1998). Word study leading to enhancement of reading vocabulary; offers many strategies to help children learn to decode and remember words.

In Closing

1. After using the activities in this section, what insights have you gained about how children acquire vocabulary? What did you discover about yourself as a teacher of literacy by teaching these activities?

2. Which of the activities in the section did you think were particularly effective for the following types of vocabulary development? Why?

   - Learning new words for new concepts
   - Enriching the meaning of known words
   - Learning new words for known concepts
   - Moving words into children's speaking vocabulary
   - Learning new meanings for known words

3. Which activities did you think best encouraged the love of language? In what ways was this manifested?

4. Which activity did you think was most successful in developing children's ability to use the context to figure out the meaning of unknown words? Why?

5. Select an activity that offered you the most insights into the level of vocabulary development of your learners. What did you discover? Cite examples of specific children with whom you worked.

6. Several of the activities used a combination of senses to help children remember words that were introduced. What might be the advantages and disadvantages of these activities? What did you learn about the learning styles of specific children through these activities?

7. Several of the activities focused on having the children use more colorful words and phrases either orally or in writing. How will such vocabulary enrichment activities help the children to become better writers? Why do you think so?

8. Certain activities asked the children to consider the fine shades of meaning of words they already knew. How is speaking and writing vocabulary enhanced as a result of these activities? Why do you think so?

9. Which activities were most difficult for your English language learners? What did you observe about their difficulties? How could you revise these activities to make them more accessible to your English language learners?

10. Identify a child who you think has a highly developed meaning vocabulary. What are the characteristics of that child? Did his or her behavior during the activities differ from that of the other children? Describe the differences, if any.

Activities to Foster Reading Comprehension

Introduction

Since before the turn of the 20th century, educators have been touting reading comprehension as an integral part of reading and have attempted to understand exactly what happens when a reader comprehends. With exciting new research into how the brain functions during reading, the interest in this phenomenon is perhaps greater than ever. But the process of comprehension itself has not changed—we simply have a more sophisticated understanding of comprehension and an even greater need for literate, critical thinkers who are prepared to participate in an increasingly complex world.

Once thought of as simply the natural result of decoding plus oral language, comprehension now is viewed as a much more complicated process resulting from an interface among background knowledge, experience, critical thinking, and interest. Comprehension currently is defined as *the construction of meaning from text* and is the ultimate goal of exemplary, balanced literacy instruction. Proficient readers and beginning readers, too, construct meaning by making connections—by integrating what they know about a topic with what they are immediately encountering in print.

Proficient readers possess a myriad of strategies from which they can select to help them interact with text and construct meaning. These strategies must be directly taught to readers through modeling, guided practice, and plenty of independent application with reading material. In addition, all children must receive the opportunity to share their personal responses to what they read, in a variety of social settings.

The activities in this section have been chosen to foster comprehension in children who are in all stages of literacy development. Some activities are appropriate for children with limited decoding skills, by promoting listening comprehension through read-alouds. Other activities require some decoding skill and are appropriate only for children who can read independently.

Story Imaging

SUGGESTED GRADE LEVEL *1–3*

PURPOSE Proficient readers "see" the characters, setting, and events contained in print by imaging. This activity gives children practice in re-creating a story using their "mind's eye," practicing crucial sequencing skills at the same time.

MATERIALS
- A story board (paper divided into six panels) for each child

PROCEDURE

1. Gather the children on the floor around you. Instruct the children to close their eyes and make their mind as empty as possible.

2. Ask them to try to recall the first event of a story they recently have read (heard). Ask them to raise their hand as soon as they can "see" the event in their mind.

3. When all hands are up, solicit responses as to what individual children have visualized, and encourage them to elaborate on their images.

4. Repeat these steps with the rest of the events in the story.

5. Working individually or in small share groups, ask the children to draw the events they have visualized, using the spaces in the story board, in order of their occurrence.

6. Have the children take turns retelling the story, using the pictures on their story boards as prompts.

VARIATION: Instead of having the children draw the events in the story, have them retell the story speaking into a tape recorder.

ASSESSMENT Make a checklist containing all the features of narrative structure as they have been taught to the children—beginning, middle, end; characters, setting, plot, events, ending, and so on. As individual children share their story boards, assess their ability to retell the story, using the checklist as a guide. Place checklists in student's files. Provide direct instruction in narrative structure to those children unable to retell the story.

SAMPLE CHECKLIST

NARRATIVE STRUCTURE

Name		Date	
		Yes	No
Beginning, middle, end of story		☐	☐
Characters		☐	☐
Setting		☐	☐
Plot		☐	☐
Events		☐	☐

Flip Book Summaries

(Adapted from Hoyt, 1999)

SUGGESTED GRADE LEVEL *1–3*

PURPOSE The ability to retell is an important component of reading comprehension. This activity asks children to retell a story in written form in the sequence in which the events happened.

MATERIALS
- 9" × 12" white construction paper, precut (see illustration)
- Markers or colored pencils

PROCEDURE

1. After reading a narrative text to the children, make four columns on the chalkboard, labeled *title, beginning, middle,* and *end*.

2. Have the children brainstorm events that occurred in each of these parts of the story.

3. Model a finished example of the flip book; explain that the title and author will go in the first box, something that happened in the beginning will go in the second box, something that happened in the middle will go in the third box, something that happened at the end of the story will be put in the final box.

4. When they flip the flap on each box, have them draw a picture that goes with the words they chose.

5. Have the children share their words and drawings with the rest of the class, telling why they chose the parts to tell about and draw.

ASSESSMENT Evaluate the finished flip book for each child on the basis of sequential order and the presence of a title page, beginning part, middle part, and ending part. With preliterate children, oral presentations regarding the illustrations can be used to determine if the children understand the basics of story structure. For children unable to complete this activity successfully, model and then have them practice retelling stories they have read, pointing out the beginning, middle, and end. Revisit the Flip Book Summaries activity.

The boy sees a dog in the clouds. He is at the beach.

The dog becomes real and the boy and dog play. The mom says to try to find the owner.

The boy gets to keep the dog.

THE SKY DOG
by
Brinton Turkle

Notes for next time . . .

_____

_____

_____

_____

_____

_____

Adapted from *Revisit, Reflect, and Retell: Strategies for Improving Reading Comprehension,* by Linda Hoyt (Westport, CT: Heinemann, 1999).

Which One Am I?

SUGGESTED GRADE LEVEL 2–3

PURPOSE Proficient readers verify their predictions as they read. Knowing that their predictions were on target provides positive reinforcement. This activity allows children to preview a story and make predictions about what the characters are like and encourages them to check their predictions after reading.

MATERIALS
- Three large poster boards, each containing a description of a character in a story
- Black marker
- Writing paper for each child in the class

PROCEDURE

1. Show the children the title of a book they are about to read and offer a two- to three-sentence preview, or the back cover synopsis.

2. Prior to the reading of the selection, write on one of the poster boards a detailed description of the internal qualities of the main character in the story. On each of the other two boards, write a detailed description that does *not* describe this character. Alternatively, you may use stories children have written during Writer's Workshop, allowing children to write the three descriptions (one correct; two incorrect) of the main character of their story.

3. Choose a child to read each of the three descriptions.

4. Have the three children come to the front of the classroom and take turns reading their descriptions aloud, then holding them up for all to see.

5. Ask the class to decide which of the three descriptions they think might describe the main character in the story they are about to read.

6. Ask the children to each write a sentence telling why they chose the description they did.

7. Ask the children to read (listen to) the story to find clues that validate or invalidate their original descriptions as they learn about the main character.

8. Following the reading, have the same three children return to the front of the class and reread the descriptions so the children can revise their opinions.

9. Lead a discussion about which clues in the story caused the children to change their mind or validate their original opinion. Have them find evidence in the story to support their revised opinions. Have them read these passages aloud to the class.

ASSESSMENT   Ask the children to write a sentence or two stating how they know the description of the main character is now correct. Encourage them to copy evidence directly from the story that documents their beliefs. Regroup children who are unable to complete this activity. Model how to refer to the text to find evidence that supports descriptive words that have been chosen.

Notes for next time . . .

Which Came First?

**SUGGESTED
GRADE LEVEL** *2–4*

PURPOSE Causal relationships are some of the most difficult to discern for early readers, especially for second language learners. The following activity will help to promote an awareness of cause and effect relationships in sentences through small group problem solving and discussion.

MATERIALS
- Chalkboard and chalk
- Ten sentence strips (see illustration)

PROCEDURE

1. Write the following sentence on the chalkboard: If it rains, we will not play ball. Discuss which event comes first, the rain or the decision not to play ball.

2. Explain that the word "if" often signals something that "causes" something else to happen, and that event is called the "effect."

3. Provide another example: I will give you a penny if you say "please."

4. Ask the children to tell you what follows the word "if." (You say "please.") Explain that this is the cause. Ask the children to tell you what the effect will be. (I will give you a penny.)

5. Read the 10 sentence strips to the children. While they watch, cut each sentence strip apart between the cause and the effect.

6. Divide the children into groups of three. Distribute two unmatched sentence halves to each group.

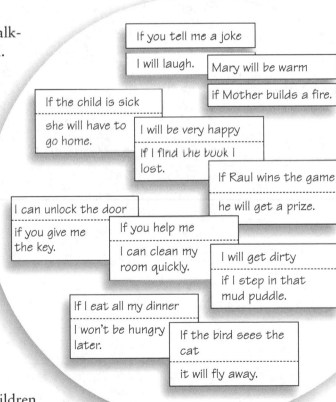

If you tell me a joke

I will laugh.

Mary will be warm

if Mother builds a fire.

If the child is sick

she will have to go home.

I will be very happy

If I find the book I lost.

If Raul wins the game

he will get a prize.

I can unlock the door

if you give me the key.

If you help me

I can clean my room quickly.

I will get dirty

if I step in that mud puddle.

If I eat all my dinner

I won't be hungry later.

If the bird sees the cat

it will fly away.

7. After they have read the nonsensical sentence they were given, ask the children to visit other groups, trying to locate the matching half of their sentence.

8. When all have found their matched sentences, ask them to read their sentence to the rest of the class, explaining which part is the cause and which is the effect.

ASSESSMENT Individually, ask the children to complete each sentence when you give them the first part, using the 10 sentences in the illustration. The endings need not be exact as long as they make sense. Then ask the children to tell you which part of each sentence is the "cause" and which is the "effect." Tally the number of correct responses. Revisit this activity, creating new cause and effect cards, for children correctly identifying fewer than 10 causes and effects, restating the explanation in step 2.

Notes for next time . . .

_____

_____

_____

_____

_____

_____

_____

_____

_____

_____

_____

_____

_____

_____

Opinionnaires

(Adapted from Readence, Bean, & Baldwin, 1998)

**SUGGESTED
GRADE LEVEL**   *3–6*

PURPOSE
This prereading structured activity provides children with a statement with which children must agree or disagree. By focusing on this statement, which is related to key ideas or issues in the passage to be read, the teacher can provide connections with the children's prior knowledge on the subject to be introduced and show the children graphically how reading, and the new information it provides, can change minds.

MATERIALS
- Overhead transparency or chart paper (showing a somewhat controversial statement)
- Two pieces of paper for each child

PROCEDURE

1. From a text that is about to be read to or by the children, create a provocative idea or piece of misinformation.

2. Write a statement, or statements, concerning this topic on the overhead transparency or chart paper and read it to the children. For example, if the passage offers the children information about garden snakes, the statement might be "All snakes are bad." The more statements used, the more predictions they will make.

All snakes are bad.

☐ I agree   ☒ I disagree

Snakes are slimy.

☐ I agree   ☐ I disagree

All snakes are poisonous.

☐ I agree   ☐ I disagree

3. Divide the children into small share groups of three to four children each and ask them to discuss the statement.

4. Ask the children who agree with the statement to form one line at the front of the room and those who disagree to form another line. Ask each child to then turn to the person behind him or her and explain why he or she agrees or disagrees.

5. Explain to the children that they will be reading (or listening to) a passage that contains information about the topic that has just been discussed. Ask them to read (or listen to) the passage to see what the author has to say about the topic.

6. Afterward, hand out to each child a paper upon which is written the same statement. Have the children reconsider the statement and write down their answer.

7. Conduct a whole-group discussion asking children if their feelings about the topic have changed after their reading. Encourage them to explain exactly what caused them to change their minds.

ASSESSMENT   Note whether the opinion of each child changed. Ask each to orally defend his or her position to you, changed or unchanged, on the basis of what he or she read (heard). For those children unable to offer one plausible explanation as to why they changed their mind, conduct a mini-lesson on providing supporting evidence for opinions.

Notes for next time . . .

_____

_____

_____

_____

_____

_____

_____

_____

_____

_____

_____

_____

_____

_____

Adapted from *Content Area Literacy: An Integrated Appraoch,* by John E. Readence, Thomas W. Bean, and R. Scott Baldwin (Dubuque, IA: Kendall/Hunt, 1998).

Response Heuristic

(Adapted from Bleich, 1998)

SUGGESTED GRADE LEVEL 2–5

PURPOSE Lack of personal involvement with text may affect the quality of children's response to literature and limit their understanding of what they have read. This activity is a structured device designed to promote children's engagement with text by inviting them to consider their personal perceptions, associations, and reactions to the text.

MATERIALS • Personal reaction sheet for each child (see illustration)

PROCEDURE

1. Initiate this activity with a small group of children to introduce them to the structure of the required responses. Read aloud a book to the class (Example: *Alexander and the Terrible, Horrible, No Good, Very Bad Day,* by Judith Viorst, 1978).

2. Ask the class to offer their perceptions of, reactions to, and associations with this book. Begin by soliciting their perceptions by asking: What did you think was important in this book? Write all their responses on the chalkboard.

3. Elicit their reactions by asking: How did the book make you feel? Write their individual responses on the chalkboard.

4. Encourage them to make personal associations with the book by asking: Does the book remind you of any experiences? Again, write all the children's responses on the chalkboard. Note: If any of the questions meet with a lack of response, you may want to model your own thoughts and feelings about the text.

5. In the next session, after a different book has been read, pass out the reaction sheets. Review the three questions on the sheet and explain to the children that they will be writing their personal responses in the spaces provided. Stress that there are no right or wrong answers.

ASSESSMENT Check each child's response sheet, looking for personal responses, accurate perceptions, and stated relationships to his or her own life. For children having difficulty with this assessment, administer a Reading Interest Inventory (Cecil, 2003; Cecil & Gipe, 2003). Match reading material to the child's interest and reading level to develop more personal involvement with text.

1. What is important in this book?

   The boy was having a bad day and everything seemed to go wrong for him. He was in a really bad mood.

2. How did the story make you feel? Why?

   I felt sorry for the boy. I didn't like when the other boy said he was not his best friend anymore.

3. Have you had any experiences that the book reminds you of?

   I had a bad day last week. I missed the bus and my sister was mad at me because she said I took her things. I didn't. My dad said I woke up on the wrong side of the bed.

Notes for next time . . .

_____

_____

_____

_____

_____

_____

Adapted from *Know and Tell: A Writing Pedagogy of Disclosure, Genre, and Membership,* by David Bleich (Portsmouth, NH: Heinemann, 1998).

Mindscape

SUGGESTED GRADE LEVEL 2–6

PURPOSE Comprehension deepens when children are able to elaborate on a text by adding information to their preexisting knowledge. This activity allows children to elaborate on a story by inferring what selected characters were thinking as they were presented in various capacities.

MATERIALS
- An outline of a head, with lines for writing inside, one for each child
- Crayons or colored markers

PROCEDURE

1. After reading a narrative text with the children, ask them to discuss their favorite parts of the story.

2. Pass out two head outlines to each child. Ask the children to choose a favorite character from the story. Explain that they will decorate the outline to match the outside of this character's head, while the inside will be used to describe what the character is thinking.

3. Pass out crayons or colored markers and encourage the children to make the outline look like their chosen character by adding the appropriate colored and styled hair, a hat, bow, or other features that symbolize the person.

4. Ask the children to revisit the story to find a favorite part that contains their character. Instruct them to copy a sentence from this part, placing it underneath the character's head.

5. Ask the children: What was [your character] thinking while this was going on? Imagine what he/she was saying to himself/herself and write your ideas on the lines inside his/her head.

Those silly children are not going to steal my broom. I'll do something mean to them.

"I'm going to make you wish you were a black cat."

6. Have the children share their Mindscape with the rest of the class, reading the excerpt and telling how they think the character was feeling at that time and why they think so.

ASSESSMENT Check for each child's ability to (1) find an excerpt that relates to his or her chosen character, and (2) appropriately infer how that character might be feeling in the situation. For children unable to complete these activities successfully, provide direct instruction in making inferences about how characters are feeling using books with which all in the group are familiar.

Notes for next time . . .

_____

_____

_____

_____

_____

_____

_____

_____

_____

_____

_____

_____

_____

_____

_____

_____

_____

_____

Consequences

SUGGESTED GRADE LEVEL   *2–6*

PURPOSE   This activity helps children to reflect on the behavior shown by a main character in stories they have read, to identify with that character's reasons for behaving a certain way, and finally, to consider the consequences of that behavior.

MATERIALS   • Chalkboard or overhead transparency

PROCEDURE

1. Place four boxes horizontally on the chalkboard or overhead transparency. Over the first box, write the word "Character." Over the second, write "Behavior." Over the third box, write "Why?" Over the fourth box, write "Result."

2. Invite the children to consider the behavior of a main character in a favorite story they have read, using this graphic organizer. For example, have the children recall Goldilocks and put her name in the first box. What words might be used to tell about the behavior of Goldilocks in the story of Goldilocks and the Three Bears? (Naughty; disobedient; she went where she wasn't supposed to.) Write these words in the second box. For the third box, ask the children to consider why Goldilocks behaved the way she did. For example, they may believe she was just bored, or that she was looking for an adventure. Accept all reasonable responses. To fill in the fourth box, ask the children to think about the result of boxes two and three. For example, if the children said Goldilocks was naughty because she was bored, what was the result of this naughty behavior? (She trespassed in the bears' house and got chased.) Write the answer in the fourth box.

Character
| Gingerbread Boy |

Behavior
| runs away |

Why?
| wants to run and play |

Result
| gets eaten |

3. Erase the boxes and begin the process again using a character from a different story. Have the children work in groups of three to consider their answers for each of the boxes. Then call on groups to contribute their responses.

ASSESSMENT   Make a checklist for each child. Include the categories "character," "behavior," "reason," and "result." Using a similar story that all the children have read, assess each child's ability to determine a reasonable response for each category. For children unable to complete this activity successfully, provide direct instruction, using a Think Aloud to show how you would respond to the four categories using characters from stories with which the children are familiar.

SAMPLE CHECKLIST

Name _____   Date _____

	Yes	No
Character	☐	☐
Behavior	☐	☐
Reason	☐	☐
Result	☐	☐

Notes for next time . . .

_____

_____

_____

_____

_____

_____

_____

_____

_____

Sentence Sharing

(Adapted from Tompkins, 1998)

SUGGESTED GRADE LEVEL 2–6

PURPOSE In this social activity, the teacher selects the excerpts for the children to read in order to introduce or review important concepts, summarize events, or focus on an element of expository structure. The activity also provides an authentic purpose for repeated reading to develop fluency, and is especially suitable for expository text.

MATERIALS
- Oaktag sentence strips containing key ideas from text

PROCEDURE

1. Ahead of time, make sentence strips on oaktag from an informational book or content-area textbook that the children have read. Include only key ideas from the text and make each sentence meaningful by itself (see examples on the next page). Optionally, have children make up the sentence strips from the text.

2. Distribute sentence strips to individual children, or have them work in pairs. Ask them to practice reading their strip (help them with difficult words) until they can read it fluently and confidently. Have them explain the facts to their partners.

3. Instruct the students to move around the classroom, stopping to read their excerpt to another child in the class. When they have chosen a reading buddy, they sit elbow to elbow, taking turns reading their excerpts to each other.

4. After the first child reads, the two children discuss the text that has been read. Then the other child reads and the two discuss the second excerpt.

5. When the partners have finished reading, they disband, search for other partners, and repeat the procedure.

6. When most children have finished, have them return to their seats. Invite volunteers to read their excerpts to the rest of the class in order and share what they have learned through the Sentence Sharing activity.

ASSESSMENT On an individual basis, ask each child to recall as much as he or she can about the text that was shared. Look for the key idea and several supporting details. Review the elements of expository structure for those children having difficulty completing this task.

Sentence Strips

Trees are the tallest and oldest living things on earth. (1)

Many redwood trees are more than 2,500 years old. (2)

A young tree may have a trunk no bigger around than your thumb. (3)

The tallest trees in the United States are the giant sequoias and redwoods in California. (4)

The trunk is attached to a big tangle of roots that are crooked and reach out in every direction. (5)

Some sequoias have such big trunks that it would take 20 men to make a circle around them! (6)

One of the most valuable uses of trees is in making houses and furniture out of the wood. (7)

The number of rings extending outward from the center of its trunk tells how old a tree is. (8)

The trunk of a tree grows longer and bigger around as the tree gets taller and heavier. (9)

The tree is made up of three parts—the trunk, the roots, and the branches. (10)

Most of a tree's roots are buried below the surface of the ground. (11)

Roots are made of wood like the trunk and the overhead branches. (12)

Sometimes you can see the top of a tree's roots above ground. (13)

Notes for next time . . .

_____

_____

_____

_____

_____

_____

_____

_____

Adapted from *50 Literacy Strategies: Step by Step*, by Gail E. Tompkins (Upper Saddle River, NJ: Merrill, 1998).

PPC Charts

(Adapted from Yopp & Yopp, 2001)

SUGGESTED GRADE LEVEL 2–6

PURPOSE This activity activates and builds upon prior knowledge and encourages active engagement with text through predictions. It also allows children to see how their peers use critical-thinking strategies.

MATERIALS
- A copy of the same book, one for each child. Suggestions:

  Catherine Called Birdy, by K. Cushman (New York: HarperCollins, 1994). 6–8.

  Shiloh, by P. R. Naylor (New York: Atheneum, 1991). 4–6.

  Smoky Night, by E. Bunting. (San Diego: Harcourt Brace, 1994). 2–4.

PROCEDURES

1. Distribute copies of a previously unread trade book, one to each child. The book must be on the instructional level of each child; fiction or nonfiction may be chosen. Tell the children they are going to "preview," "predict," and "confirm."

2. Allow each child five minutes to preview, or skim the first chapter of the book, looking at chapter titles and illustrations. Then have the children close their books.

3. Ask the children to brainstorm some words they would expect to be in the chapter and also explain their reason for thinking so as you write their ideas on the chalkboard, under a column labeled, "Word Predictions." For example, a child might predict the word "veterinarian" might be in the book *Shiloh* because he or she sees a picture of the dog limping; another child might guess that the word *nickname* might be in the book *Catherine Called Birdy,* because it seems from the title that the main character is called something other than her real name.

"Shiloh"	
Word Predictions	Appeared in text
veterinarian	yes
canine	no
rural	yes
violent	no
shotgun	yes

4. When all who wish to have made predictions of words they think will be in the book, the children read, or listen to, the book.

5. When the book has been read, invite the children to return to the chart. Guide them to note and discuss which words were confirmed—i.e., the word was found in the text—and those that were not. Provide a new column, labeled "Appeared in Text" and write "yes" or "no" after each word.

ASSESSMENT   After this activity has been conducted several times, encourage the children to make their own individual PPC charts before reading books they have chosen. Individually, ask them why they predicted the words they did to identify the match between the language and content of the text and the language and background knowledge of the child. Place their PPC charts in their files. Compare with charts completed with other stories later in the school year.

Notes for next time . . .

_____

_____

_____

_____

_____

_____

_____

_____

_____

_____

_____

_____

_____

Adapted from *Literature-Based Reading Activities,* 3rd edition, by Ruth Helen Yopp and Hallie Kay Yopp (Boston: Allyn & Bacon, 2001).

Polar Opposites

(Adapted from Yopp and Yopp, 2000)

SUGGESTED GRADE LEVEL   *2–6*

PURPOSE   This activity dealing with antithetical personality traits (sometimes antonyms) is ideal for helping children begin to see fictional characters as three-dimensional and beginning to think of word choices with subtler shades of meaning.

MATERIALS
- A book with which all the children are familiar
- A list of personality traits and their opposites
- Chart paper

PROCEDURE

1. Choose a character from a story with which all the children are familiar, preferably one that the whole class has just enjoyed.

2. Help the children to develop a list of personality traits and the opposite quality for each and write them on opposite sides of a chart. For example, quiet, thoughtful, brave, industrious, and considerate might be on one side of the chart, and boisterous, rash, fearful, lazy, and inconsiderate might be on the other side.

3. Place three to five blank spaces between each set of words, suggesting that a person, or character, can have a personality anywhere in between (see illustration).

4. Introduce each of the descriptive words by suggesting how a person with each of the character traits—and their opposites—might behave.

5. Select a character from the chosen story, such as Nat from *Miss Maggie* by Cynthia Rylant.

6. Say to the children: Let's think about the words "brave" and "fearful." Where do you think Nat would fall on this chart? Is he more like brave, or is he more like fearful? Why do you think so?

7. Solicit responses from individual students and ask them to give examples from the story to support their rationale for placement on the chart. Encourage the children to document their answers from the story, if differences of opinion arise.

8. Repeat the procedure with other major characters from the book.

NAT

quiet	_____X_____	boisterous
thoughtful	_____X_____	rash
brave	_____X___	fearful
industrious	_____X_____	lazy
considerate	_____X_____	inconsiderate

ASSESSMENT As a follow-up to this activity, prepare individual Polar Opposites activity sheets for every member of the class. Using the same words and their antonyms, ask the children to determine where they would fall on each of these personality traits. One by one, have the children explain their choices to you, demonstrating that they do or do not understand the words. For children having difficulty with this assessment, provide direct instruction in documenting beliefs about characters by finding evidence in the story.

Notes for next time . . .

_____

_____

_____

_____

_____

_____

_____

Adapted from *Literature-Based Reading Activities, 3rd ed.,* by Ruth Helen Yopp and Hallie Kay Yopp (Boston: Allyn & Bacon, 2000).

Sentence Pantomimes

SUGGESTED GRADE LEVEL *3–5*

PURPOSE   Research and observation have determined that certain language structures, especially those with indirect objects or adverbial clauses, may cause comprehension difficulties, especially for children for whom English is a second language. Reflecting on their knowledge of language and focusing on these structures, as this language activity does, can improve children's comprehension of difficult sentences.

MATERIALS   ● Ten sentence cards containing sentences with clauses and indirect objects (see illustration)

PROCEDURE

1. Divide the children into groups of three.

2. Read all of the sentences to the children without explaining their meaning, just to be sure the children can properly decode all the words. Discuss how punctuation must be noted in order to interpret a sentence correctly.

3. Distribute one sentence card to each group and ask the groups to discuss how they might act out their sentence for the rest of the class. Have each group select one group member to read the sentence while the other two act it out.

4. Call on the groups, one at a time, to come up to the front of the room and act out their sentence card for the rest of the class as one member of their group reads it.

5. Ask the rest of the class to show, by a "thumbs up" or a "thumbs down" signal, whether they think the actors correctly interpreted the meaning of the sentence.

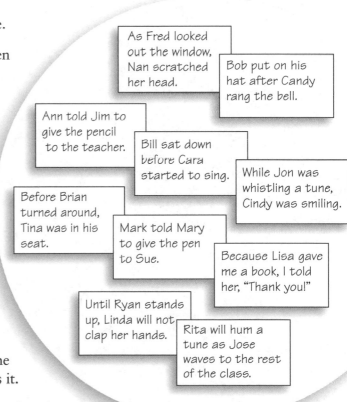

As Fred looked out the window, Nan scratched her head.

Bob put on his hat after Candy rang the bell.

Ann told Jim to give the pencil to the teacher.

Bill sat down before Cara started to sing.

While Jon was whistling a tune, Cindy was smiling.

Before Brian turned around, Tina was in his seat.

Mark told Mary to give the pen to Sue.

Because Lisa gave me a book, I told her, "Thank you!"

Until Ryan stands up, Linda will not clap her hands.

Rita will hum a tune as Jose waves to the rest of the class.

6. If any children disagree with the interpretation, invite them individually to reenact the sentence as they think it should be. Discuss their interpretation.

ASSESSMENT This can be used as an informal evaluation of receptive language for children in their "silent period" of language development. Ask individual children to act out each sentence as you say it. Particularly note problems that English language learners encounter. Place this information in the child's file. Provide practice acting out simple commands, such as in "Simple Simon," for children unable to act out more than three sentences.

Notes for next time . . .

_____

_____

_____

_____

_____

_____

_____

_____

_____

_____

_____

_____

_____

_____

_____

_____

_____

Other Ideas & Activities

- **MIX-UP.** Print the main ideas of a story on oaktag strips and place the strips in incorrect order in a pocket chart. Ask the children to read each strip aloud while putting the strips in the correct order according to the sequence of events in the story.

- **TRUE OR FALSE?** Prepare several statements about a story that has just been read, some true and some false. Give each child two cards—one labeled *true* and the other labeled *false*. As you read each statement aloud, ask the children to hold up the appropriate card.

- **RATE IT.** Encourage the children to think critically about the books they have read. With your guidance, invite the children to establish their own rating system for books they have read—from poor (a sad face) to excellent (a happy face).

- **PROBLEM SOLVING.** In small groups, have the children respond to the following questions concerning problems of the main characters in stories they have recently read: What problem did the main character face? How did he/she solve the problem? How would you have solved the problem?

- **FAVORITE SCENES.** Have the children depict scenes from books they have read, using papier-maché, fabric, construction paper, clay, or other materials. Encourage each child to share his or her creation with the class, describing the events that led up to the scene as well as those that followed it.

- **INFERENCES.** Bring in an old gardening or driving glove. Ask the children to make inferences about who might have owned it by examining it (e.g., if it is for the right hand, a right-handed person may have taken it off to pull a weed and lost it; if it is large, it may belong to an adult man, etc.).

- **PICTURE DIARY.** Have the children make a picture diary for their favorite character in a story that has been read recently, by drawing four things that happened in the story in order, folded into four parts on construction paper.

- **CONTRAST CHART.** Give each child a paper containing two columns, one labeled *likenesses* and the other *differences*. Have the children compare two stories that were read recently, considering factors such as setting, number of characters, mood, difficulty, and others.

- **MAIN IDEA DRAWINGS.** Ask the children to use just one drawing to best tell what a story they have just read or heard is about. Invite them to share their drawing with the class, telling how their drawing captures the main idea of the story.

- **SHADOW PUPPETS.** With tagboard and black markers, have the children trace the main characters from a book they have read, cut them out, and tape straightened-out paper clips to the back. Using the overhead projector, have them retell the story with the help of these shadow puppets.

- **TAPED BOOK CHAT.** Ask the children to tape-record their reactions to a book they have read. Encourage them to tell just enough to interest their classmates and make them curious but not so much that they don't need to read the book for themselves.

- **PREDICT THE ENDING.** Read a provocative book aloud to the children. Stop at the most exciting part. Ask the children to brainstorm what they think will happen next. Have them listen to confirm or refute their hunches.

- **STORY-PICTURE SEQUENCING.** Prepare a sequence of pictures that tell a story from discarded basals or trade books. Read the story to children and then have them arrange the pictures and retell the story in the correct sequence.
- **INTERVIEWS.** Have the children pretend to be reporters and interview a favorite movie star, sports star, recording star, and so forth. Ask them to create a list of five questions they might ask and then predict the answers the person might give.

Children's Literature List

Appelt, Kathi, illustrated by Keith Baker. *Elephants Aloft.* (New York: Harcourt Brace, 1993). An adventurous journey of two elephants named Rama and Raja from India to Africa to visit their aunt. One adjective on every two-page spread describes what is happening. An excellent book for a read/listen and retell. K–2

Bridwell, Norman. *Clifford and the Big Parade.* (New York: Cartwheel/Scholastic, 1998). Popular Clifford again saving the day in his own unique way. Children will enjoy guessing what will happen as Clifford and Emily participate in their town's birthday celebration. An ideal book for having children predict the outcome. K–2

Dumphy, Madeleine, illustrated by Alan James Robinson. *Here Is the Arctic Winter.* (New York: Hyperion, 1993). A beautifully illustrated expository text explaining how some animals are strong enough to survive the cold, dark Arctic winter while others are not. An excellent model for young readers of an expository text using comparison and contrast. 1–3

Flournoy, Valerie. *Tanya's Reunion.* (New York: Dial, 1995). The travels of Tanya and her grandmother to an old farm in Virginia to attend a family reunion is a pencil-and-watercolor-illustrated picture story book. Because the story's dialogue is so rich in rural African-American dialect, the story is great for creating a Readers Theatre. 4–6

Wildsmith, Brian, and Wildsmith, Rebecca. *Wake Up, Wake Up.* (New York: Harcourt, 1993). Practice with cause and effect relationships. Rooster wakes one animal, which wakes up another animal, and so on until the last animal wakes up the farmer, who feeds them all. K–2

Other Resources for Fostering Comprehension

Asking Better Questions: Models, Techniques, and Activities for Engaging Students in Learning, by Norah Morgan and Juliana Saxton (York, ME: Stenhouse Publishers, 1996). Simple examples showing K–8 teachers how they can pose well-thought-out questions to children and in turn encourage children to ask themselves better questions. Teachers learn to use questions to acquire information about students, build common knowledge, and increase comprehension.

Better Books! Better Readers! How to Choose, Use, and Level Books for Children in the Primary Grades, by Linda Hart-Hewins and Jan Wells (York, ME: Stenhouse Publishers, 1999). Based on the authors' belief that using real books and real writing experiences help children not only become literate but also lovers of reading. Offers practical guidelines for creating classrooms that foster language learning and critical thinking.

Content Area Literacy: An Integrated Approach, by John E. Readence, Thomas W. Bean, and R. Scott Baldwin (Dubuque, IA: Kendall/Hunt, 1998). Explores the development of reading comprehension strategies throughout the curriculum. Though most are suitable for older students, some are appropriate for grades 2–3.

50 Active Learning Strategies for Improving Reading Comprehension, by Adrienne Herrell and Michael Jordan (Upper Saddle River, NJ: Prentice Hall, 2002). This text incorporates the strongest and most current research available to help teachers actively involve their students in the reading comprehension process. Teachers receive expert guidance in a step-by-step format that clearly states and fully illustrates each of the 50 strategies.

50 Literacy Strategies: Step by Step, by Gail E. Tompkins (New York: Merrill, 1998). Some of the best-known and most effective strategies for teaching reading and writing K–6 in an easy-to-follow format. Spiral bound.

Guided Comprehension in Action: Lessons for Grades 3–8, by Maureen McLaughlin and Mary Beth Allen (Newark, DE: International Reading Association, 2002). The Guided Comprehension Model is a step-by-step teaching framework that encourages students to become active, strategic readers by providing direct and guided strategy instruction, numerous opportunities for engagement, and a variety of texts and instructional settings.

Keeping It Together: Linking Reading Theory to Practice, by Ian Morrison (Bothell, WA: Wright Group, 1996). Especially for early elementary students, links proven classroom practices with a consistent theory of reading and comprehension in a practical way.

Reading Strategies That Work: Teaching Your Students to Become Better Readers, by Laura Robb (Jefferson City, MO: Scholastic Professional Books, 1998). A set of more than 30 strategies that proficient readers use. Included are strategies for predicting, summarizing, rereading, inferring, and noting cause and effect.

Revisit, Reflect, and Retell: Strategies for Improving Reading Comprehension, by Linda Hoyt (Westport, CT: Heinemann, 1999). A highly practical collection of more than 130 strategies and 90 reproducibles for any teacher attempting to evoke high-quality responses to literature.

Striking a Balance: Best Practices for Early Literacy, by Nancy Lee Cecil (Scottsdale, AZ: Holcomb Hathaway, 2003) and *Literacy in the Intermediate Grades: Best Practices for a Comprehensive Program,* by Nancy Lee Cecil and Joan P. Gipe (WScottsdale, AZ: Holcomb Hathaway, 2003). Companion texts to this activities book, these books present major research in and a theoretical overview of early and intermediate literacy in an easily understandable, reader-friendly style. The books include numerous strategies as well as many practical tools for teaching and assessing literacy.

Tell Me: Children, Reading, and Talk, by Aidan Chambers (York, ME: Stenhouse Publishers, 1996). An approach for discussing books so children learn to find the heart of a story, make sense of a string of facts, and understand important ideas. Practical information about book talking, explaining some of the processes and outlining the ground rules developed by teachers and others who work with children and books.

Ultimate Guided Reading How-To Book, by Gail Saunders-Smith (Tucson, AZ: Zephyr Press, 2003). The author makes integrating guided reading into a prescribed reading program easier than ever. Using cues, strategies, behaviors, and skills, the text shows how to develop children's literacy, taking them from prereading to higher levels of comprehension.

In Closing

○ ○

1. After using the activities in this section, what insights have you gained about how children develop reading and listening comprehension skills? What did you discover about yourself as a teacher of literacy by teaching these activities?

2. Which of the activities in this section did you find were particularly effective in teaching the following comprehension strategies? Why?

   - Making predictions
   - Visualizing
   - Tuning in to prior knowledge
   - Making personal connections
   - Monitoring understanding
   - Generalizing
   - Evaluating
   - Asking and answering questions

3. Choose an activity that was particularly easy and one that was difficult for the children with whom you worked. Why do you think it was easy/difficult? What, if any, adaptations would you make next time you teach the lesson? Why?

4. What did you discover about the need to determine what children already know about a subject before beginning an instructional activity? How did the assessment suggestions at the end of each activity provide you with insights into the strengths and limitations of your teaching of comprehension strategies?

5. Select an activity that offered you the most insights into the general knowledge background of the children with whom you worked. What did you discover about the importance of children having background knowledge about a topic before reading? Cite examples of specific children with whom you worked.

6. Several of the activities asked the children to retell narratives after reading. What comprehension strategies are reinforced and assessed through the use of these activities? What did you learn about your learners' comprehension as a result of doing these activities?

7. Certain activities encouraged the children to figure out deleted words by using the context of the sentence. What might be the advantages and disadvantages of these activities? What did you learn about a specific child's use of comprehension strategies based upon these activities?

8. Some activities asked the children to revisit a favorite character after reading and write something about that character. How do you think reading comprehension can be developed through the use of these activities? Why? Give examples of specific children and what you think they learned as a result of this activity.

9. Which activities seemed especially difficult for your English language learners? What did you observe about their difficulties? How could you revise these activities to make them more accessible to your English language learners?

10. Identify a child you think has a highly developed ability to use comprehension strategies. What are the characteristics of that child? Did his or her behavior during the activities differ from that of other children? Describe the differences, if any.

Activities to Inspire Young Writers

Introduction

Reading and writing provide the major paths to literacy for all children. Children learn the value of communication through the written word early on—long before they enter school—as they struggle to make sense of print in their environment. From posters on nursery room walls, to before-bedtime story books, to billboards inundating the community, letters and words soon become part of the consciousness of children. Their need to know what the words say compels them first out of curiosity, quickly replaced by the desire to communicate themselves. The acquisition of reading and writing then enables children to develop into individuals capable of communicating in unique and personal ways.

Early attempts at writing provide opportunities for children to experiment with print and extend their understanding of text. It follows that emergent writing—if much experimentation is encouraged—has been found to play a pivotal role in children's learning to read. Experimentation provides children with invaluable practice with segmenting sounds into words, leading to an understanding of the relationship between sounds and letters, or phonics.

In older children, writing activities should go beyond the skills and mechanics and can be the catalyst for the natural interaction of language acquisition and development. Moreover, writing activities following reading can enhance and improve reading comprehension, as composition is an interactive process that challenges the writer to construct meaning for an intended audience. The author/reader relationship contained in writing is essential to reading comprehension because the author is responsible for making the writing comprehensible to others. That relationship is enhanced as children go through the stages of the writing process: prewriting, drafting, sharing, revising, editing, and publishing.

The following activities have been selected to accommodate all children's wishes to communicate by providing them with authentic opportunities to participate in motivational writing purposes.

The Busy Bee

SUGGESTED GRADE LEVEL   *K–3*

PURPOSE   The aim of this daily writing activity is to provide a model for writing and to begin the editing process, focusing on the importance of the mechanics, including spelling, grammar, and punctuation. The children also are given a model of the thinking involved in making editing decisions as they occur in writing.

MATERIALS
- Overhead projector
- Transparency of The Busy Bee
- Optional: editing sheet on p. 202

PROCEDURE

1. Lead a general discussion about what is going on in the lives of the children, at home or at school.

2. As the children share, summarize each idea in one sentence. Ask each child if your sentence summarizes what they shared.

3. Write the summary of what each child said on the transparency of The Busy Bee. Note: How the sentence will be written depends on the child's level and skill.

4. Write four or five sentences on the transparency in this manner.

5. Later that day, give the children copies of The Busy Bee—this time with some glaring errors in punctuation, spelling, or grammar.

6. In pairs, have the children edit the sentences. When finished, compare the edited copies with the original on the overhead transparency.

The Busy Bee

Bree got a new puppy for her birthday.

LeRoy's mother had a baby boy named Eddie.

Hoa brought her toy dinosaur to school.

We are all happy to have a new classmate named Joshua.

Abby is going to her cousin's house to spend the night this weekend.

7. Have a child rewrite the edited The Busy Bee and publish it as part of a class book. Or send home weekly the edited versions of this activity as part of a class newsletter.

ASSESSMENT   Evaluate the children on the basis of their ability to successfully edit the sentences. Note: Be sure to model the editing as a whole class before having pairs assume this responsibility. More proficient writers can write the sentences themselves, to be edited in pairs. For emergent writers, you may simply model the writing and focus on sounds within the words.

Name _____   Domain _____

Assignment _____   Date _____

EDITING SHEET

Self Edit

1. I have included all the parts of the assignment.   _____

2. All sentences have the correct punctuation.
   (. , ; : " " ' ? !)   _____

3. All sentences begin with a capital letter.   _____

4. No two sentences begin with the same word.
   (then, and, I)   _____

5. Spelling is correct to the best of my ability.   _____

My signature _____

Partner Edit

1. All parts of the assignment were covered.   _____

2. All sentences have correct punctuation.   _____

3. All sentences begin with a capital letter.   _____

4. A variety of words are used at the beginning
   of sentences.   _____

5. Spelling is correct to the best of my ability.   _____

Partner's signature _____

Teacher's signature _____   Date _____

What Do Writers Do?

SUGGESTED GRADE LEVEL *K–6*

PURPOSE This is an activity to help all children understand the writing process and to give the teacher some insight into how students think about writing and what it entails.

MATERIALS
- Bio of children's literature author
- Chart paper

PROCEDURE

1. After reading an enjoyable piece of children's literature to the children, spend some time discussing the author. Personalize this person by telling children where he or she is from, summarize the plots of other books he or she has written, and provide any other interesting biographical details you have researched. Optional: Invite a local author to talk to children.

2. Have the children brainstorm all the things they think the author had to do to write the book. Ask them specifically: What do good writers do? Do *all* writers do these things?

3. On the chart paper, write all the ideas the children offer, discussing them one at a time. Connect the ideas to their own writing.

4. Leave the chart in a prominent place in the classroom so the children can refer to it when they are writing. Review the ideas on the chart before the children are to be engaged in creative writing assignments.

5. Encourage the children to add new ideas to the chart as they think of them.

What Do Good Writers Do?

Writers think of ideas.

They make you interested in what they have to say.

They plan their story for an audience.

Good writers get suggestions from somebody.

They try to write so others can read what they wrote.

Authors have a beginning, a middle part, and an ending.

They use lots of juicy words.

Good writers use complete sentences.

They make you feel happy or sad because of their writing.

ASSESSMENT   With this activity, you can clearly see if children are beginning to see themselves as writers and understand the tasks involved in writing. Use this activity primarily to give you perspective on the direction your writing instruction has to take to promote awareness of the various facets of the writing process. Follow up with a Writing Attitude Survey (Cecil, 2003) to see if these understandings have had a positive impact on each child's perception of him or herself as a writer. Use the activity several times during the year to measure the children's progress in understanding the writing process.

Notes for next time . . .

_____

_____

_____

_____

_____

_____

_____

_____

_____

_____

_____

_____

_____

_____

_____

_____

Five Senses

SUGGESTED GRADE LEVEL *1–2*

PURPOSE This activity provides the visual stimulation to allow learners, especially English language learners, to think about words to complete sentence stems that tell how a balloon looks, feels, tastes, smells, and sounds.

MATERIALS
- Enough balloons for each group of five children
- String to tie the balloons
- Sentence stems for each of the five senses (see illustration)
- Overhead projector and blank transparency

PROCEDURE

1. Place the children into groups of five. Give each group one balloon that has been blown up and tied at the end.

2. Give each group five sheets of paper. On each sheet of paper is written a sentence stem for one of the five senses. Read each of the sentence stems with the children.

3. Begin with the sense of sight. Ask each child to take turns holding the balloon and thinking of words that tell about how it looks. Assign one child from the group to that sense and determine which word(s) will be used to complete the sentence stem.

4. Using the overhead projector, demonstrate how the children are to write the word(s) to complete the sentence, sounding out the word they wish to use.

5. Go to the next sense, hearing. Ask the children to pass the balloon around in their group and brainstorm words that tell how the balloon sounds. Assign a different child within the group to decide which word(s) or phrases to use and finish the sentence.

6. Repeat this procedure until the balloon has been considered using all the five senses.

7. Have each group share its ideas with the rest of the class.

8. Make class books about balloons and the five senses, encouraging each child to illustrate his or her contribution.

My Balloon

My balloon looks like ___a blue pickle.___

My balloon sounds like ___a squeaky old door.___

My balloon smells like ___a new baby doll.___

My balloon feels like ___a smooth stone.___

My balloon tastes like ___yucky bubble gum.___

ASSESSMENT Use a clipboard to observe the contributions of each child in each group. Note whether each child understands the concept of each sense and if each is able to think of appropriate words to describe that sense. Finally, invite each child to read his or her group's contributions to you, asking the child to track while reading the new words and the sentence stems. Place your observations in each child's file.

Notes for next time . . .

_____

_____

_____

Descriptive Recodes

○○○○○○○○○○○○○○○○○○○○○○○○○○○○○○○○

4

SUGGESTED GRADE LEVEL *1–3*

PURPOSE This is an enjoyable way to allow children to take the basic writing of decodable texts and make it more descriptive and interesting through the use of enhanced vocabulary and more sophisticated phrasing.

MATERIALS
- Decodable text at the children's independent reading level
- Paper
- Writing instruments
- Overhead projector
- Overhead transparency of a page from a decodable text

PROCEDURE

1. Select a paragraph at random from a decodable text, project it on the overhead projector and read it with the children.

2. Model aloud how you would revise several sentences from the text, making them more descriptive and interesting by adding juicy words to replace the tired ones and by adding dialogue, emotions, phrases, and other details to make the writing more vibrant.

3. After you have modeled several paragraphs, elicit suggestions for revising from the children.

4. Read the new page of text and compare it with the original. Solicit opinions as to which is more interesting. Why?

5. Assign a page (a sentence for emerging writers) of decodable text to pairs of students. Ask each pair to rewrite their page (sentence), adding descriptive phrases, juicy words, and other more interesting details.

6. When each group has finished, ask the children to practice reading their revised page (sentence) of text.

(Original)

Nat was Sad

Nat sat on the mat. Nat was sad.

A rat sat on the mat. The rat was sad.

A fat cat sat on the mat.

Was the cat sad? The cat was not sad.

The cat ate the rat. Nat saw that the cat ate the rat. Nat was sad!

7. Invite one child from each pair to read their new page (sentence) to the whole group, in order.

8. Discuss how the additions made the text more interesting, and why.

Optional: Use nondescriptive stories the children have written that you have saved from past school years.

ASSESSMENT   As pairs of children are working on this lesson, observe and take anecdotal notes of each child's participation. Afterward, have individual children tell you a juicy word or phrase he or she remembers that made the story more interesting and have him or her tell why. During subsequent individual writing time and conferencing with the children, check to see if they are incorporating more description in their writing. Regroup children who are still not incorporating description. Repeat the activity, offering individual assistance.

Notes for next time . . .

_____

_____

_____

_____

_____

_____

_____

_____

_____

_____

_____

_____

Quick Write

(Adapted from Cunningham & Allington, 1999)

SUGGESTED GRADE LEVEL   2–6

PURPOSE   Writing that takes place before reading can help young children clarify what they already know and helps them respond later to what they have read. Writing before reading also encourages children to think about what they are reading, and assimilate new knowledge with old.

MATERIALS
- Timer
- Writing instruments
- Writing paper

PROCEDURE

1. Before introducing the children to an expository piece on a topic such as cows, tell them that you are going to give them two minutes to write down everything they know about cows (preliterate children may draw pictures illustrating their knowledge).

2. Tell the children to list as many ideas as they can think of and not to worry about spelling, handwriting, or creating complete sentences.

3. Set the timer for two minutes and tell the children to begin writing.

4. When the time is up, ask the children to draw a line after their last idea and then count the total number of ideas they wrote down about the topic.

5. Have the children read or listen to the expository piece to find out more about the topic.

6. After the reading/listening, tell the children they will have three minutes to add to their list.

7. When the time is up, ask the children to label the first part of the list "before" and the second part "after" (see illustration).

COWS

Before

Cows are animals. They live on farms. They eat grass and hay. They have babies called calves.

4 ideas

After

Cows have two stomachs. They chew their cuds. They never eat meat. Black and white cows are called Holsteins, and they give the most milk. Daddy cows are called bulls.

6 ideas

---

8. For a greater challenge: Ask the children to write two short paragraphs about cows, using the ideas from both lists. Give them lined paper with sentence stems for each paragraph. Tell them that this time they will create complete sentences from the ideas on their lists and self-edit for spelling and correct punctuation.

ASSESSMENT   Evaluate the children's quick writes based upon the difference in quantity of ideas in the first and second lists. Were the children able to augment their lists after reading (hearing) the story? Were the children able to correctly identify details in the story? Was the summary of the text accurate? Place the quick write in the child's file. Use it for determining writing growth when compared with quick writes done later in the school year.

Optional: Evaluate the children's short paragraphs using the Writing Conventions Rubric in Appendix D.

Notes for next time . . .

_____

_____

_____

_____

_____

_____

_____

_____

_____

_____

_____

_____

Adapted from *Classrooms That Work: They Can All Read and Write,* 2d edition, by Patricia M. Cunningham and Richard L. Allington (New York: Longman, 1999).

Picture Paragraphs

SUGGESTED GRADE LEVEL   2–6

PURPOSE   One of the most difficult skills to teach children is how to turn groups of sentences into a cohesive paragraph. This activity demonstrates to children how they can read their own work and, using their own drawings, determine which sentences go with which key concepts.

MATERIALS
- A writing draft from each child
- Colored pencils
- Drawing paper
- Scissors
- Paste
- Sturdy cardboard

PROCEDURE

1. Ask the children each to procure a draft of a story on which they are currently working.

2. Invite the children to make a series of rough sketches that tell about each of the events in the story.

3. Ask the children to reread their piece to decide which sentences could go together and tell about the first picture.

4. When they have selected the sentences, have them draw a circle around each sentence that might go with that picture, using the same colored pencil.

5. Have them repeat these steps for each of their drawings, using a different colored pencil for each of the pictures.

6. Explain that each group of sentences that accompanies a drawing is called a paragraph, a group of sentences that all are about the same topic.

7. Provide scissors, paste, and sturdy cardboard so the children can rearrange their sentences and paragraphs by cutting and pasting as they find a more logical sequence for them.

ASSESSMENT   Assess the children's ability to determine the main ideas of paragraphs in stories by the pictures they draw. Assess their ability to determine supporting

The Dog's Adventure

Once there was a little dog that wandered off into the dark forest. He didn't know where he was going. He didn't know where his home was.

Soon the dog came upon a little man who seemed kind. The dog asked, "Mister, do you know where I live?" The man answered, "No, I sure don't."

Then the man reached down and picked up the dog. The dog trusted him. But guess what? The man took the dog right to the pound!

details by the sentences they select to go with these pictures, as well as the topic sentences they choose. Observe them as they reorder the sentences and pictures to determine if they are able to detect the sequence in the story. For children experiencing difficulty finding main ideas or reordering, provide a mini-lesson on these areas.

Notes for next time . . .

_____

_____

_____

Provocative Paintings

SUGGESTED GRADE LEVEL   3–6

PURPOSE   Fine art can be a delightful stimulus to writing if children are asked provocative questions and are allowed to respond in their own words about their reactions. This activity shows how to integrate art with writing to create a rich blend of the two.

MATERIALS
- Reprints of fine art paintings (suggestions: Kahlo, Rivera, Monet, Cassatt, O'Keefe, Picasso)
- A notepad for each child

PROCEDURE

1. Introduce a fine art painting to the children, telling a bit about the artist, his or her life and times, and the title of the piece.

2. Do the same with five paintings over several days.

3. When all the paintings have been introduced, hang them, gallery-style, in a prominent place in the room.

4. Tell the children they are to become "art critics" and will write down their reactions to their favorite painting. Write a list of questions on the board and read each one with the children.

5. Invite the children to walk around and study the paintings. Ask them to select their favorite, and jot down some words and phrases about their selection in response to the following questions:

   Which painting is most like your life and experiences? What does it remind you of?

   What would you name this painting?

   What in your life does the painting remind you of?

> **Contrast Frame**
>
> Water Lilies and Hand with Flowers are different in a few ways. First, <u>Water Lilies doesn't have people and Hand with Flowers has two people's hands in it.</u> Second, <u>Water Lilies has soft colors in it while Hand with Flowers has bright colors in it.</u> But the way the paintings are most different is that <u>Water Lilies looks real while Hand with Flowers looks like a cartoon.</u>

What are some people, places, or things the painting makes you think of?

What would you do differently if you had painted this picture?

Write down some words or phrases that you think of when you see this painting.

6. When the children have finished jotting down their thoughts, have them choose a partner who has selected a painting different from theirs.

7. Have them use a Contrast Frame to compare the two paintings (see illustration) using their lists of words and phrases.

8. Encourage pairs of students to read their Contrast Frames to the rest of the class, with one child reading while the other points to the appropriate painting.

ASSESSMENT   The Contrast Frame provides a scaffold that enables children with even rudimentary writing abilities to compose a paragraph. Evaluate paragraphs on the basis of complete thoughts and contrasting ideas, while adjusting expectations of complexity to each child's developmental capabilities and/or linguistic stages, for English language learners. Place paragraphs in each child's file.

Notes for next time . . .

_____

_____

_____

_____

_____

_____

_____

_____

_____

_____

_____

Triangular Triplets

(Adapted from Cecil, 1994)

SUGGESTED GRADE LEVEL 2–3

PURPOSE In this motivational introduction to writing poetry, children practice rhyming while creating simple three-line poems.

MATERIALS
- One sheet of plain white paper for each child
- One sheet of colored construction paper for each child
- Scissors
- Paste
- Scrap paper
- Pencils

PROCEDURE

1. Distribute colored construction paper and a sheet of plain white paper to each child.

2. Ask the children to draw a picture of themselves in the center of the white paper, engaged in their favorite activity.

3. Demonstrate how to draw a triangle around their drawing, cut it out, and paste it near the top of their construction paper.

4. Read the sample poem to the children (see illustration). Discuss how the ending words all rhyme and how each line tells something about the activity in the triangle.

5. Guide them to use the picture in their triangle as inspiration for a three-lined rhymed poem.

6. Have them write drafts of their poem on the scrap paper while you offer suggestions for easy rhyming words.

My Bike

I like to ride my bike each day.

I'd rather ride than run or play.

I meet a lot of friends this way!

7. When they finish their poems, have them write one line on each side of the triangle to form a "running commentary" about the activity occurring inside the triangle.

ASSESSMENT   Check to see that the poems have (1) three lines, (2) three words that rhyme at the end of each line, and (3) each line corresponding to the picture. Conference individually with children who have difficulty with the poem in any of these three areas.

Notes for next time . . .

_____

_____

_____

_____

_____

_____

_____

_____

_____

_____

_____

_____

_____

_____

_____

_____

_____

Adapted from *For the Love of Language: Poetry Scaffolds for Every Learner,* by Nancy Lee Cecil (Winnipeg, Manitoba: Peguis Publishers, 1994).

Add-On Stories

SUGGESTED GRADE LEVEL *2–6*

PURPOSE With this unique writing activity, children can participate in creating a narrative piece regardless of their level of writing proficiency. Narrative structure is reinforced, and the children see, graphically, that many plots are possible from a single beginning sentence.

MATERIALS
- Writing paper
- Writing instruments
- Story Starters (see illustration)

PROCEDURE

1. Group children into three each and distribute writing materials. Explain that each group will be writing a part of shared stories.

2. Write a story starter on the board and read it to the children. Ask them to copy it on the top of their papers.

3. Tell the children they will now have 10 minutes to begin a story using the lead-in sentence they have just written on their papers. When the 10 minutes are up, ask them to finish the sentence they are writing and pass their paper to the person sitting to their left in the group and receive the paper of the child to their right. *Note:* You will need to "float" around to read writing that appears illegible to fledgling readers.

4. Explain that they will now read the story beginning from the person on their right and then add a middle part.

5. When 10 minutes have passed, ask them again to pass their paper to the person sitting to their left and receive the paper from the child on their right. This time they will read the

Sample Story Starters

The puppy was looking in at the warm fire and whimpering.

I opened the front door and there was a large box sitting on the doorstep.

I was shocked when I noticed my hands were growing large and hairy.

There he was on my desk, the tiniest little pony you ever saw.

My friends said the old house was haunted and I just had to find out.

"Three wishes," said the wise lady, "and use them with care."

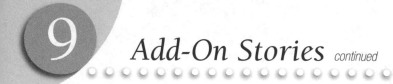

paper before them and create an original story ending for it. Explain that sometimes a person will have written no more than a sentence and that is okay; the idea is to keep to the idea started by the previous writer.

6. When the story endings have been completed, collect them and read them to the class, remarking on the diversity of stories made possible by one lead-in sentence! Return the stories to the groups for group editing, illustrations, and incorporation into a class book.

ASSESSMENT   As you are helping struggling writers with this activity, check to see if they are able to create story beginnings, middles, and endings. Further, ask group members to identify the "somebody," "wanted," "but," and "so" of their shared stories. Provide direct instruction in the use of story grammars for those children *not* able to identify narrative structure.

GROUP MEMBERS: **STORY TITLE:**

_____   _____

_____   Date: _____

_____

Somebody: _____

Wanted: _____

But: _____

So: _____

Notes for next time . . .

_____

_____

_____

_____

What's News?

(Adapted from Norton & Norton, 2003)

SUGGESTED GRADE LEVEL *4–6*

PURPOSE Besides learning to write an accurate and informative news story, the concept of writing for a specific purpose and audience will be reinforced through this motivational activity.

MATERIALS
- Local newspapers
- School newspapers
- News magazines
- Writing materials

PROCEDURES

1. Ask the children to look through class, school, local, or national newspapers for an article that interests them. Have them bring these articles to class.

2. Invite the children to read their articles aloud as other children listen for the purpose of the article and who the article has been written for. Point out the use of the five W's (what, who, when, where, why) in every article.

3. On the board or overhead projector, create four columns as follows:

    Type of Article   Purpose   Information   Audience

4. Lead a discussion with the children about the purposes, types of information contained in the article, and who the targeted audience was. Fill in the grid for each article brought in by the children.

5. With the children, brainstorm some recent school and/or local events that might be considered "newsworthy," e.g., a community member who won an award, the result of a school sports event, a classmate's new baby sister, the results of a science experiment, and so forth.

6. Invite the children to select one event and write it as a news article for a classroom newspaper, reminding them to include the five "W's"—what, where, why, who, and when—as well as considering their purpose and audience.

7. Have peer editors edit and proofread each other's news articles. Duplicate them for the class newspaper. Optional: Create an online newspaper by submitting articles to the website "Create Your Own Newspaper" (http://crayon.net).

ASSESSMENT   Children's news articles should be assessed on the following criteria: clear purpose, clear and concise information, targeted audience, five "w's" included, and correct spelling and grammar. Place news articles in each child's writing folder.

SAMPLE CHECKLIST

News Article

Name _____   Date _____

	high range	mid range	low range
Clear purpose	☐	☐	☐
Clear and concise information	☐	☐	☐
Specific audience is targeted	☐	☐	☐
The five "W's" have been included	☐	☐	☐
Correct spelling and grammar	☐	☐	☐

Notes for next time . . .

_____

_____

_____

_____

_____

Adapted from *Language Activities for Children,* 5th edition, by Donna E. Norton and Saundra E. Norton (Upper Saddle River, NJ: Merrill, 2003).

Other Ideas & Activities

- **LISTS.** Encourage the children, in small share groups, to list five ideas on a topic, such as: Five Things To Do Last, Five Things Not to Say to a Shark, or Five Things We Don't Like To Do.

- **WHAT HAPPENS NEXT?** Read a short story to the children and stop at the most exciting point. Discuss with the children what they think might happen next. Ask the children to write an ending using one of the brainstormed ideas or another idea of their own choosing.

- **PEN PALS.** Find another class of students in a neighboring school or in another city or state. Introduce friendly letter writing by having your students initiate correspondence with the students there by telling about themselves. Provide a template letter for emergent writers.

- **CLASSIFIEDS.** After reading the children some advertisements from the classified advertising section of a newspaper, ask them to think how they might sell themselves. Have them create a small classified ad for selling themselves by listing their most positive features and qualities.

- **MAIL SERVICE.** Put a mailbox in your classroom where children can write messages to you or to each other (only "good" and "true" messages). Utilize the "service" to tell children when they have behaved well.

- **I AM . . .** Have the children draw pictures of themselves, including any physical characteristic they think makes them different from others. Ask them to finish the sentence: I am . . . at least five times at the bottom of the drawing. Provide a time when children can share their drawings and "I am . . ." statements.

- **PICTURE PERFECT.** Take pictures of each child in the class and hang them around the room. Invite other classmates to write "good and true" comments about other children on paper positioned under each picture. You can contribute, too!

- **SLOGAN STATEMENTS.** Have the children keep a list of slogans they notice on people's tee-shirts and on bumper stickers. Discuss these and what they say about the person who has them. Encourage the children to each write a personal slogan telling something about themselves.

- **SILLY EVENT.** Ask the children to write an invitation to a humorous, fictitious event, such as a crocodile hunt, a tiddly winks contest, an animal marriage, and so on.

- **PICTOBIOGRAPHY.** Ask the children to bring in old and recent pictures of themselves, their family, their pets, friends, and so forth. Give them long sheets of paper on which to paste the pictures. For each picture, have them write one sentence telling about the part of their life shown in that picture.

- **HAND-OUT.** Have the children trace their hand on a piece of paper. On the outline of their hand, ask them to write all the things they can do with their hands.

- **PLAYGROUND WATCH.** Ask the children to watch a person they don't know on the playground for 10 minutes. Then have them write what they think the person was thinking. Extra challenge: Have them hypothesize a name for the person and describe the person's daily routine.

- **SALESPERSON.** Select as many items from the classified ads as there are children in your class. Allow each child to select an item and, using descriptive language and an illustration, create a poster convincing others to buy it.

- **PROVOCATIVE QUESTIONS.** Use provocative questions such as "What if animals could talk?" or "What if everyone looked exactly alike?" to generate a discussion. Then make a list of advantages and disadvantages to such an event occurring. Finally, have the children write a brief paragraph stating their personal opinion about the topic.

Children's Literature List

Anholt, Catherine, and Laurence Anholt. *All About You.* (New York: Viking, 1991). A series of questions asking children to tell about themselves. Possible illustrated answers are included. Provides preparation for writing an autobiographical piece. 1–6

Asch, Frank. *Ziggy Piggy and the Three Little Pigs.* (New York: Kids Can, 1998). A take-off on a familiar story. Ted, Frank, and Ned warn their brother Ziggy about the Big Bad Wolf. They tell him he should build a house to keep himself safe but Ziggy builds a raft instead. He saves the day for his brothers. Children can create similar take-offs on other familiar fairy tales. K–3

McDonnell, Flora. *I Love Animals.* (New York: Candlewick, 1994). Drawing and words showing why a little girl loves all animals. Repeated lines provide opportunities for choral or shared reading. Structure provides an ideal model for writing. K–3

Numeroff, Laura, illustrated by Felicia Bond. *If You Give a Pig a Pancake.* (New York: Geringer/HarperCollins, 1998). A circular tale that takes the reader/listener through a day in the life of a girl and her pig that happens to love pancakes. Using this scaffold with another animal and object (e.g., "If you give a dog a bone . . ."), children can be invited to write their own circular tale. K–3

Simon, Semour, illustrated with photos. *Autumn Across America.* (New York: Hyperion, 1993). Seasonal changes from east to west across America captured in striking photographs. Simon points out how animals and plants also change with the seasons. The photos can be used as provocative writing prompts. 3–6

Other Resources for Teaching Writing

Children's Writing: Perspectives from Research, by Karin L. Dahl and Nancy Farnan (Newark, DE: International Reading Association, 1998). Explores the beliefs teachers have shared about classroom practices and children's writing processes. The authors highlight representative research studies, describing them with a focus on classroom application. Timely topics such as writing workshops and writing and technology are included.

Classrooms That Work: They Can All Read and Write, 2d edition, by Patricia M. Cunningham and Richard L. Allington (New York: Longman, 1999). A plethora of ideas for developing readers, writers, and thinkers using a variety of authentic narrative and expository texts. The authors share the viewpoint that phonics instruction is necessary, but it is not enough to create joyful readers who construct their own meaning from text.

For the Love of Language: Poetry Scaffolds for Every Learner, by Nancy Lee Cecil (Winnipeg, Manitoba: Peguis Publishers, 1994). Ideas to help children explore many types of poetry. Each poetry activity includes a description, an easy-to-follow pattern, and a lead-in activity to help motivate children and help the teacher prepare for the session. Also includes samples of poetry written by children.

Fresh Takes on Using Journals to Teach Beginning Writers: Five-Minute Mini-Lessons, Skill-Building Strategies, and Irresistible Activities That Inspire Children to Write, by Jim Henry (Jefferson City, MO: Scholastic Professional Books, 1999). A model of journal writing that helps beginning writers become engaged, proficient authors of poetry, fiction, and prose. Journal writing becomes dynamic through sharing, demonstration lessons, and independent writing time.

Getting the Most Out of Morning Message and Other Shared Writing Lessons, by Carleen daCruz and Mary Browning Schulman (Jefferson City, MO: Scholastic Professional Books, 1999). Photos, samples of student work, classroom dialogues, and lesson plans to illustrate innovative techniques for teaching beginning writers by writing with them. Also includes tips on creating hands on literacy resources such as Word Walls, Big Books, and slide shows.

Know and Tell: A Writing Pedagogy of Disclosure, Genre, and Membership, by David Bleich (Portsmouth, NH: Heinemann, 1998). Intended for English teachers, but adaptations of concepts can be made for much younger students. The author stresses that all writing must be viewed in the context of the immediate social scene, the writer's interests and feelings.

LanguageActivities for Children, 5th edition, bu Donna E. Norton and Saundra E. Norton (Upper Saddle River, NJ: Merrill Prentice Hall, 2003). A practical book that includes many opportunities for the integration of the language arts across the curriculum, emphasizing oral and written language.

Reading–Writing Connections: From Theory to Practice, 3d edition, by Mary F. Heller (New York: Longman, 2000). An opportunity to look inside the classroom and see how theory and research can be transformed into practical, developmentally appropriate literacy instruction. The text offers effective teaching of the reading–writing connection through direct instruction and child-centered activity, encouraging children to become lifelong readers and writers.

25 Mini-Lessons for Teaching Writing, by Adele Fiderer (Jefferson City, MO: Scholastic Professional Books, 1999). A wealth of samples of children's writing so students can see good writing by peers. The lessons focus on writing skill elements such as choosing pertinent topics, organizing ideas, writing clearly, and learning how to edit.

Untangling Some Knots in K–8 Writing Instruction, edited by Shelley Peterson (Newark, DE: International Reading Association, 2003). This compilation presents the research, thinking, and practice of educators and researchers who have successfully overcome challenges they have faced when teaching writing. Chapters offer new ideas for the process approach to teaching writing, suggestions for students from diverse backgrounds, and ideas for using technology, drama, and poetry to teach writing.

In Closing

1. After using the activities in this section, what insights have you gained about how children learn to use the writing process? What did you also discover about yourself as a teacher of writing by teaching these activities?

2. Which of the activities did you think were particularly effective for reinforcing the following components of the writing process? Why?

   - Prewriting
   - Drafting
   - Sharing
   - Revising
   - Editing
   - Publishing

3. Which of the activities did you think was the most effective for developing the following literacy goals? Why?

   - Awareness that writing is constructing meaning
   - A positive attitude toward writing and its conventions
   - An appreciation of self as writer
   - Development of self as editor and collaborator
   - Interest in experimenting with writing in a variety of formats

4. What did you discover about the children's need to choose a topic of interest to them so as to become fully engaged in the writing process? Which activity best underscored this need?

5. Select an activity that offered you the most insight into the writing abilities of your learners. What did you discover? Cite examples of specific children with whom you worked.

6. Several of the activities asked you to provide the children with scaffolds or templates to help them to begin writing on a certain topic. What might be the advantages and disadvantages of using these devices? How might using such a device allow children to achieve more than they might without that device?

7. Certain activities had children use their senses before they began writing. How was writing encouraged as a result of these activities? Give examples of specific children and how they responded as a result of the activities.

8. Some activities began with oral discussion or brainstorming. How do you think these precursors to writing provided children with ideas? Give examples of specific children and how they were engaged in writing as a result.

9. Which activities were most difficult for your English language learners? What did you observe about their difficulties? How could you revise these activities to make them more accessible for your English language learners?

10. Identify a child you think has highly developed writing ability. What are the characteristics of the child? Did his or her behavior during the activities differ from that of the other children? Describe and explain the differences, if any.

Activities to Develop Literacy in the Content Areas

Introduction

ontent area literacy refers to the use of reading, writing, speaking, listening, viewing, and visually representing as tools for learning subject matter. Often children are expected to learn subject matter through reading; taking notes and outlining; listening to the teacher; or viewing, for example, a documentary, but are never taught exactly *how* to learn in these various ways.

Learning from informational text is different from reading or writing stories. A major part of the difference lies in the fact that stories are narrative material while informational text is generally expository material, and both have a unique structure. When teaching children to learn from informational, or content area text, it is necessary to use expository material for modeling, demonstration, and practice to ensure children can apply appropriate strategies to other informational texts they come across.

The following activities are designed to show children how to access content area material through the vehicles of reading, writing, speaking, listening to one another, viewing, and visually representing. Many different subject areas are addressed, but all require children to use expository material to move from "learning to read" to "reading to learn."

Categories

SUGGESTED GRADE LEVEL   2–6

PURPOSE   This study skill activity will encourage the use of a variety of reference material so necessary in the intermediate grades. The activity correlates well with any subject area when words from that area are the chosen classifications. The activity can be adapted for most grade levels.

MATERIALS
- Photocopied grids, one for each pair of children
- Access to several reference materials
- Internet access (optional)

PROCEDURES

1. Write a five-letter word, such as "GAMES," on the top of the grid set up like a bingo card. Note: Avoid words with the letters q, y, z, or double letters.

2. For the horizontal rows, write large classifications such as rivers, countries, birds, famous people, mammals, geometric shapes, rocks, and so forth. These should be written on the left side (see diagram). Use fewer and simpler categories for younger children.

3. Put the children in pairs. Distribute the grids, one to each pair of children.

4. Using reference materials, when necessary, have children fill in the blank cells of the diagram with an answer that corresponds to the letter at the top of the diagram.

5. When the children have finished, have them share their answers and where they obtained the information.

6. In scoring, give five points for an answer no one else has; if two pairs have the same answer, three points; one point for an answer three or more pairs have.

ASSESSMENT   After having conducted this activity with pairs, create a new grid and distribute to each member of the class. Evaluate each child's ability to use reference material to locate information through their accurate completion of the exercise. Provide direct instruction in the use of reference materials for children experiencing difficulty completing the grid.

SAMPLE CLASSIFICATION GRID

	G	A	M	E	S
RIVERS	Ganges	Amazon	Missouri	Elbe	Snake
COUNTRIES	Ghana	Austria	Malta	Ethiopia	Syria
BIRDS	goldfinch	auk	mynah	ern	sparrow
FAMOUS PEOPLE	Gandhi	Pamela Anderson	Marilyn Monroe	Ralph Waldo Emerson	Arnold Schwarzenegger
ANIMALS	gerbil	aardvark	mouse	eel	skunk
COLORS	green	amber	maroon	ebony	silver

Notes for next time . . .

_____

_____

_____

_____

_____

_____

_____

Classified Giving

2

SUGGESTED GRADE LEVEL 3–5

PURPOSE   This activity will provide children with authentic practice in solving math problems, evaluating and prioritizing needs, making judgments, assessing the monetary value of goods, and interpreting abbreviated forms of communications in classified advertisements. The activity will also require children to orally defend their choices.

MATERIALS
- Copies of classified ads from the local newspaper, enough for each child (Optional: department store catalogues)
- Play money
- PowerPoint for the presentation (optional)

PROCEDURE

1. Read one classified advertisement from the local newspaper with the children. Discuss abbreviations as they are used and explain those that are unfamiliar to the children.

2. Explain to the children that they will be given $500 to spend on a needy family that contains a husband, his wife, a 10-year-old boy, and a five-year-old girl. They are to use the play money to buy helpful gifts that are advertised in the classifieds, for each member of the family.

3. Divide the children into groups of four. Select a chair for each group who will see that all members participate in the discussion and agree on a final decision. Select a recorder who will create the shopping list for the group. The math calculator will keep track of the "budget," and the illustrator will draw a picture of each purchase. Optional: The final presentation can be prepared in PowerPoint.

4. The group must decide how to spend the money so that each person in the family has something he or she may need, but they must make sure not to go over the $500 limit. They must keep track of their math calculations and list their purchases.

5. When each group has finished, they present to the class:

   a. The list of their presents

   b. The justification for their choices

   c. The illustrations of the presents

   d. Their math calculations, in brief

ASSESSMENT Evaluate each member of the group on their participation in the group, the efficacy of the final choices, and the final presentation. For individual assessments, do the activity at a later date giving each child a budget, a scenario, and a classified section of the newspaper or a catalogue. Assess each child's mathematical calculations, as well as his or her reasons for the purchases. Place each child's work in his or her file.

Notes for next time . . .

_____

_____

_____

_____

_____

_____

_____

_____

_____

_____

_____

Fantasy Destinations

SUGGESTED GRADE LEVEL   3–6

PURPOSE   This activity integrates math, geography, art, computer skills, and creative writing by having the children discover a place they would like to go, use resources to find information about the place, and create a brochure to "sell" the place to their classmates in an oral presentation.

MATERIALS
- Access to computers and the Internet
- Business stationery
- Poster board and colored markers
- Sample vacation brochures
- Encyclopedias
- Informational trade books featuring different countries

PROCEDURE

1. Obtain some brochures from various vacation destinations to which you or friends have been. Share them with the children. Explain that they are going to choose a travel destination, find out everything they can about it, find out how much it will cost them to stay there for a week, and create a brochure to interest other children in their discovery.

2. Divide the children into pairs. After conferring with their partner, have them select a destination.

3. Ask the children to write to the Chamber of Commerce for the destination to get information about hotels, restaurants, and specific places of interest.

Grand Canyon Features

- Panoramic Views
- Hiking Trails
- Mule Rides
- Guided Tours

Grand Canyon Expenses

- Hotel $100.00 a night
- Food $50.00 a day
- Mule Ride $100.00 per person

4. Allow time for each pair to explore the Internet, peruse trade books and magazines, and consult the library to find at least 10 facts about their chosen destination that make it a desirable vacation spot. Tell the children they must consult at least three different resources.

5. Have the children estimate how far their destination is from their city and calculate how much it would cost to go there using various means of transportation. Also, have them figure in motels or campgrounds, food, and other costs.

6. Encourage each pair to create a brochure, using a PowerPoint presentation or other media of their choosing, highlighting the special features of their destination and how much it will cost to go there. (If PowerPoint is not available, this can be done with posters.)

7. Have the pairs share their fantasy destinations with the rest of the group.

ASSESSMENT   Evaluate according to the criteria presented in the sample checklist.

SAMPLE CHECKLIST

Name _____   Date _____

	high range	mid range	low range
Accuracy of factual information	☐	☐	☐
Interesting facts provided	☐	☐	☐
Reasonable estimate of cost	☐	☐	☐
Creativity of presentation	☐	☐	☐
Number or resources	☐	☐	☐
Clarity of oral presentation	☐	☐	☐

Notes for next time . . .

_____

_____

_____

_____

Current Event Bumper Stickers

(Adapted from Cunningham & Allington, 1999)

SUGGESTED GRADE LEVEL   3–6

PURPOSE   This activity will encourage children to critically read an article or editorial from the newspaper and summarize the main idea or message to create a bumper sticker.

MATERIALS
- Copies of newspaper clippings
- Overhead of a newspaper editorial
- Poster board in a variety of colors
- Colored markers
- Bumper stickers

PROCEDURE

1. From the newspaper, clip an editorial, by-line column, or feature story. (Straight news stories should NOT be used for this activity.) Duplicate a copy for each member of the class.

2. Display several examples of bumper stickers. Discuss their meaning and the fact that they must summarize a complex opinion in a few words. Examples:
   - My favorite people are dogs.
   - Visualize whirled peas.
   - Money worthless? Give it to me!
   - MIAs—does anybody care?

> My favorite people are dogs.

> Visualize whirled peas.

> Money worthless? Give it to me!

> MIAs—does anybody care?

3. As a class, read an editorial from a current newspaper on the overhead projector. Discuss how the ideas could be summarized into a bumper sticker. Write down all the children's ideas.

4. Divide the class into groups of three. Distribute newspaper clippings. Explain that they will read the newspaper article silently and then coauthor a bumper-sticker-type saying that embodies the main idea or message of the writer.

5. When the groups have completed the task, have each group read their saying to the entire class. Encourage them to also express why the particular saying is a concise statement of the main idea or the writer's message.

ASSESSMENT   Note how each child contributed to the group's discussion of the article. For individual accountability, select a new editorial or feature story. Ask the children to read it silently and create a summarizing saying for the article. Evaluate how completely each child was able to summarize the author's main message. For children experiencing difficulty with this activity, regroup for a mini-lesson on finding the main idea in a newspaper article.

Notes for next time . . .

_____

_____

_____

_____

_____

_____

_____

_____

_____

_____

_____

Adapted from _Classrooms That Work: They Can All Read and Write,_ 2d edition, by Patricia M. Cunningham and Richard L. Allington (New York: Longman, 1999).

Math Talk

SUGGESTED GRADE LEVEL 3–6

PURPOSE Through this activity, children will discover that the language of mathematics, far from being just used in school, is a part of our everyday life. They will also practice putting math symbols into words.

MATERIALS
- Several current newspapers
- Colored construction paper
- Paste
- Empty bulletin board

PROCEDURE

1. Clip two or three articles from today's print media in which some type of mathematics is discussed, for example, statistics, comparison of numbers, or percentages.

2. Paste the clippings on colored construction paper and draw a line under each mathematical term. Print the math word near its position in the article and place on the bulletin board.

3. After studying your examples, invite the children, in pairs, to find clippings in which mathematics have been used in articles in the newspaper.

4. Have the children place their articles on the bulletin board, underlining the math figure and writing the math word near its position in the article. As a group, discuss the meaning of the terms.

5. When the children have been alerted to how often "math talk" is used in the paper, they will find more than they can use in the project. Challenge them to then find these (and other) unfamiliar math terms, the meanings of which can be discussed in class:

Polls	Surplus
Average	Thrift
Inflation	Deficit
Mortgage	High yield
Statistics	Economy

Consumer debt soars to record level while savings drop

By Eileen Alt Powell
ASSOCIATED PRESS

NEW YORK—As the bills from holiday spending sprees arrive, Americans are finding that the mountain of debt they've built has gotten even higher.

Consumer debt has more than doubled in the past 10 years to record levels, making it hard for many families to cope.

For Bruce and Lorraine Esbensen of Clifton Heights, Pa., trouble started when they spent lavishly on their wedding six years ago. They soon found themselves falling behind on their bills.

"Creditors were calling, and I knew if I paid one, I couldn't pay the other," Lorraine Esbensen remembers. "It was so painful I got to the point where I didn't want to answer the phone."

Credit counselors helped the couple work out a repayment plan, but it still took more than four years to pay down their debt.

Consumer debt hit a record $1.98 trillion in October 2003, according to the most recent figures from the Federal Reserve. That debt—which includes credit cards and car loans, but not mortgages—translates to some $18,700 per U.S. household.

At the same time, the government says the nation's savings rate dropped to just 2 percent of after-tax income in the first half of the year. That means many people lack the means to deal with financial emergencies, much less their eventual retirement.

Experts worry about the impact not only on individual families but also on society as a whole.

"The Depression generation is passing on, and we're losing their values," said Howard Dvorkin, president of the nonprofit Consolidated Credit Counseling Services in Fort Lauderdale, Fla. "Now we've got an entire generation that doesn't know anything about thrift and careful spending. It's tearing the fabric that made this country great."

Just how did American consumers get so deeply in debt?

Robert D. Manning, a sociology professor at the Rochester Institute of Technology who wrote "Credit Card Nation—The Consequences of America's Addiction to Credit," says the problem dates back to the 1980s, when financial institutions began issuing credit cards and making loans to people who wouldn't have qualified in the past.

Source: Reprinted with permission of The Associated Press.

ASSESSMENT Informally, ask the children to jot down 10 math figures, and their corresponding words, they found in the newspapers. Additionally, ask them to name two unfamiliar math terms that they learned the meaning of as a result of completing this activity.

Notes for next time . . .

_____

_____

_____

What's This Food?

SUGGESTED GRADE LEVEL *3–6*

PURPOSE
Children will practice using descriptive language and "showing rather than telling" to write about a food they have researched, discovering in the process its food group membership, nutritional value, and place of origin. The written piece can be used as a topic in Writer's Workshop.

MATERIALS
- Discarded food and/or health magazines
- Access to the Internet, trade books, encyclopedias, and other resource materials

PROCEDURES

1. Discuss the four major food groups (food pyramid with upper grades) and why it is important to have adequate servings from each every day. Optional: Invite a health care professional to visit the class for this discussion.

2. Gather pictures of common food from discarded magazines, identified with a label, and give one to each child in the group. (Do not allow children to see one another's pictures.)

3. Explain that the children are to find out everything they can about the food they have been assigned to, but minimally the following:
   - Its food group membership
   - Its nutritional value
   - Where it originated
   - When it is usually eaten
   - How it is often prepared (recipes can be included)
   - How much it costs, roughly

4. When the children have completed their research, ask them to write a short paragraph describing their food without actually naming it, including the above factual information, as well as providing a detailed physical description of the food.

5. When every child is finished, have the children take turns reading their paragraph aloud, while the other children try to guess the name of the food.

ASSESSMENT   Evaluate the paragraphs on the accuracy and richness of the words used in the description. Assess the research on the inclusion of the six factors: food group membership, nutritional value, origination, when eaten, preparation, and cost. Work individually with those children who failed to find research on one or more of the factors. Provide peer editing for the paragraphs in Writer's Workshop, using the editing sheet from "The Busy Bee" activity. Place finished products in children's files.

Notes for next time . . .

_____

_____

_____

_____

_____

_____

_____

_____

_____

_____

_____

_____

_____

Historic Conversations

SUGGESTED GRADE LEVEL   *4–6*

PURPOSE   To complete this activity, children must go beyond simple research to imagine how a historical figure might respond to today's world. Children must use critical thinking and inferencing skills to make these decisions.

MATERIALS
- Biographies of famous historic figures, enough for half the class
- Access to costumes
- Packs of 3" × 5" cards, one for each group member
- Film clip of a historic figure, such as Martin Luther King, Jr., Amelia Earhart, Cesar Chavez, Diego Rivera, Golda Meir, or Thomas Edison

PROCEDURES

"I have a dream."

1. Show the clip of the historic figure, for example, Amelia Earhart. Discuss why she is still considered important today. Ask the children how they think she might respond to the following questions:
   - What has changed since you were alive?
   - What is better in the world?
   - What is worse?
   - What would you like to tell people of today?

2. Divide the class into pairs. Ask each pair to select a famous historic figure. Besides studying the persons' biography, invite them to research the person using trade books, encyclopedias, the Internet, and any other available resources.

3. When research has been completed, have the partners discuss how their historic figure might respond to the above questions, as well as how the person might have talked, thought, and made gestures.

4. Then have each pair, using the 3" × 5" cards, create questions for the historic figures chosen by the other class members, devising at least one for every person.

5. On a selected day, have one of the pairs dress in a costume appropriate for their historic figure while the other child in the pair introduces the figure and confers with him or her when answering questions.

6. Invite other members of the class to take turns asking questions from their cards. The child portraying the historic figure tries to answer the questions as that figure might, according to the research the pair has done.

7. This activity, which may take a couple of weeks to complete, is finished when every pair has had the opportunity to be interviewed and answer questions.

ASSESSMENT This activity demands that children go beyond simply factual knowledge to understand the greatness of a historic figure and to identify his or her vision. Evaluate, using anecdotal notes, how well each pair has been able to think critically and creatively about the person's point of view, according to their research. Also, take anecdotal notes on the insightfulness of questions asked by the other members of the class. Place notes in the children's files.

Notes for next time . . .

_____

_____

_____

_____

_____

_____

_____

_____

The Top Five

SUGGESTED GRADE LEVEL *4–6*

PURPOSE To ensure that children come away from their content area reading with an awareness of important subject area terminology, this activity focuses on helping children connect a particular vocabulary with a particular area of study.

MATERIALS
- Textbook
- Paper
- Pencils

PROCEDURES

1. Following the reading of a content area textbook section, ask the children to look back over the material and choose about 10 words they think are the most important to the section.

2. Working in pairs, have the children discuss the words they have chosen and reduce the number to the five most important words (number of words may vary according to the difficulty of the text material). Encourage the children to discuss the words' meaning and their relative importance to the topic. Explain to them that the narrowing down to five words will necessitate some compromise.

Ten most important words from "The Birth of Our American Flag" (made-up):

sew	American Revolution
needle	thirteen
banner	handwoven
stripes	history
stars	flag

<u>Top Five</u>

flag

American Revolution

thirteen

handwoven

history

3. Ask each pair to present their list and the reasons behind their choices to the rest of the class.

4. Follow with further discussion to develop a whole-class Top Five list of words for the selection.

5. Discuss the relationship of certain words that could in turn help children see that some words are subsumed within others.

ASSESSMENT   Evaluate each pair's ability to select the most critical words in the section as well as their ability to define the words. For those children not able to complete this activity, provide direct instruction on finding the main ideas in expository text.

Notes for next time . . .

_____

_____

_____

_____

_____

_____

_____

_____

_____

_____

_____

_____

_____

_____

_____

_____

_____

_____

Greatest Hits Parts of Speech

(Adapted from Cunningham & Allington, 1999)

SUGGESTED GRADE LEVEL *4–6*

PURPOSE Children will practice recognizing parts of speech through listening to vocal music from popular recording artists.

MATERIALS
- CDs containing vocal music; contemporary, but screened for appropriateness
- CD player

PROCEDURES

1. Review the parts of speech with the children.

2. Explain that you will be playing music that may be familiar to some of them, but that they will be listening for a particular part of speech, for example, adjectives.

3. Play a song for the children as they listen for the assigned part of speech. Ask them to make a list of all the words they hear that pertain.

4. When the song is finished, write down their contributions on the board. Discuss any contributions that are not the assigned part of speech and how they can tell.

5. Continue this activity, changing the part of speech sought. Create Word Walls using the parts of speech from the songs.

6. Segue the lesson into an assignment after all parts of speech have been covered. Ask the children to listen to the radio or their own CDs at home and make a list of the words they hear, an example of how they were used, and to categorize them by parts of speech. On an assigned day, have each child read his or her list to the class, which decides on the accuracy of the choices.

7. Variation: Have the children listen to vocals for metaphors and similes.

ASSESSMENT Evaluate each child's list for the number of parts of speech found and the accuracy of each item, according to the context they provide. For children unable to identify parts of speech, provide a mini-lesson on parts of speech, using items and events in the classroom as examples.

Notes for next time . . .

_____

_____

_____

_____

_____

_____

_____

_____

_____

_____

_____

_____

_____

_____

_____

_____

_____

Adapted from *Classrooms That Work: They Can All Read and Write,* 2d edition, by Patricia M. Cunningham and Richard L. Allington (New York: Longman, 1999).

Other Ideas & Activities

- **COMMUNITY FIELD TRIP.** Arrange a visit to a reconstructed log cabin, pioneer village, or museum exhibit in your community if such resources are available. Have the children develop questions to ask docents beforehand and, after the visit, have the children write thank-you notes.

- **MAP IT.** Have the children draw a simple map of their backyard, neighborhood, or the school yard. Ask them to bring the map home and see how many flowers and trees they can find and mark on the map. Using resources, have the children find the names of the flowers and trees, write them on the map, and share their findings with the rest of the class.

- **TREE HOTEL.** Find a tree near the school and gather your students around it. Ask the children to watch and listen for animals and insects. Talk about the residents you can't see that live in tunnels and burrow beneath the ground and around the tree's roots.

- **LITTER HUNT.** Plan a 30 minute "litter hunt" around the school grounds and ask the children to work in pairs to gather litter to fill plastic bags. Note: Check first for the presence of any unsanitary or hazardous material. Follow up with a discussion about why the litter may have dropped, how we can prevent littering, and invite the children to create posters exhorting others not to litter.

- **CAREER AWARENESS CENTER.** Create a career awareness center in the classroom. Place several "career kits" in the center. Each kit should be a box containing items appropriate to a given job or career opportunity. Be sure to represent the entire spectrum of careers, including custodian, taxi driver, field-worker, and so on. Have each child give a paragraph about which career appeals to him or her and why.

- **SEASONS.** Use a calendar to name the months in each season and discuss the names winter, spring, summer, and fall. Discuss the kinds of weather common to each season. Assign pairs of students to create and share a diorama of one of the seasons, including paper dolls dressed in appropriate clothes.

- **TELEPHONE TALK.** Provide two toy telephones. Divide the class into pairs. Print subjects for telephone conversations on 3" × 5" cards, such as reporting a fire, taking a message, or calling the doctor in an emergency. Have the children practice such conversations and then present them to the class using the toy telephones.

- **TASTE AND TELL.** Conduct a group discussion of different tastes in foods in different cultures and different families. Ask each child to bring in a favorite family recipe and to be prepared to tell the background of the food and why it has become a family favorite. Have each child use a word processing program to type the recipes into a special book to take home.

- **WHOSE BAG?** Give each child a plain brown grocery bag and tell them to take the bag home and fill it with five items that best tell the story of their identity. The next day, have the children take turns sharing their items and explaining how they are reflective of their personalities.

- **WATER USE.** Invite each child to collect pictures of the many ways we use water, including transportation, recreation, production, and how animals depend on water for their homes. Summarize by having the children write an essay entitled, "What life would be like without water—could we survive?"

- **CONSERVATION COUNTS.** Lead a group discussion on the importance of developing good conservation habits and on the consequences to all people if this is not done. Aid children in making plans to promote conservation in their neighborhood by creating a conservation manual, posters, talks to other classes, and so forth.

- **NUMBERS GAME.** Write a social security number on the board. Discuss what it is, why it is needed, how it is obtained, and the purposes for which it is most often used. Make a list of other numbers that may be researched by the children to increase their understanding of the use of numbers in our society.

- **SILENT NAMESAKES.** Make a list of buildings, streets, stadiums, parks, schools, etc., that have been named after important people. Assign pairs of students to research one place on the list to determine why and how the name was chosen, by whom, when, and what ceremony was involved, if any. Share orally with the class.

- **UNCLE SAM'S FAMILY.** Discuss the meaning of the word "citizenship." Ask the children to pretend they have just arrived in this country from a country of their choice and want to become citizens. Have them work in pairs to discover what information is required, the length of the waiting period, the monetary cost, and what the privilege and demands will be.

Children's Literature List

Bare, Colleen Stanley. *Never Grab a Deer by the Ear.* (New York: Cobblehill, 1993). The author uses beautiful color photographs to show young readers the difference between two kinds of deer that are native to North America, the white-tailed deer and the mule deer. 2–4

Cassidy, John. *Earthsearch.* (San Francisco: Klutz, 1994). Billed as a "children's geography museum in a book," this volume inspires children to read to learn. The book puts the concept of ecology in a broader context and shows how the actions of human beings have a profound effect on the planet. 4–6

Lewis, Barbara. *The Kid's Guide to Social Action: How to Solve the Social Problems You Choose—And Turn Creative Thinking into Positive Action.* (Minneapolis, MN: Free Spirit, 1991). Lewis's guide presents some of the steps to take when you and your students have identified a problem critical to your school or neighborhood. Lists of tips in each section assist in this. 4–6

Moore, Kay. *. . . If You Lived at the Time of the American Revolution.* (New York: Scholastic, 1997). This intriguing picture story book, in question-and-answer format, tells the story of the American Revolution from the point of view of the British and the Americans who fought in it. 4–6

Taylor-Cork, Barbara. *Weather Forecaster.* (New York: Watts, 1992). This book introduces atmosphere, days, seasons, air pressure, cloud formation, warm and cold fronts, and climates around the world, among other phenomena. Directions for projects, such as making a barometer, are included. 4–6

Other Resources for Developing Literacy in the Content Areas

Content Area Literacy: An Integrated Approach, by John E. Readence, Thomas W. Bean, and R. Scott Baldwin (Dubuque, IA: Kendall/Hunt, 1998). Explores the development of reading comprehension strategies throughout the curriculum. Though most are suitable for older students, some are appropriate for grades 2–3.

Social Studies Excursions, K–3, by Janet Alleman and Jere Brophy (Portsmouth, NH: Heinemann, 2002). *Social Studies Excursions, K–3* has been developed primarily for teachers who are looking for a supplement or a substitute for their primary-grade textbook. Teacher educators will find it a one-of-a-kind resource.

Think Nonfiction! Modeling Reading and Research, by Stephanie Harvey and Anne Goudvis (Portland, ME: Stenhouse Publishers, 2003). In this book, the focus is on comprehension for content area material—specifically, noticing new learning, asking questions, and determining the importance of information. Nonfiction readers are taught to merge their thinking with the new information to learn, understand, and remember.

The Teacher's Complete Guide to the Internet, 2nd edition, by Anne Heide and Linda Stillborne (New York: Teachers College Press, 2002). This invaluable book offers teachers a resource on how to integrate the Internet into their classroom, providing classroom projects and activities and relevant Internet sites.

The Story of Ourselves: Teaching History through Children's Literature, by Michael O. Tunnell and Richard Ammon (Portsmouth, NH: Heinemann, 1993). *The Story of Ourselves* focuses on the need for a stimulating history curriculum with the application of children's trade book literature as an indispensable ingredient for such a curriculum.

Using Children's Literature to Teach Math and Science in the Elementary Grades, by Lynn Columba, Cathy Kim, and Alden Moe (Scottsdale, AZ: Holcomb Hathaway, 2005). Math and science introduce children to concepts that are challenging and often abstract. This book advocates using children's trade book literature to make these concepts relevant to children and help them connect the concepts to their own lives. Over 50 activities provide specific techniques for using children's literature to facilitate learning in math and science.

In Closing

1. After using the activities in this section, what have you learned about how children use literacy to learn about the world? What did you discover about yourself as a teacher of literacy by teaching these activities?

2. Which of the activities did you find particularly helpful in teaching literacy in the following content areas?
   - science
   - social studies
   - mathematics
   - music
   - art
   - health and nutrition
   - computer skills
   - current events

3. Choose an activity that was particularly easy and one that was particularly difficult for your children. Why do you think it was easy/difficult? What, if any, adaptations would you make the next time you teach the lesson? Why?

4. What did you discover about the need to determine the background knowledge of the children before beginning an activity? How did the assessment suggestions at the end of each activity provide you with insights as to the strengths and limitations of your teaching of literacy in the content areas?

5. Select an activity that offered you the most insights into the general knowledge background of the children with whom you worked. What did you discover about the importance of providing information to your learners before leading a discussion? Cite specific anecdotal information.

6. Several of the activities asked the children to use a newspaper or other medium to gather information. What content area literacy skills are reinforced and assessed through the use of such activities? What did you learn about your learners' content area literacy skills as a result of doing these activities?

7. Some activities asked the children to do research on a topic using the Internet and/or other sources. What were some problems and successes associated with having children do research? What did you learn about a specific child's ability to do research as a result of these activities?

8. Some activities required the children to use the Internet or listen to their favorite music in a different way and then share their findings with the rest of the class. How do you think critical thinking can be enhanced through these activities? Give examples of specific children and what you think they learned as a result of one of these activities.

9. Which activities seems especially difficult for your English language learners? What did you observe about their difficulties? How could you revise these activities to make them more accessible to English language learners at each stage of language acquisition?

10. Identify a child you think is successful with content area literacy. What are the characteristics of that child? Did his or her behavior during the activities differ from that of the other children? Describe the differences, if any.

Activities to Promote Recreational Reading

10

Introduction

There is probably no one single more important task teachers can perform than that of developing students' motivation to read and instilling a lifelong habit of reading and writing. We not only want children to be able to read and to read to learn, but certainly we want them to *want* to read. Research, in fact, suggests significant advantages in terms of decoding ability, comprehension, and vocabulary acquisition for those children who choose to read in their spare time. But how can books compete with the other omnipresent forms of entertainment, such as video games, television, and computers in this age of technology?

In the following activities, the emphasis is on two critical areas: the affective aspects of literacy, or developing positive attitudes and interests for reading and writing, and authentic literacy experiences, or guiding children to see the value of literacy in one's daily life. Most of the activities involve motivational literature response activities that occur in the classroom situation but are designed to help children develop a more positive response to literature. The attitudes will hopefully transfer to recreational reading beyond the classroom and last a lifetime. Other activities involve exposing children to various genres of literature so they may find new interests in reading to explore.

Literacy Center

SUGGESTED GRADE LEVEL *K–6*

PURPOSE   Children need an inviting place to read and write where the materials have already been gathered for them. Also, the existence of such a place in the room makes a statement to children about how much the teacher values literacy.

MATERIALS
- Various literacy materials
- Comfortable places to sit (e.g., beanbag chairs, large pillows)

PROCEDURES

1. Explain to the children that they will be designing a corner of the room to be used for reading and writing when they have free time.

2. Write to the parents, explaining the purpose of the corner and ask for their help in supplying used furniture, carpet, shower curtains, discarded reading material, and other items to make the area pleasant and private.

3. Fill the area with items that will "turn the children on" to reading and writing including, but not limited to:

   - A variety of books spanning all genres, interest levels, reading levels, and representing many ethnic and cultural groups
   - Pamphlets
   - Catalogues
   - Many types of writing instruments and paper
   - Comic books
   - Books children have written
   - Read-along tapes and earphones

- Baseball and football cards
- Newspapers
- Provocative pictures to inspire writing

4. Discuss with the children the rules to be followed when they are using the Literacy Center. Post these. The following are some examples:

   - Use six-inch voices.
   - Don't bother someone when he or she is reading or writing.
   - Put materials away when finished.

5. Build in times during the day when children may use the center; for example, after lunch, before and after school, when finished with assignments, and so forth.

ASSESSMENT   Take anecdotal notes on who uses the Literacy Center and in which activities they participate. For more specific empirical data, administer a Reading Interest Inventory (Cecil, 2003; Cecil & Gipe, 2003) before the implementation of the Literacy Center, and once again at the end of the school year.

Notes for next time . . .

_____
_____
_____
_____
_____
_____
_____
_____
_____
_____
_____

Interest Groups

SUGGESTED GRADE LEVEL *1–6*

PURPOSE Comprehension and appreciation of expository text will increase when children meet together to discuss a common interest and consider ways to find out more about their hobby. Additionally, by organizing and sharing this information, they will expand the reading interests of other children.

MATERIALS
- Informational books on a variety of topics
- Specialty magazines
- Internet access (optional)

PROCEDURES

1. Administer a Reading Interest Inventory (Cecil, 2003) to the group.

2. From the results, create five or six interest groups within your classroom, such as:
   - A sports team
   - Computers
   - A music group
   - Horses, dogs, cats, etc.
   - Collections or hobbies such as stamps, model trains, etc.
   - Specific reading series, such as *Harry Potter*

3. Encourage the children to join one of the groups.

4. Have the groups meet and gather more information about their special interests through available resources amassed in the classroom.

5. Direct the children to set up special displays featuring products, books, articles, pictures, or other materials that may influence others to also develop the interest.

6. Finally, have the groups prepare oral reports to inform others of their interest using the following outline:

- What is your topic?
- List the major ideas or facts you want others to know.
- Provide pictures, models, objects, or other things to help others understand your topic.
- Show and summarize two books or articles on the topic.
- Describe a website that has information on the topic (optional).
- Decide how to begin the presentation to grab everyone's attention.
- Conclude the presentation by telling others how exciting, interesting, enjoyable, etc., the topic is.

For younger children, the outline can be simplified.

ASSESSMENT Evaluate the displays and presentations on the basis of the number and quality of resources used. Informally note the increase in actual reading about the topics by those in each interest group. Note the number of books read by each child and place in the child's file.

Notes for next time . . .

_____

_____

_____

_____

_____

_____

_____

_____

_____

_____

Read to Find the Ending

SUGGESTED GRADE LEVEL   *1–6*

PURPOSE   Children can be enticed to read an entire book when a section of the text has been read to them and they have been introduced to the characters, setting, and style. If left at a critical point, children will want to see how the story turns out.

MATERIALS   ● Narrative text appropriate for the grade level:

Shiloh (4–6)

The Wave (2–4)

Elvis the Rooster Almost Goes to Heaven (1–3)

The First Strawberries (1–3)

PROCEDURES

1. Find a book with much dramatic intensity, such as the ones suggested above.

2. Obtain several copies of the book.

3. Motivate the children to read the book by connecting the theme of the book to their own experiences.

4. Introduce the main characters in the book through the use of shadow puppets or large drawings of them.

5. Discuss the setting through the use of maps and/or a sharing of information from the Internet.

6. Read the book aloud, stopping at a very exciting part of the text.

7. Brainstorm with children what they think might happen next. Invite them to respond orally or in written form.

8. Tell them they may borrow the book to finish reading at home.

9. Try this activity with many different genres, at least once a month to encourage recreational reading.

ASSESSMENT   Note how many children actually request the book and finish it. Ask those students to informally tell about the ending of the book and how they would have ended it. For those who cannot tell about the ending of the book, provide direct instruction on narrative structure, focusing on the possible ways stories can end.

Notes for next time . . .

_____

_____

_____

_____

_____

_____

_____

_____

_____

_____

_____

_____

_____

_____

_____

_____

Swap Meet

**SUGGESTED
GRADE LEVEL**   *2–6*

PURPOSE   Children will practice oral reading skills as they read the blurbs on the back cover of favorite books from home to entice others to read.

PROCEDURES

1. Bring in a copy of a book that was among your favorite as a child. Read the children the blurb on the back cover and then add why the book was a personal favorite of yours.

2. Encourage the children to bring in two paperback books that they have already read and would like the others to read. (Note: A note home to the parents explaining the purpose of the swap meet and asking for permission for the children to trade one book is suggested. Also, you should be prepared with several books to offer those children who have no books at home.)

3. On the assigned day, invite each child to "sell" their books by (a) reading the blurb on the back and (b) offering a personal response to the book.

4. As each child is finished, the other children keep track of their first, second, and third choice books of those that have been presented.

5. Have the children turn in their book choice list. Most children will end up with a book that is on their list; popular choices can be circulated in the classroom library.

ASSESSMENT   Evaluation of this activity is long term and may be reflected through more positive attitudes on an end-of-the-year reading attitude survey compared with one conducted at the beginning of the year. Positive attitudes may also be reflected in greater circulation of books in the classroom library.

Notes for next time . . .

_____

_____

_____

_____

_____

_____

_____

_____

_____

_____

_____

_____

_____

_____

_____

_____

_____

_____

Book Bytes

(Adapted from Yopp & Yopp, 2001)

SUGGESTED GRADE LEVEL *2–6*

PURPOSE This activity provides a brief preview of a book. Short sentences featuring interesting passages from a text will make many children eager to read the whole book.

MATERIALS
- 3" × 5" cards on which are written sentences and phrases from a book the teacher wants children to read
- Several copies of the book

PROCEDURES

1. Select a book with much dramatic intensity, such as *Toughboy & Sister* by Kirkpatrick Hill. Be sure to have enough copies available for half the students in the class.

2. From the text, cull sentences and phrases that suggest some of the most interesting events in the book, writing one sentence on each card, and creating as many cards as there are children in the class. Examples:

   > "'Daddy, don't go! I'd get scared to be up here at camp, just us.'"

   > "Sister made Toughboy leave the radio on all night so she wouldn't feel so lonesome."

   > "He was afraid the bear would come back."

3. Give each student a book byte and have them read and reflect on it.

4. Ask the children to wander around the room, reading their book byte to others.

5. When the children have heard all the book bytes, have them write a short quick write, describing what they think the book is about.

> "Daddy, don't go! I'd get scared to be up here at camp, just us."

> Sister made Toughboy leave the radio on all night so she wouldn't feel so lonesome.

> He was afraid the bear would come back.

6. Put the children in pairs. Have them discuss their quick writes.

7. Give a copy of the book to each pair. Have them sit, shoulder to shoulder, and take turns reading the book aloud to each other.

8. Allow time for class discussion after each reading session, preferably a chapter per session.

ASSESSMENT Evaluate quick writes on the presence of narrative structure: Have children create characters, a problem, a resolution, and an original story ending from the book bytes they encountered. Also, informally gauge the interest level in reading this book after sharing small sections of it.

Notes for next time . . .

_____

_____

_____

_____

_____

_____

_____

_____

_____

_____

_____

_____

_____

Adapted from *Literature-Based Reading Activities,* 3rd edition, by Ruth Helen Yopp and Hallie Kay Yopp (Boston: Allyn & Bacon, 2001).

Quotations

**SUGGESTED
GRADE LEVEL**   *3–5*

PURPOSE   This activity is excellent for getting children to see how famous people and others they admire value reading and literacy. It is especially helpful to show children that people value literacy in a variety of ways, for a variety of reasons.

MATERIALS
- Large poster paper for each child
- Several books of quotations, such as *Bartlett's*

PROCEDURES

1. Check out several books of quotations from the public library. Besides *Bartlett's*, be sure to include some books with quotes by more contemporary people.

2. If you have a local sports team, find out if they support any literacy activities and obtain some relevant quotes about literacy, and the value of books, from them. (Several NBA stars, for example, have made TV ads highlighting the value of books in their lives.)

3. Peruse the books and find several quotations to share with the children. Discuss their meaning.

4. Introduce the children to the reference books of quotations and explain their purpose and use.

5. Invite the children to search through the books, select a quote about literacy from a person they admire or just a quote that appeals to them.

6. When children have selected their quotes, have them write the quotes on the poster paper and then illustrate their interpretation of the meaning of the quotation.

7. Encourage the children to share their posters in front of the class and then display them around the periphery of the classroom or in the halls of the school for other children to admire and read.

ASSESSMENT Have the children write a short paragraph about the quotation they selected and what they think reading means to the author of the quote. Ask them whether they agree or disagree with the quotation, and why. For children whose paragraphs reveal a negative attitude toward reading, administer a Reading Interest Inventory (Cecil & Gipe, 2003). Use the results to match each reader with a book he or she might enjoy.

Notes for next time . . .

_____

_____

_____

_____

_____

_____

_____

_____

_____

_____

_____

_____

_____

_____

_____

_____

_____

Newspaper Scavenger Hunt

SUGGESTED GRADE LEVEL 3–6

PURPOSE Children will become familiar with the newspaper and what types of interesting information can be found in it.

MATERIALS
- One current newspaper for each pair of children in the class

PROCEDURES

1. Duplicate the following questions, one for each child in the class:

   - If you had $50 to go shopping today, what would you buy?
   - If you could choose a job from the classified ads, which would you want?
   - Find a happy story from the newspaper. What is the headline?
   - Find a sad story from the newspaper. What is the headline?
   - Find someone's opinion (editorial). Do you agree or disagree?
   - Cut out the picture you think is the best one in the paper. Write your own caption for it.
   - What is the funniest cartoon in the paper?
   - What is the least expensive car you can find?
   - Find an article about someone close to your age.

   What's In the Newspaper?

   What is the Headline?

   Do you agree or disagree?

   What is the funniest cartoon?

   THE TIMES

2. Place the children in pairs. Give each pair a newspaper.

3. Instruct each pair of children to answer the questions on the sheet by leafing through the newspaper. Encourage discussion about interesting items the children find.

4. When each pair has finished, invite the children to share their answers with the rest of the class.

5. Using the children's findings, create a bulletin board entitled, "What's in the Newspaper?"

6. Encourage the children to bring in items of interest from the newspaper from home and build in a regular time to share them.

ASSESSMENT Ask the children to do a quick write in response to the following prompt: What can you find in the newspaper that is of particular interest to you? Check to see that each child has discovered at least one section of the newspaper that is of interest to him or her.

Notes for next time . . .

_____

_____

_____

_____

_____

_____

_____

_____

_____

_____

_____

_____

_____

_____

_____

_____

Imaginary Diaries

**SUGGESTED
GRADE LEVEL**   3–6

PURPOSE   Children will extend and deepen their understanding and appreciation of main characters in literature by creating a diary of the thoughts and feelings they imagine the characters might have while experiencing specific events in the book.

MATERIALS
- Fictional texts children have read, such as:

  Bridge to Teribithia, by Katherine Paterson (Crowell, 1978)

  Maniac Magee, by Jerry Spinelli (Little/Brown, 1991)

  Dear Mr. Henshaw, by Beverly Cleary (Morrow, 1984)

  Cassie Binegar, by Patricia MacLachlan (Scholastic, 1982)

PROCEDURES

1. Ask the children if they have ever kept a diary. Ask the children who have done so to discuss what kinds of writing they put in a diary.

2. Read to the children *Dear Mr. Henshaw.* Discuss the types of diary entries and their length and content, and how each reflects events in the main character's life.

3. Have each child select a book he or she has recently read in which there is a main character with whom he or she strongly identifies. (Optionally, this activity could be used in conjunction with fiction used in Literature Circles.)

4. Ask each child to create a 10-entry diary that corresponds to the events experienced by the character in one chapter from the book, using the entries from *Dear Mr. Henshaw* as a guide.

5. Invite the children to share their favorite diary entries with the rest of the class.

ASSESSMENT   Review the entries the children have written and assess them using a five-point rubric for expressive writing. Place them in each child's file.

Sample child's entry as Cassie Binegar in *Cassie Binegar*

"I don't know why we had to move to this place. The house is so old and dingy and there is only one tree in the yard—and it is a poor excuse for a tree at that. I miss the order of every thing at my old house and especially my own SPACE! I had space up in the attic, but then they put so much junk up there that I couldn't even go there to get any peace. Why couldn't things just stay the way they were? Everything was sweet. I HATE change!!"

SAMPLE RUBRIC

Expressive Writing

Name _____ Date _____

_____ Vivid and precise language is used to express the character's thoughts and feelings. (5 points)

_____ Character's feelings are described adequately. (4 points)

_____ Character's thoughts and feelings are sometimes expressed. (3 points)

_____ Limited expression of character's thoughts and feelings. (2 points)

_____ Sentences lack meaning; no thoughts or feelings expressed. (1 point)

Other Ideas & Activities

- **READING FESTIVAL.** Invite people from the community to spend an hour reading their favorite books to the children. These role models can show children that they value reading and that it leads to success.

- **BOOK SERIES.** Introduce the children to the first book in a series by reading the first one aloud to children and then having the others available. Also, introduce them to prolific authors, such as Judy Blume, in this way.

- **HOLIDAY READING.** For appropriate holidays, set up a display of books concerning the holiday and its history. Include a range of religious holidays.

- **BOOK CHARACTERS.** Have pairs of children trace each other's figure on large paper and then decorate them to look like their favorite book characters.

- **READ-IN.** Plan a special Friday evening sleep-over at the school where every child gets to stay up late as long as they are reading. Award prizes for the most books read.

- **BOOK REVIEWS.** Make a cumulative book review by collecting one-sentence comments from the children as they finish books from your classroom library.

- **SCHOOL SURVEY.** Have the children take a survey to determine which books are favorites throughout the school. Invite the children to help you set up a display of the winners.

- **LOTS OF LANGUAGES.** Arrange a display of familiar books written in several different languages. Invite the children to read these books in their home languages for the others in the class.

- **READING TO YOUNGER CHILDREN.** Have each child read and reread a picture storybook in preparation for reading it to younger children. The repeated readings will enhance fluency.

- **READING STARS.** Include small incentives for reading a specified number of books, as documented by parents. Highlight success on a bulletin board mentioning the "reading stars."

- **READ TO CHILDREN!** Children of *all ages* enjoy being read to. Fill in odd moments of the day by modeling "book worm" behavior of getting back to an exciting book at every opportunity.

- **BOOK FAIR.** Contact a local bookstore to display books on consignment in your cafeteria or multimedia room. Most stores will offer a discount.

Children's Literature List

Bruchac, Joseph. *The First Strawberries*. (New York: Penguin Puffin, 1993). This Cherokee legend explains the origins of strawberries on earth. A quarrel between a man and his wife leads to the woman walking away. The sweetness of strawberries reminds the woman of the happiness in her marriage. 2–4

Cazet, Denys. *Elvis the Rooster Almost Goes to Heaven.* (New York: HarperCollins, 2003). Elvis thinks that his growing is responsible for making the sun come up each morning. Then a bug flies into his throat and the sun comes up anyway. He is ready to give up but his friends don't let him. K–3

Hill, Kirkpatrick. *Toughboy & Sister.* (New York: Puffin Books, 1990). Every summer Toughboy and his sister stay at their isolated family fishing camp on the Yukon River, but their mother dies and their father vanishes, leaving the two of them to fend for themselves. 3–5

Hodges, Margaret. *The Wave.* (Boston: Houghton Mifflin, 1964). The people of a village in Japan are threatened by a destructive tidal wave. An old man sees the danger and attempts to warn the villagers by burning his own rice fields. 4–6

Naylor, Phyllis Reynolds. *Shiloh.* (New York: Atheneum, 1991). A young boy growing up in West Virginia discovers that a neighbor is abusing his dog. In his efforts to save the dog, the boy encounters a series of moral dilemmas. 4–6

Other Resources for Promoting Recreational Reading

Fostering the Love of Reading: The Affective Domain in Reading Education, edited by Eugene H. Cramer and Marietta Castle (Newark, DE: International Reading Association, 1994). The authors believe that increasing the proportion of readers who read widely ought to be as much a goal of reading instruction as increasing the number of competent readers. The suggestions in this book will help teachers inspire children to read widely, and well.

Even Hockey Players Read, by David Booth (Portland, ME: Stenhouse, 2000). This comprehensive overview of the challenging issues surrounding boys and reading includes strategies and practical solutions for helping struggling readers and, in the process, uncovers assumptions and stereotypes parents and educators hold about boys.

Reading Reasons: Motivational Mini-Lessons for Middle and High School, by Kelly Gallagher (Portland, ME: Stenhouse, 2003). Gallagher offers a series of mini-lessons specifically tailored to motivate children to read and, in doing so, to help them understand the importance and relevance of reading in their lives. This book introduces and explains nine specific "real-world" reasons why children should be readers.

Lively Discussions! Fostering Engaged Reading, edited by Linda Gambrell and J. Almasi (Newark, DE: International Reading Association, 1996). The authors of this compelling text all believe that a love for reading can be enhanced through reader response and stimulating discussions that start in class, but lead to more recreational reading at home.

Promoting Volunteer Reading in School and Home, fastback no. 225, by Leslie Morrow (Bloomington, IN: Phi Delta Kappa Education Foundation, 1985). The quest of all teachers is finding ways to get children to read because they see it as a pleasurable chosen activity. This book provides many ideas for achieving this goal.

Lost in a Book: The Psychology of Reading for Pleasure, by Virginia Nell (New Haven, CT: Yale University Press, 1988). This book underscores the motivational and behavioral factors that make children choose reading over other activities, helping teachers to consider how to appeal to the varied learners in a classroom.

Through the Eyes of a Child: An Introduction to Children's Literature, by Donna E. Norton (Upper Saddle River, NJ: Merrill/Prentice Hall, 2003). To inspire children to read requires matching the appropriate book to the appropriate reader. This comprehensive introduction to children's literature provides information about current and classic books from all genres and for all ages and interest levels, complete with classroom activities.

Language Arts Activities for Children, 5th edition, by Donna E. Norton and Saundra E. Norton (Upper Saddle River, NJ: Merrill/Prentice Hall, 2003). Stimulating activities for the language arts increase interest in both reading and writing beyond the classroom. This user-friendly book provides a year's worth of motivational activities to promote recreational reading development.

Easy Reading: Finding Joy and Meaning in Words, by Laura Rose (Tucson, AZ: Zephyr Press, 2001). The clearly designed activities provided in this book can significantly improve students' comprehension, enjoyment, and personal involvement at any grade level.

Literature-Based Reading Activities, 3rd edition, by Ruth Helen Yopp and Hallie Kay Yopp (Boston: Allyn & Bacon, 2001). The premise of this book is that quality children's literature, and the opportunity to discuss it and respond to it, will create better readers who enjoy reading beyond the classroom doors. All activities include children's literature references.

Striking a Balance: Best Practices for Early Literacy, by Nancy Lee Cecil (Scottsdale, AZ: Holcomb Hathaway, 2003) and *Literacy in the Intermediate Grades: Best Practices for a Comprehensive Program,* by Nancy Lee Cecil and Joan P. Gipe (Scottsdale, AZ: Holcomb Hathaway, 2003). Companion texts to this activities book, these books present major research in and a theoretical overview of early and intermediate literacy in an easily understandable, reader-friendly style. The books include numerous strategies as well as many practical tools for teaching and assessing literacy.

In Closing

1. After using the activities in this chapter, what insights have you gleaned about what makes children enjoy reading? What did you discover about your role in motivating the children to read?

2. Which of the activities in this section did you think were particularly helpful in the following areas? Why?
   - Motivating children to read in school
   - Motivating children to read at home

- Motivating children into different genres
- Motivating children to respond to literature

3. Which activity did you feel worked best to promote interest in reading? In what way did this happen?

4. Which activity did you think was the most successful at reaching the children who are the most reluctant readers? Why?

5. Select an activity that offered you the most insight into the reading interests of your learners. What did you discover? Cite specific examples of specific children with whom you worked.

6. Several of the activities invited the children to make predictions about what might happen next, or what the book might be about. How do you think such predictions help to motivate the children to read?

7. One activity (*Swap Meet*) asked the children to bring in books they have read and "talk them up." Why might the children's responses to their books be more motivational than the teacher's opinion?

8. One activity (*Quotations*) encouraged the children to become familiar with what famous people have had to say about the value of reading in their lives. Do you feel such an activity might have an effect on the way the children view reading? Why or why not?

9. Which activities were particularly difficult for English language learners? What did you observe about their difficulties? How can you revise these activities to be more accessible for your English language learners?

10. Identify a child who particularly enjoys reading. What are the characteristics of that child? What do you think has caused this child to be so motivated to read? What special activities can you provide to assure that the child expands his or her reading interests?

Activities for Working with Parents

11

Introduction

I t is not always fully appreciated just how much communication and sensitivity are needed to make the relationship between the child, the parents or caretakers, and the teacher work optimally so that there is a true synergy between home and school. Teachers often need to be the prime movers, envisioning innovative ways to get the parents—from all cultural and linguistic backgrounds— aware of how best to help their child with literacy. Teachers need to make parents feel at ease by talking to them in clear terms about the progress of their son or daughter, and find ways to explain the most effective ways to reinforce the goals of a balanced and comprehensive literacy program at home.

The activities in the following chapter are designed to recruit parents as partners in their child's education. Some activities concern ways to communicate about the literacy curriculum so that parents can most effectively help their child at home; others are specifically designed to reach the parents that may have been turned off to the educational system, and fear the usual negative reports about their child. These activities address ways to gain rapport with the parents by pointing out the positive aspects that every child possesses. You may also find the sample cover sheet for a homework packet (provided in Appendix E) useful as a model for involving parents in their children's homework assignments.

Finally, encountering a child whose parents cannot read or cannot read English is not uncommon. Also, we may occasionally teach children who have no telephones in their homes, and for many families, Internet access is largely through the public libraries. These situations should be kept in mind when selecting parent involvement activities. One method of contact will not reach all children; the individual needs of families and parents must always be considered.

Note: For the sake of readability, the term "parent" is used throughout this chapter. This term should be understood to encompass the concept of caretaker as well—a family member or other committed adult who may have primary responsibility for the care of a child.

Happy Gram

**SUGGESTED
GRADE LEVEL**   *K–6*

PURPOSE   You can gain parents' trust and confidence before you have to enlist their help if a problem should arise by making the first note home a positive one.

MATERIALS   • Stationery lined like telegrams

PROCEDURES

1. Early in the school year take the time to share good news with parents to begin to cultivate good rapport.

2. Once a week, write letters to the parents of several of your students, telling them something positive, such as:

   A child accomplished an academic goal

   A child finished reading a challenging book

   A child did particularly well on a homework assignment

   A child helped you or someone else

   A child read to a younger child

   A child led a group

3. The good news can be written on preprinted paper patterned after a telegram form.

4. The good news can be a handwritten note or a certificate or award format.

5. Keep track of Happy Grams you send out so every student occasionally receives one.

6. Engage an older child or community resource person to help you translate the message for parents who do not speak English.

HAPPY GRAM

To: Mrs. Jones

From: Mr. Kronberg

Re: Your daughter, LeTasha

LeTasha did a terrific job reading Where the Wild Things Are to a group of kindergarten students. I was very proud of her and I am sure you are, too!

Notes for next time . . .

_____

_____

_____

_____

_____

_____

_____

Postcard Previews

SUGGESTED GRADE LEVEL   K–6

PURPOSE   A postcard sent to the child and his or her parents at the beginning of the school year, outlining some exciting books that will be read and topics that will be studied, will make children and their parents feel welcomed and build bridges.

MATERIALS
- Blank postcards, one for each child who will be in your class in the fall

PROCEDURES

1. In the summer, get the names and addresses of the children who will be students in your class in the fall.

2. Obtain a set of blank postcards that can be sent to each family.

3. Write a brief note to each child, beginning with, "Dear Richard, I am very excited to have you in my class in the fall and I am looking forward to meeting you!" or "Estimado Ricardo, Estoy muy alegre que estarás en mi clase este año. Estoy anticipando de conocerte."

Estimado Ricardo,
Estoy muy alegre
que estarás en mi
clase este año.
Estoy anticipando
de conocerte.

4. Follow this introduction with an outline of some activities that the child can look forward to. Examples:

   Books that you will be reading to them or together

   Topics to be studied

   Field trips to be taken

   Special classroom activities

   Awards or contests

5. If you are aware of linguistic differences of some of your future students, be sure to find community resource people to translate your message so that it is accessible and welcoming to *all*.

Notes for next time . . .

_____

_____

_____

_____

_____

_____

_____

_____

_____

_____

_____

_____

_____

_____

_____

_____

_____

_____

_____

Parent Volunteers

**SUGGESTED
GRADE LEVEL**   K–6

PURPOSE   Once parents start coming to the classroom and feel they are welcome—and
have something to contribute—many become interested in actually helping out.

MATERIALS   • Teacher-Created Parent Recognition Certificate

PROCEDURES

1. Send a letter asking parents if they have the time
and interest in volunteering in the classroom.

2. For those who respond, hold an informal
briefing session on your teaching goals
and strategies, the type of classroom cli-
mate you are trying to create, and your
expectations for them. As well, encourage parents to share their ideas,
experiences, and expectations.

3. Show the volunteers around the
school. Answer questions such as
where should they park? Can they use
the teacher's lounge? Should they
check in at the office? Should they call
if they are ill?

4. Discuss possible roles and what the volunteers would be most comfortable doing. Some
suggestions:

   • Tutors. Listening to children read and reading
   to them.

   • Aides. Supervise reading time or free time.

   • Field trip assistants. Have them help organize the field trips.

   • Room parents. Have them help with special parties and school activities.

   • Clerical helpers. They can photocopy material, make teaching aids, and correct papers.

5. Working parents may also want to be involved. They can be involved at home, at their convenience, in the following ways:

   • Making learning games

   • Sewing puppets or costumes

   • Baking for parties and special events

6. Recruit parents from other cultural and language groups to enrich your classroom by asking them to share:

   • a song in their language

   • special arts and crafts

   • a traditional food

   • a story or folktale

7. Develop an all-purpose Parent Recognition Certificate to show your appreciation to parents who help out in any way. Optional: Hold a volunteers' tea, or have the children plan a special activity to honor the parents.

Notes for next time . . .

_____

_____

_____

_____

_____

_____

_____

_____

_____

_____

_____

_____

Homework Contracts

**SUGGESTED
GRADE LEVEL**   2–6

PURPOSE   Homework is the most common link between home and school life. Children who are frustrated by assignments that are too difficult, however, can benefit from a negotiated homework contract created by parents, teacher, and the child.

MATERIALS   • Individual Homework Contracts

PROCEDURES

1. Identify those children who consistently "can't do" or "forget" to do their homework.

2. Bring parents and child together in a conference. Discuss the situation in a straightforward, friendly manner, listening carefully to each person's explanation of what the problem is. Explain the benefits of homework. Provide translators for parents from other language groups.

3. Set realistic goals for completion of homework for a specified time in the future appropriate to the age of the child, for example, the next three weeks.

4. List the contract's objective, the follow-up actions you or the parents will take (signatures, phone calls, further meetings) and the consequences of not meeting the terms of the contract (e.g., limiting television time; shorter recess).

5. Include rewards for contracts completed. At home, this might be a special privilege; at school this may mean a new leadership responsibility and special recognition.

HOMEWORK CONTRACT	
FOR:	Kendall Nguyen
OBJECTIVE:	Kendall will turn in his homework every day
FOLLOW-UP ACTION:	We will have a telephone conference in two weeks on March 12, to discuss Kendall's progress.
CONSEQUENCES:	Parents will reduce computer time by 1/2 hour a day if Kendall neglects to turn in his homework on more than one occasion.
REWARD:	Kendall will assume the role of hall monitor if he consistently turns in his homework for three weeks. Parents will reward Kendall with a book of his choice.

Notes for next time . . .

_____

_____

_____

_____

_____

_____

Sunshine Calls or Emails

SUGGESTED GRADE LEVEL   K–6

PURPOSE   The most frequent and effective way teachers can use telephones is to report on positive progress and behavior. Such a routine habit will enhance the relationships you are building with the parents of your students.

MATERIALS
- Telephone (or email access)

PROCEDURES

1. Get into the habit of calling at least one parent a week to relay good news. Keep track of these Sunshine Calls or emails by putting a check next to names on your class roster.

2. If making a phone call:
   a. Before calling, make notes about what you want to say. (Note: Be sure you know the parent's name, as it may not be the same as the child's.)
   b. Introduce and identify yourself, and ask if this is a good time to talk for 5 or 10 minutes. If not, arrange for a more convenient time.

3. Keep your message short, simple, and straightforward, avoiding jargon.

4. Offer a positive comment about the child. Listen carefully and use "I messages."

5. Conclude on a positive note, and invite response ("I am glad we have had this chance to chat. If you need to call or see me about anything . . .").

6. For parents who speak other languages, enlist the aid of a staff resource person who speaks the language, or an older child in the family. If making a Sunshine Call, rehearse the above steps with them and have them explain that they are calling on your behalf.

Sunshine call or email

To: mandsdevries@aol.com

From: Hannah Lowenbaum
<hlowenbaum@mail.milwaukee.k12.wi.us>

Subject: Robert's enthusiasm for reading

I am thrilled with the enthusiasm Robert has been showing for reading since he has discovered *Harry Potter.* Last week he completed the second in the series, staying in during recess to finish it!

Notes for next time . . .

_____

_____

_____

_____

_____

_____

_____

_____

Dial-a-Teacher

**SUGGESTED
GRADE LEVEL**   K–6

PURPOSE   Parents can use your recorded messages to obtain information on homework assignments, tips for working with children at home, and even daily inspirations.

MATERIALS   • Personal answering device or class web page

PROCEDURES

1. Offer parents a special number connected to an answering device that they may use to get information when school is closed, or when you are unable to be reached by phone. Send a note to your students' homes explaining the purpose of this number.

2. Record a message to parents on the machine to keep them informed about such things as:

   • Homework assignments
   • Spelling words for the week
   • Books their children may like to read
   • Books to read aloud to children
   • Tips on reading aloud
   • Tips on writing with children
   • At-home suggestions for supplementing a unit

3. Change messages on a regular basis, and make them available at a regular time each day or week.

4. Make messages short and to the point.

5. Messages pertaining to children's work should include suggestions for how parents can help.

6. Enlist the aid of a translator in recording your messages in other languages if you have children with parents who speak limited English.

Optional: Create a class website to provide this information.

Notes for next time . . .

_____

_____

_____

_____

_____

_____

_____

_____

_____

_____

_____

_____

_____

_____

_____

_____

_____

_____

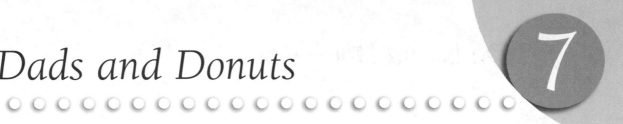

Dads and Donuts

SUGGESTED GRADE LEVEL	*K–6*

PURPOSE   Male role models who care about reading are critical in motivating children to read, yet the person who has been most conspicuously absent at school is the father. This is a program specifically designed to reach out to the male caretakers in children's lives.

MATERIALS
- Coffee and donuts
- Flyers to send home with children

PROCEDURES

1. If you, like many teachers, have had difficulty reaching the fathers of your students, you might start with an informal survey addressed to the male caretaker in the lives of each of your students. Be sure to be inclusive of older brothers, cousins, grandfathers, pastors, or other significant male figures in your students' lives.

2. In the survey, ask what specific provisions might allow the male figure in the home to attend a school function; for example, weekend events? evening hours? interactive meetings? informal get-togethers?

3. From the information received, schedule an event geared specifically for your students and their "fathers," such as the popular Saturday morning "Donuts and Dads," where fathers and other male caretakers can come and *read to their children* and learn how to better develop their child's literacy skills.

4. Send out colorful flyers, especially designed to recruit fathers and other male caretakers.

5. Make the get-together informal, with time to build a rapport with the parents, time for the "dads" to get to know one another, and light refreshments.

6. Plan one activity to share with the "dads," such as how to choose an appropriate book for the child, how to do a "Think Aloud," or how to ask "why" questions to deepen comprehension.

7. Enlist the aid of older children or community resource persons to ensure that flyers are printed in all languages spoken by parents of children in the class; similarly, have translators available to translate instructions for the activity and other pertinent information.

Notes for next time . . .

_____

_____

_____

_____

_____

_____

_____

_____

_____

_____

_____

_____

_____

_____

_____

_____

_____

_____

Newsletters

SUGGESTED GRADE LEVEL *K–6*

PURPOSE Surveys of parents show that they read school newsletters and consider them a useful source of information. Parents indicate that *classroom* newsletters would be even *more* helpful.

MATERIALS
- Desktop publishing program
- Copy of the newsletter for the family of every child in your class
- Translators for every home language in your class

PROCEDURES

1. Decide upon a format for a monthly newsletter. One idea is to place a one-page newsletter on the back of a monthly school calendar.

2. Create a consistent format, or logo, so the newsletter becomes instantly recognizable.

3. Keep the format clean and uncluttered and avoid using jargon. Date each issue.

4. Include information that will help parents to help their children in literacy. Some suggestions:
   - List of books children might enjoy
   - Riddles to share with children
   - Highlights of community resources
   - Frequently asked questions and answers
   - Reminders
   - Children's writing
   - Announcements of upcoming events
   - Lists of items parents could collect for class projects
   - Possible activities parents and children could do at home together

5. Although frequency can vary depending upon what you are trying to accomplish, try to send the newsletter home on a certain day of the week each time so parents can be looking for it.

6. Locate translators so the newsletter can be translated into the home language of every family with whom you work.

**SAMPLE
NEWSLETTER**

Mr. Tan's Fifth Grade News   November, 2004

Dear Parents and Guardians,

We have had quite a week! Our school book fair was a huge success. Our class bought 87 books—more than any other class in the school—and we also have 12 new additions to our classroom library. Thanks to all of you who participated.

In Social Studies, we have been practicing study skills. Using a method known as SQ3R, students practice the most effective way to preview, skim, read, and study content area subjects, such as science and social studies. This week, please ask your child to demonstrate this method while reading a chapter about the California Gold Rush. You will be amazed!

Best regards,

Kenneth Tan

Notes for next time . . .

_____

_____

_____

_____

_____

_____

Specific Suggestions to Offer Parents

Note: The following activities can be done in English or the child's home language.

- **WHAT WAS YOUR FAVORITE PART?** After reading a story to your child, or after he reads one to you, ask what his favorite part was. Listen carefully to the answer, for this will give you an indication as to whether he can determine the main idea, or if he tells you everything without telling the central thought.

- **SURVEY FIRST!** Help your child develop the habit of surveying materials before she reads them by noticing the pictures, major headings, and reading the summary before reading the book or chapter.

- **FOLLOW DIRECTIONS.** The next time you put a toy or model together according to written directions, have your child help you. Ask him to read some of the directions to you, or point to the diagram that illustrates the direction you are reading.

- **FEELINGS.** As you read to your child, or as your child reads to you, ask her how different characters are feeling. Have her tell why she has drawn this conclusion by pointing to significant facts or events in the story. Have her reread these parts.

- **TELL ME WHY.** One of the most important things you can do to help your child think is to talk to him about the things he sees. For example, as you take a walk or ride in a car, ask him why cars have tires, why we have stop signs, or why trees need rain.

- **LET'S FIND OUT.** Topics such as insects, plants, animals, or events may come up as you are watching television or working in the yard with your child. Use encyclopedias or the Internet to locate the answers and "think aloud" so your child will see how you are locating the information.

- **HOW TO.** Many "how to" books are available for learning things such as how to knit, play sports, bind books, cook, and make paper animals. If your child is interested in learning any of these skills, obtain a book for her to read about it. If she is unable to read it, read it to her.

- **HOW DO YOU SPELL . . .?** As your child develops an interest in writing words, he will ask you how to spell them. Sometimes respond simply by telling him the letters. Other times, ask him to listen to the sounds in the word and think of the letters that make those sounds.

- **DISCUSSING STORIES.** Reading to your child is an invaluable activity. As you read, ask your child questions about the pictures, characters, and events in the story, usually starting with "Why do you think . . .?" and "What would *you* do if . . .?" to help your child make personal connections with the story.

- **USING THE CONTEXT.** As your child is reading and she comes to a word she does not know, tell her to skip it and read the rest of the sentence to see if she can determine what the word might be. If she can't, tell her the word, but also help her to look at the sounds of the word.

- **HOW MANY WORDS CAN YOU MAKE?** Provide your child with several plastic alphabet letters or letters you have written on index cards. Ask him to see how many words he can make using the letters. Make the activity more enjoyable by taking a turn at making words that you can introduce to your child.

- **SUBSCRIBE TO CHILDREN'S MAGAZINES.** Many birthday and holiday presents are broken before the special day is over, but for a reasonable cost you can get your child a magazine subscription to *Cricket* or *Ranger Rick* that will last throughout the year. Ask your child's teacher for suggestions.

- **FRIDAY NIGHT READ IN BED.** Establish a routine that, on a specified weekend night, you allow your child to stay up as long as she wishes, as long as she stays in bed and is reading something. This routine plants the seeds for future "book worm" behavior.

- **DEVELOP THE LIBRARY HABIT.** Take advantage of the library story hours, book clubs, plays, in addition to checking out books for your child and yourself. Ask the children's librarian what books and activities she recommends most highly for your child.

- **FOLLOW DIRECTIONS.** The next time you are cooking, planting, or carrying out a household chore, have your child write down the steps followed to carry out the activity.

Children's Literature List for Parents

Albert, Richard E. *Alejandro's Gift*. (New York: Chronicle, 1994). This book provides an insightful look at wilderness and how humans can observe its wonders with more than just their eyes. The glossary includes illustrations and brief descriptions of plants and animals that inhabit the Southwestern United States. K–3.

Bunting, Eve. *Dandelions*. (New York: Harcourt Brace, 1996). This is the story of a family moving from Illinois to Nebraska during the westward migrations in the United States during the mid-1800s. Dandelions are a metaphor for this family that endures the hardships of change and yet continues to try to build a better life. 4–6

Gerstein, Mordecai. *The Story of May*. (New York: HarperCollins, 1994). The colors of earth tones and sky tones guide the reader to the story of May, a fanciful character and a "little month of a girl." May is the daughter of April, an earth mother much like the Greek goddess Demeter, and of December, the earth father she seeks. K–2.

Loredo, Betsy. *Faraway Families*. (New York: Silver Moon, 1995). The author offers helpful ideas to help family members feel closer to loved ones far away. She suggests creating family trees, sending photos, handmade pictures of family members and family activities, letters, videotapes, and customized "care packages." 4–6.

Parker, Steve. *It's an Ant's Life*. (Pleasantville, NY: Reader's Digest Children's Books, 1999). In this first-person journal, the author (an ant) provides a wealth of information about ants. The journal makes use of diagrams, clippings, maps, and a glossary to explain an ant's life. 3–5.

Viorst, Judith. *Alexander and the Terrible, Horrible, No Good Very Bad Day.* (New York: Atheneum, 1972). Alexander has a terrible day when one thing after another goes wrong for him. Provides a great stimulus for discussing moods. K–3.

Other Resources for Working with Parents

Raising Readers: Helping Your Child to Literacy, by Steven Bialostok (Winnipeg, Canada: Portage & Main Press, 1992). This book answers all that parents ask about their children's reading. It helps make parents partners, not adversaries, by explaining how current ways of teaching reading correspond to the way children acquire language.

From Your Child's Teacher: Helping Your Child Learn to Read, Write, and Speak, by Robin Bright (Winnipeg, Canada: Portage & Main Press, 1999). Getting parents involved in their child's education is the important theme of this book. It is an excellent resource for teachers who want to give parents hints for helping their children with homework, making reading part of their lives, and developing them as writers.

Ways with Words: Language, Life, and Work in Communities and Classrooms, by Shirley Brice Heath (New York: Cambridge University Press, 1983). In this classic study, the author describes her groundbreaking work with one community as she studied their literacy habits and their impact on their children's success in school.

Many Families, Many Literacies: An International Declaration of Principles, by Denny Taylor (Portsmouth, NH: Heinemann, 1997). In this edited text, the variety of home practices in diverse cultures is explored as well as the current trend toward family literacy programs.

Growing Up Literate: Learning from Inner-City Families, by Denny Taylor and C. Dorsey-Gaines (Portsmouth, NH: Heinemann, 1988). For any teacher working in an inner-city environment, this book is a must. The authors help teachers to realize the literacy assets that children bring to school, rather than focusing on the deficits.

Families at School: A Guide for Educators, by A. Thomas, L. Fazio, and B. L. Stiefelmeyer (Newark, DE: International Reading Association, 1999). The authors urge us to consider the wide range of literacy practices that may occur in the homes of a variety of diverse youngsters. They suggest that doing so will allow us to build more effectively upon the literacy experiences that children bring with them to school.

Family Literacy: From Theory to Practice, edited by Andrea DeBruin-Parecki and Barbara Krol-Sinclair (Newark, DE: International Reading Association, 2003). This book fills an important void in the largely unstudied field of family literacy, providing teachers with the full scope of family literacy issues, from discussion of theoretical perspectives and descriptions of actual practices and strategies to examination and evaluation of diverse family literacy programs and participants.

In Closing

1. After reviewing the activities in this chapter, what insights have you gained about the importance of keeping parents informed about their children's literacy development?

2. Which of the activities did you think were particularly effective for:
   - Informing parents about their child's literacy development
   - Giving parents tools to help their child with literacy
   - Getting parents to come to school to learn about how to work with their child in literacy
   - Fostering positive relationships between home and school

3. What activities did you feel would be helpful in diminishing negative feelings that parents may have developed about schools and/or education?

4. Select an activity that offered you the most effective way to showcase your literacy program for parents. In what ways was this effective?

5. Several of the activities suggested differing ways to communicate with parents, such as using the answering machine and providing a class newsletter. What do you see as the advantages and disadvantages of using these approaches compared to more traditional conferences?

6. One activity (*Parent Volunteers*) suggests that you recruit parent volunteers to participate in the class activities either in the classroom or at home. How do you think such participation benefits both parents and children?

7. One activity (*Dads and Donuts*) suggests particularly recruiting fathers and male caretakers. Do you think this specific gender targeting has any merit for helping to motivate children to read? Why or why not?

8. One activity (*Postcard Previews*) asks teachers to write to the child and his or her family before the school year has even begun. Do you think such a proactive message could help to create more positive relationships between the family and the school? In what way(s)?

9. Which activities would be particularly difficult for parents who speak languages other than English to participate in? How might you revise these activities to make them more accessible for parents who speak other home languages?

10. Identify a child whose parents are very involved in his or her literacy development. How does the child's attitude toward school differ from those of children whose parents are minimally involved? Describe the differences, if any.

Video Self-Assessment

(With permission from Linda Current)

Making a video of a lesson you teach to a class is an outstanding way for you to gain heightened awareness of what you do well and in what areas you may need improvement. Be aware that the first few times you view the tape, you may find yourself focusing on the superficial—your "bad hair day," your clothes, or the pounds you wish you could lose. This is normal and to be expected but, of course, not the purpose for the taping.

After viewing the tape in a general way a few times, play it again, this time focusing more intently on the specific behaviors listed below. You might have to view the tape separately for each behavior because it is difficult to concentrate on everything you are doing in one viewing.

In the spaces below, write down any observations, insights, or feelings you have about your lesson and your teaching behaviors. Particularly be on the lookout for any behavior patterns.

Note: Optionally, a friend or colleague may observe your teaching and respond to the following questions. This could replace your video self-assessment or serve as additional feedback.

1. How does my voice sound? Pitch? Volume? Expression? Pace?

_____

_____

_____

2. How does my face and body language convey my enthusiasm for the lesson? Do I smile? Do I make eye contact with the children?

_____

_____

_____

3. Do I move around the room appropriately as I teach? Do I make nonverbal connections with children during the lesson?

_____

_____

_____

4. Do I reflect "with-it-ness?" Do I project awareness of what is happening in all parts of the classroom with all the children? Do some children glance up at me to determine if I am "with-it" or not?

_____

_____

_____

5. What is the approximate ratio of teacher talk compared to student talk?

_____

_____

_____

6. Are the children on-task? Who is not? Do I notice? What do I do about it?

_____

_____

_____

7. Is the noise level appropriate for the lesson? Do I set noise level expectations in advance?

_____

_____

_____

8. Do I lead into the lesson in a stimulating way? Do I set a purpose for the lesson?

_____

_____

_____

9. Am I aware of how my second language learners are able to access the lesson? What specific provisions do I make to add comprehensible input into the lesson?

_____

_____

_____

10. Do I appear to have a clear objective for my teaching? Do I reach my objective? How?

_____

_____

_____

11. Do my procedures follow a logical sequence?

_____

_____

_____

12. Do I give the children clear instructions and check that they understand what they are to do?

_____

_____

_____

13. How do I use praise? Count the number of instances of positive reinforcement and the instances of negative reinforcement. What are my interpretations of these numbers?

_____

_____

_____

14. On what area of classroom management do I need to focus?

_____

_____

_____

15. What are the strengths of the lesson?

_____

_____

_____

16. What are the strengths of my teaching performance?

_____

_____

_____

17. What are the problems, if any, with the lesson?

_____

_____

_____

18. What would I change in the lesson next time?

_____

_____

_____

19. What would I change in my teaching performance next time?

_____

_____

_____

B

Instruction and Reflection Profile

This profile contains two separate parts. The first part comprises the reflection a teacher must do when planning a lesson, before actually teaching it. Teachers must make the following decisions when planning a lesson:

What outcomes are to be achieved?

What grouping configuration shall I use?

What methods are most appropriate?

Which activities will best help me meet my goals?

What materials will be most beneficial?

How will I determine whether children have met my objectives?

The first part of the profile is to be completed before you do your lesson to help you consider each of these important questions.

The second part of the profile is to be completed after you have completed your lesson. Teachers continually learn about the effectiveness of their lessons and the effectiveness of their own teaching performance by the reflecting they do after each lesson. During this second reflection, they revisit the decisions they made to design their lesson and determine, by considering the same questions, if they have met their instructional goals.

Complete Part I before you teach your lesson. Complete Part II after your lesson.

Part I

GOALS

What are your goals for student learning for this lesson? Why have you chosen these goals? How do you expect the students to behave differently as a result of your teaching?

_____

_____

_____

_____

GROUPING

How will you group your students for instruction? Why?

_____

_____

_____

_____

METHODS

What teaching method(s) will you use for this lesson?

_____

_____

_____

_____

ACTIVITIES

List the activities you have planned and the time you have allocated for each.

_____

_____

_____

_____

MATERIALS

What instructional materials will you use? Why have you chosen these materials?

_____

_____

_____

_____

ASSESSMENT

How and when do you plan to assess student learning on the content of this lesson? Why have you chosen this form of assessment?

_____

_____

_____

_____

Part II
GOALS

Did all the children achieve the learning goals you had set for them? How do you know that?

_____

_____

_____

_____

GROUPING

How would you group your students for this lesson in the future? Why?

_____

_____

_____

_____

METHODS

In what ways were your teaching methods effective? Why do you think so?

_____

_____

_____

_____

ACTIVITIES

In what ways did your activities help you to meet your goals? Might you use other activities instead in the future? Why?

_____

_____

_____

_____

MATERIALS

In what ways were your materials effective/ineffective? Why do you think so?

_____

_____

_____

_____

ASSESSMENT

Did anything occur during this lesson to change your assessment plan? If so, how has it changed? How will your assessment inform future instruction?

_____

_____

_____

_____

Lesson Plan Format

Teaching often is considered both an art and a science. The "art" element in teaching is the special magic teachers bring to the classroom through the force of their personality, creativity, and caring for the children, as well as the personal way they orchestrate the activities that take place in the classroom.

The "science" element of teaching is in the reflection that occurs while designing lessons to be motivational and to meet the developmental needs of all learners, and also while considering the strengths and weaknesses of the lesson after it has been taught.

This instrument may be used as is, or with modifications, to help you design an effective literacy lesson for children. Space for self-reflection is included at the end. Use the space provided or use additional paper to complete your self-evaluation.

1. **PURPOSE OF THE LESSON**

    Why have I chosen to teach this lesson?

    _____

    _____

    _____

2. BEHAVIORAL OBJECTIVES

What will children be able to do/do better as a result of this lesson?

_____

_____

_____

3. MOTIVATION

What will I do/say to get the children engaged in what I want them to do?

_____

_____

_____

4. PROCEDURES

Lesson development: What steps will I use to develop this lesson in an organized fashion?

_____

_____

_____

5. ASSESSMENT

Evaluation of the lesson: How will I know that children have met my objectives for the lesson? What exactly do I expect them to be able to do/do better as a result of my lesson?

_____

_____

_____

6. SELF-EVALUATION OF LESSON

How do I think the lesson went? What happened that I did not expect? What worked well? What did not work well? What would I do differently? How has my assessment informed future instruction?

_____

_____

_____

Writing Conventions Rubric Grades 4-6

	HIGH RANGE	MID RANGE	LOW RANGE
Sentence Structure and Paragraphing	☐ Students vary the length and structure of their sentences ☐ Paragraphs purposely express and explore ideas	☐ Some sentence variety appears ☐ Paragraphs focus on a main idea and change appropriately	☐ Simple or incomplete sentences dominate ☐ A single paragraph dominates
Spelling	☐ Spelling is accurate	☐ Commonly used words are spelled accurately ☐ Expanded vocabulary words may be spelled phonetically or closely guessed	☐ Frequent spelling errors appear
Mechanics	☐ A wide variety of punctuation enhances the meaning of the text	☐ Mid and end sentence punctuation marks are used accurately ☐ Capital letters are used appropriately	☐ Punctuation marks may be missing or inaccurate ☐ Capital letters may be missing or used inappropriately

Cover Sheet for a Homework Packet

Name _____ Homework Packet # _____ Due Date _____

First Grade Homework Packet

Homework packets are given out on Monday. Students are to complete at least one page each night and return the entire packet to school on Friday. Please monitor your child's daily progress so that work is not completed in one sitting. Do not return individual assignments each day.

Please remind your child to bring his or her book home at least twice a week.

Read from Book 1, "Too Much Noise." Be sure your child's finger is under each word as it is read. Read the story at least twice. Make sure your child returns the book to school the very next day.

Practice vocabulary words from "Too Much Noise." Cut them apart. Examples of use:

1. Put in alphabetical order.
2. Make sentences with word cards and write the sentence.
3. Practice learning the words by sight.
4. Keep these words in an envelope labeled with the name of the story.

Please do not expect your child to be able to do all of the above activities. Children learn at their own pace, so please select activities appropriate for your child.

Please remember to check the bottom of this paper and then sign on the line when the packet is complete.

Room 6 students are to be in portable 1-A. Room 5 students are to be in portable 1-B. Thursday will be a minimum day, and there will be no school on Friday due to conferences.

BOOK ORDERS. Select books you wish to purchase. Fill out order and send a check to "See Saw Books" in an envelope labeled with your child's name, book order, and room number. Be sure your child's name is on the order form.

SUPPLEMENTAL READING. Read daily with your child. Check as completed.
☐ Monday   ☐ Tuesday   ☐ Wednesday   ☐ Thursday

My child has completed this week's homework.   _____

Parent's signature

305